D1546308

BURKE IN THE ARCHIVES

Studies in Rhetoric/Communication
Thomas W. Benson, Series Editor

BURKE IN THE ARCHIVES

Using the Past to Transform the Future of Burkean Studies

Edited by

DANA ANDERSON *and* JESSICA ENOCH

THE UNIVERSITY OF SOUTH CAROLINA PRESS

© 2013 University of South Carolina

Published by the University of South Carolina Press
Columbia, South Carolina 29208

www.sc.edu/uscpress

Manufactured in the United States of America

22 21 20 19 18 17 16 15 14 13   10 9 8 7 6 5 4 3 2 1

Library of Congress Cataloging-in-Publication Data

Burke in the archives : using the past to transform the future of Burkean
studies / editors, Dana Anderson and Jessica Enoch.
    pages cm. — (Studies in Rhetoric/Communication)
    Includes bibliographical references and index.
    ISBN 978-1-61117-238-6 (hardbound : alk. paper) — ISBN 978-1-61117-239-3 (ebook)
    1. Burke, Kenneth, 1897–1993—Criticism and interpretation. I. Anderson, Dana,
    1971– editor of compilation. II. Enoch, Jessica, editor of compilation.
    PS3503.U6134Z59 2013
    818'.5209—dc23

                                                        2013011378

CONTENTS

SERIES EDITOR'S PREFACE

In 1974 Penn State University purchased the first of several sections of the archives of Kenneth Burke. Further acquisitions have extended that first purchase—first twelve linear feet of letters and other papers; then in 2000 to 2005 another twenty-five linear feet. Most recently another eighteen linear feet of materials, including correspondence, manuscripts, notes, reviews, and related materials were added to the collection. Kenneth Burke's long and productive life as one of the most important literary and rhetorical theorists of the twentieth century—perhaps the most important—is enriched in the archives by his lively correspondence with major intellectual figures over the decades.

For years Penn State professor of English Jack Selzer, the author of important studies of the work and life of Kenneth Burke, has taught a graduate seminar based on the Burke archives at Penn State. Recently he has been joined in that effort by Debra Hawhee, once a student in the seminar and now professor of English at Penn State.

The editors of the present volume, Dana Anderson and Jessica Enoch, have brought together a remarkable group of research scholars from English and communication, many of them graduates of Jack Selzer's famous Burke seminar, with their own reports of the research the archives have made possible. The result is a fascinating reexamination of Burke's work, raising new questions about archival research, about the Burke archives, about Burke's relations with his contemporaries, and about Burke's theories of rhetoric, technology, and language. The essays take Burke seriously, but they avoid the hazards—which Burke warned against—of piety, and they sometimes take Burke to task. Sandra Stelts, the curator, and Jeanette Sabre, the collections processor of the Kenneth Burke Papers at Penn State University, describe the history of the archive. Ann George offers a lively revisionist account of the reception of Burke's *Permanence and Change* (1935), contesting the claim that Burke's work was ignored in his own time by invoking a lively set of previously undiscovered reviews, notes, and correspondence from the archives. George shows how very much Burke was in and of his time.

Ned O'Gorman and Ian Hill pursue an undeveloped hint from the archives about the work of Burke and Lewis Mumford on "the poetics of technology," finding common intellectual ground and a common concern for methodology. Dave

Tell reconstructs a frustrating debate between Frederic Jameson and Kenneth Burke, which began with a keynote address by Jameson to the 1977 English Institute. Burke, present at the 1977 meeting, was deprived of a chance to reply to what he thought a seriously mistaken attack on his own work; his reply came later in the journal *Critical Inquiry* with "Methodological Repression and/or Strategies of Containment." Tell finds rich evidence in the archives about Burke's agitated state of mind in the face of Jameson's criticism, but he faults Burke for failing in his response to live up to his own standards, at the same time calling it both tragic and instructive and arguing that though there were "no winners" in the exchange, it demonstrates "the necessity and the limits of logology."

Keith Gibson has found in the archives a 1956 Burke interview with Swedish radio that offers new reflections on Burke and technology. Jeff Pruchnic explores Burke's correspondence and his manuscript drafts to investigate the way Burke negotiated the relations of his private beliefs and public voice. Michelle Smith uses the archives to revisit the 1982 Conference of the Eastern Communication Association, at which Burke was present to hear and then respond to papers by Bernard Brock and Herbert Simons on his work. Burke surprised the panel and an overflow auditorium by telling the panelists they had it wrong.

Jodie Nicotra investigates a Burkean encounter with mysticism. Scott Wible explores Burke's teaching career at Bennington College. Debra Hawhee, refashioning a notion from Kenneth Burke, suggests "historiography by incongruity" as an archival methodology, using the archive not so much to pin down the indefinite as to unsettle the tidy.

In the afterword Jack Selzer describes his own archival adventures, at Penn State and elsewhere, including how he got hooked, and describing human relationships derailed by editorial elisions and unsent letters as well as friendships cemented by visits to Burke's place in Andover, New Jersey. Of his years of working with the archives, Jack has written, "What teachers Kenneth Burke and his colleagues have been!"

Thomas W. Benson

PREFACE

As doctoral students at Penn State University over a decade ago, we both took a graduate seminar with Jack Selzer on Kenneth Burke. A key (and renowned) part of the course was Jack's introduction of graduate students to the Kenneth Burke Papers held at the Paterno Library. We both remember it well.

Early in the semester, Jack walked the class to the archive and gave us a tour. He introduced us to Sandy Stelts, curator of rare books and manuscripts. He showed us what was available, explained how to find and access materials, and generally encouraged us to just poke around. Box after box of Burke's letters were already out on the reading tables, and we paced curiously from one to the next, paging through them, dwelling on whatever caught our attention. Many of the participants in the course had just started to study Burke, and the texts of this eclectic panoply of notes and exchanges were among the first that we came to know. Jess remembers vividly the laughter that punctuated our silent reading, indicating that someone had stumbled upon one of Burke's famous playful spellings or turns of phrase. Dana recalls his unease as he thumbed through these often very personal documents while the legendary bust of Kenneth Burke in the Rare Books Room looked over his shoulder.

Most seminarians anchored their semester's work in their archival discoveries, visiting Burke's papers almost daily to pursue questions we developed as a class about his thinking and writing. None of us knew much about archival research, but Jack guided us beyond that first field trip and well after it, prompting us to return to Burke's papers, to take a look at this, to cross-reference it with that, and then, thankfully, to stop researching and try to write about what we found and what we were thinking.

Of course our experience with Jack is not unique. His Burke course and its concomitant archival research has become a veritable rite of passage at Penn State. If you enter the graduate program, you take this course, and then, if you're lucky, you publish from it. The list of publications that began in Jack's courses is long and distinguished. Articles on Burke and the Bureau of Social Hygiene, Burke at Bennington College, Burke and Nietzsche, Burke and sociologist Dell Hymes, Burke and communism, Burke on *Towards a Better Life*, Burke and general semantics, Burke and ecology, Burke and progressive education, Burke and human agency, and Burke and cybernetics have landed in journals such as *Rhetorica, Rhetoric Society Quarterly, Quarterly Journal of Speech, Rhetoric Review, Philosophy and Rhetoric,* and *College Composition and Communication,* just to name a few (see articles by Jack, Wible, Hawhee, Jordan, Sheriff, Van Dyk, Nicotra, Seigel, Enoch, Anderson, and Pruchnic). Put another way, the course has become a rich opportunity for junior scholars to enter the Burkean parlor and put their oars in.

We open this collection with our reflections not to wax nostalgic about the good old graduate-school days, but instead to offer an orientation to *Burke in the Archives: Using the Past to Transform the Future of Burkean Studies.* Several years after taking Jack's course—appropriately enough at the 2005 Burke and His Circles conference at Penn State—we began talking about how significant it had been to encounter Burke in the context of his archives at such an early point in our careers. We agreed that Jack's introduction of us to the archive and his mentorship throughout our work with Burke's documents had, in Burkean terms, *oriented* us to Burke's work in unique ways and had shaped our *attitudes* not just toward Burke's oeuvre but also toward archival methodologies writ large. Probably most important of all, as mentors of graduate students ourselves, we were now in a position to truly appreciate both the genius and the effort behind Jack's seminars. So we began to imagine a way that we might recognize Jack's work by engaging the larger scholarly community in relation to the role of the archive in forwarding Burke scholarship.

Burke in the Archives is the result of our imaginings. In this collection we join with thirteen other contributors to explore how the archives inform—and even transform—the study of Burke. In doing so we and all of the authors in this collection hope to make good on various personal and intellectual debts that we owe: to Kenneth Burke himself, of course; to the generous community of scholars that carries his insight and energy forward; and for his work in this community, and especially for his dedication to the scholars he has guided toward it, to Jack Selzer.

WORKS CITED

Anderson, Dana. "Questioning the Motives of Habituated Action: Burke and Bourdieu on *Practice." Philosophy and Rhetoric* 37.3 (2004): 255–74.

Betts Van Dyk, Krista K. "From the Plaint to the Comic: Kenneth Burke's 'Towards a Better Life.'" *Rhetoric Society Quarterly* 36.1 (2006): 31–53.

Enoch, Jessica. "Becoming Symbol-Wise: Kenneth Burke's Pedagogy of Critical Reflection." *College Composition and Communication* 56.2 (2004): 279–96.

Hawhee, Debra. "Burke and Nietzsche." *Quarterly Journal of Speech* 85 (1999): 129–45.

Jack, Jordynn. "'The Piety of Degradation': Kenneth Burke, the Bureau of Social Hygiene, and *Permanence and Change." Quarterly Journal of Speech* 90.4 (2004): 446–68.

Jordan, Jay. "Dell Hymes, Kenneth Burke's 'Identification' and the Birth of Sociolinguistics." *Rhetoric Review* 24 (2005): 264–79.

Nicotra, Jodie. "Dancing Attitudes in Wartime: Kenneth Burke and General Semantics." *Rhetoric Society Quarterly* 39.4 (2009): 331–52.

Pruchnic, Jeff. "Rhetoric, Cybernetic, and the Work of the Body in Burke's Body of Work." *Rhetoric Review* 25.3 (2006): 275–96.

Seigel, Marika. "'One Little Fellow Named Ecology': Ecological Rhetoric in Kenneth Burke's *Attitudes toward History*." *Rhetoric Review* 23.4 (2004): 388–404.

Sheriff, Stacey. "Resituating Kenneth Burke's 'My Approach to Communism.'" *Rhetorica* 23 (2005): 281–96.

Wible, Scott. "Professor Burke's Bennington Project." *Rhetoric Society Quarterly* 38.3 (2008): 259–82.

ABBREVIATIONS FOR
WORKS BY KENNETH BURKE

ATH   *Attitudes toward History*
CS   *Counter-Statement*
GM   *A Grammar of Motives*
LSA   *Language as Symbolic Action*
PC   *Permanence and Change*
PLF   *The Philosophy of Literary Form*
RM   *A Rhetoric of Motives*
RR   *The Rhetoric of Religion*

JESSICA ENOCH *and* DANA ANDERSON

INTRODUCTION

Retrospective Prospecting—Notes toward a Future

The future of Burke studies: Efforts to secure it have been pronounced since even before Burke's passing. In 1966, for example, Burke himself expressed his concern for such a future. In a new foreword written that year for the second edition of *The Philosophy of Literary Form*, he penned his hope that his insights into human symbol use might "meet the tests of 'long-pull investment'" (vii). More than two decades later, in 1989, the title alone of the collection *The Legacy of Kenneth Burke* (Simons and Trevor) suggested that his work had indeed passed those tests. Another important collection, published just months before Burke's death in 1993, endowed this legacy with the material permanence of landmarks—*Landmark Essays on Kenneth Burke* (Brummett), erecting guideposts out of the sprawling secondary literature to orient generations of scholars to come. And the November newsletter of the Kenneth Burke Society, appearing only two weeks after Burke's demise, delivered what were as of yet the strongest assertions of a lasting Burkean tomorrow. Leavening its encomium with divination, its reassurances of Burke's enduring influence crossed over into the otherworldly. "As we knew we must lose him, we can be equally sure that the Burke of the texts survives," Don Burks wrote. "Future generations of Burkeans will be enriched by those works as we are . . . future Burkeans will come to know the text, and to feel that they know the writer, that his spirit is with them" (2).

The most recent addition to these earnest prognostications about the Burkean future appears in what is itself a newer landmark of the Burkean legacy, *KB Journal*. In their 2008 editors' essay, "The Future of Burke Studies," Mark Huglen and Clarke Rountree frankly address what might seem to be the most formidable limitation to the continued study and application of Burke in a century he never saw—the fact that "we no longer have Burke producing new works." The obvious potential problem they see here is one of redundancy, of "scholars retracing work done by their predecessors" in a slide toward "the point of diminishing returns for our scholarly efforts." But hope remains. As they optimistically counter, given that "one might view the Burkean oeuvre as containing as many meanings as there are contexts, language chains with ethnographic traces, constraints of persuasive situations, motivations and strategic choices, and people in the world, . . . scholars ought to be able to continue unpacking Burkean concepts indefinitely." Maybe such an unreachable horizon will indeed prove to be the future of Burke studies, one of engaged, enriching, and perhaps even—to cite yet another future-minded collection—*Unending Conversations* (Henderson and Williams).

If the sheer desire for a future of Burke studies is any measure, then the matter of whether there is to be one seems resolved.[1] The question that remains, however, cannot be answered so easily: *What kind of future should this be?* The essays of this collection mount a singular contribution to this discussion, one that, in a fitting perspectival incongruity, approaches the future by way of the past. Looking back in order to look forward, the contributors to this volume go to a resource perhaps too infrequently consulted in our deliberations about the Burkean tomorrow: they go to the archives. Engaging the stunning array of primary materials both by and about Burke that have been preserved, they consider the many roles these materials might play in shaping what we hope will be informed and inspiring years of scholarship to come. Their essays explore Burke's relationship with figures such as Fredric Jameson, Lewis Mumford, and Barbara Bate; they reconsider Burke's ideas regarding logology, epistemology, the pentad, mysticism, humanism, and postmodernism; and they rewrite Burke as an educator, a techie, and even a celebrity. Their archival excursions offer us an enlivened understanding of both well-known texts such as *Permanence and Change* and less influential essays such as "Methodological Repression and/or Strategies of Containment." And their work displays the challenge and the promise of using Burke's work to engage twenty-first-century issues and conversations, linking Burke studies to studies of disability, ontology, affect, and critical inquiry, for instance. Together, their essays suggest an orientation to the future of Burke studies that bespeaks the transformative potential of archival resources and methodologies. As we briefly discuss now in more fully introducing those essays, it is an orientation that might best be described as *impious*.

SCRUTINIZING PIETIES IN ARCHIVAL RESEARCH AND BURKE STUDIES

Archives are inevitably pious places, realms of rules, revelations, and timelessness. Unlike other scholarly resources that can be conjured in mere clicks, archives typically demand that we make the sacrifice of going to them. The process of ensuring that a particular archive holds the promise of what we seek, securing funding for travel (at a time when acquiring such funding is itself the stuff of miracles), and then setting off on the journey cannot help but evoke an air of pilgrimage. Upon our arrival at their doors, the archives ask more of us still before we are granted entry: in acts akin to ritual cleansing, we must purge ourselves of pens, beverages, backpacks—otherwise benign accompaniments that here are potential defilements.

We may be asked to wear gloves or even be barred from touching altogether, ever under the eyes of guardians of these irreplaceable artifacts. With each hopeful advance through "the next box, the next folder, the next file" in pursuit of whatever "elusive find" we seek (Phelps 1), we confirm anew the eternal truth at the heart of all archival work: coming here was an act of faith. Belying simple root meanings of "record" or "storehouse," it is hardly surprising that archives often feel much less like libraries and much more like reliquaries.

Scholars from across the range of academic disciplines have testified to the affective, even mystical responses that archives have the power to invoke. We read of archival pleasure (Burton), archival anxiety (Steedman), archival surprise (Kirsch, Gold), and even archival fever (Derrida). Rhetorician Robert Connors has wistfully described archives as places where "storage meets dreams" (223), and historian Antoinette Burton has compellingly foregrounded one "crucial constituent of the archive experience" that often escapes our acknowledgment: "desire" (11). Archives uniquely enable a kind of tactile vicariousness where, gloved hands or not, we feel we literally "get in touch with" and "experience the worlds in which [our] subjects lived" (Sutherland 29). Such moments when "archival discoveries . . . bring one into contact with the past" may even be, in language of unmistakably pious trappings, "rapturous" (Burton 8). "Aura" and "allure" (Freshwater), "seduction" and "intoxication" (Bradley): one could hardly expect more from objects whose existence is so dependent upon acid-free folders and plastic sheet protectors.

Beyond—or perhaps even *because* of—their allure and liminality, archives are pious in other ways that bear directly on their scholarly use. As theater scholar Helen Freshwater makes clear, archives inspire a certain reverence by way of the "authenticating function" they perform in scholarly work (732). Special trips to archives in the service of research projects, accompanied by meditations on the support that their rarities afford, are true bastions of academic *gravitas*. Mention of having consulted archival sources is for many the highest form of proof, for the use and interpretation of these materials can only be seriously challenged by accessing them for oneself. As sociologist Thomas Osborne writes, the "*providential* credibility" we thus ascribe to archival work endows scholars with the "right to make statements [not only] about the past, about history, about change, [and] about fate" but also, "by extension, . . . about the future" (54). It seems our authority to declare the shape of things in the archive may also empower us to declare the shape of things to come. What greater height of piety than prophecy?

Those who have studied Burke's archival materials, including the contributors to this volume, can surely attest to both the bewitching character of these resources and the authenticating weight they carry in Burke studies. The primary archival resource for Burkean research—and the primary focus for this volume—is the Kenneth Burke Papers at Pennsylvania State University.[2] Most who conduct research there concur that, in both content and size, the archive indeed inspires genuine awe. As

Jack Selzer and Robert Wess write, "the papers, amazing in their comprehensiveness and sheer volume, are the most significant repository of materials related to Burke's career in existence" (xi). Spanning more than eight decades from 1906 to 1993, the archive contains over fifty-five linear feet of materials relating to Burke and his work, holding letters to and from Burke, notes on published materials, manuscript drafts, transcripts of radio interviews, minutes from department meetings Burke attended at Bennington College, scribblings on cocktail napkins, Christmas cards, and much, much more. Selzer and Wess provocatively summarize this richness by simply noting that there is "no place to stop" (xii). Given that Burke is often regarded as one of the more arcane rhetoricians of our time, such portals into his life and thinking naturally invoke what is perhaps the most pious response of all: the hope that we might, once and for all, use these materials to get Burke *right*.

But amidst these pieties, we believe Burke's work invites us to consider our archival approaches and attitudes from a different perspective. Indeed, to articulate that perspective, we might look to the concept of piety itself as Burke develops it. In the work that contains his most sustained meditation on piety, *Permanence and Change*, Burke explores piety as the very basis for how humans forge coherence from an otherwise chaotic existence. "Piety is a system builder," he asserts, "a desire to round things out, to fit experiences together into a unified whole." Grounding and organizing this pious systematization is "an altar," a center around which this rounded-out, fitted-together, and unified whole of experience takes shape. Just as concentric spinnings bind disparate strands into a web, so this anchoring center radiates "pious linkages" to connect otherwise disconnected elements, establishing "what properly goes with what." The result is "a complex interpretative network" that "br[ings] all the significant details of the day into coordination, relating them integrally with one another" (74–75). For Burke, this inevitably pious process of system building underlies all human meaning making, engendering everything from individual texts to the parade of historical epochs that contain them.

As one such realm of meaning making, Burke studies is itself a modest, yet robust system, and one with its own pious acts and attitudes of participation within it. Exactly what altar should stand as the organizing center of those acts and attitudes deserves to be the subject of at least some of our unending conversations about the Burkean future.[3] What might it mean, then, as we suggest, to anchor Burke studies in impiety as its organizing center? What roles might archival resources and practices play as part of such an impious orientation, and how can they help us envision the kind of future that this orientation would make possible?

The essays in this volume speak directly to these questions. In doing so, they draw support from the ways that archival scholarship itself has lately been the subject of its own impious reconfiguration, especially within rhetorical studies. In 2006 for example Charles Morris observed that the field of rhetorical studies had begun to take what he described as an "archival turn." Even though archives had obviously already been "long-standing habitat[s] of the rhetorical critic" prior to Morris's observation, he yet asserted that the "disciplinary relationship with the archive has deepened recently" ("Archival Turn" 113). As scholars turn now to archives to extend rhetorical scholarship, they are, like the contributors to this volume, reflecting more critically (and impiously) on their research methods and methodologies, considering how a range of archival practices shapes the work they do.

Recent scholarship in rhetorical studies abounds with such critical scrutiny of the nature, role, and "proper" functions of archival work. In addition to large-scale efforts such as collections and special journal issues dedicated to archival methodologies,[4] individual scholars are also advancing this conversation. And it may be a surprise to learn that many are doing so with markedly Burkean overtones. Wendy Sharer for example prompts rhetoric scholars to realize their own occupational psychosis by calling attention to the work of archivists and the "powerful evaluative practices" (120) they employ through their practices of "acquisition, appraisal, collection management, description, indexing, preservation, oxidation, and deaccession" (124). Although we may not acknowledge it, these archival practices, Sharer argues, "affect the corpus of historical records we use to compose our histories" (124). Pursuing this line of inquiry further, Cara Finnegan equates archival classification systems with terministic screens and considers how they "simultaneously revea[l] and concea[l] 'facts,' at once enabling and constraining interpretation" (117–18). Morris engages similar questions by investigating a particular kind of archival screen he encountered when attempting to recover the work of queer rhetors. He writes of the "pietistic process of categorization and indexical naming" that "serves to deflect queer inquiry" by not identifying and cataloging historical figures as gay ("Queer" 146–47). Taking a different tack, Cheryl Glenn and Jessica Enoch use Burke's pentad to analyze what they term the "drama of the archives," with the goal of challenging and revising the traditional historiographic methods that typically inform archival research in rhetorical studies. And finally Liz Rohan, Patricia Bizzell, and Jacqueline Jones Royster examine the ways that researchers might better reflect on the "emotional attachments" they make with their archival subjects (Royster 246)—attachments that, again, for Burke, are at the very essence of piety.

Thus for rhetoricians taking part in this "archival turn," including the authors in this volume, archives are places of invention and production; they are "dynamic site[s] of rhetorical power" (Morris, "Archival Turn" 115). Rather than presenting us with unmediated "access to the past," archives offer us opportunities, as Freshwater writes, for the "reinterpretation," "recontextualization" and "reanimation" of that past (739). Foucault makes a similar assertion when he, sounding much like Burke, suggests that archives are *systems* that enable the "formation and transformation of statements" (qtd. in Freshwater 752). Forming and transforming knowledge in the archive, scholars engage in an imaginative wrestling between past materials and present intentions, an "agonism" that, Osborne contends, "is internal to the very principle of the archive" (55). Directly challenging what might be the most defining piety of traditional archival research, such scholarship asks that we see archival work not as the end of interpretation, but as yet one more beginning. This attitude toward the resources of the past has much to say to the present of Burke studies, and just as much to offer us in our efforts to figure its future.

THE CONTENTS OF THIS COLLECTION

Through wide-ranging archival engagements that together manifest just such an agonistic, reanimative approach to the past, the contributors to this volume invite a future for Burke studies where even our most accepted understandings open themselves to renewed inquiry and transformation. Indeed it is transformation itself that such an impious orientation would regard as the guiding center of the Burke studies system. For in Burke's analysis, transformation is not just an act but an attitude as well.[5] Transformation signifies the processes of symbolic alchemy whereby "A may become non-A" (*GM* xix); but it also names the openness to the possibility of such dramatic reversals, the willingness to contemplate both the means and the ends of such substantial reconstitutions. An attitude of transformation is the unflagging readiness to question "what properly goes with what," including, reflexively, the proprieties of Burke studies in which this attitude itself is rooted.

The essays in this volume pursue a wide variety of subjects and questions in service of this aim, by way of an equally wide variety of archival materials and practices. They ask, What kinds of "coherence," "coordination," and "rounding-out" do these materials and methods enable? How do these archival arguments thus shape the present—and the potential future—of Burke studies? *Burke in the Archives* foregrounds these questions, providing the field with a focused meditation on archival practice that it has not yet engendered. Given this focus, one especially salient contribution of this volume is methodological: in each essay, authors articulate the particular ways they have used archival materials to forward their arguments about Burke and his work. The guiding principle here is not merely to underscore the simple fact *that* scholars go to the Burke archives but rather to investigate *what* scholars do once they get there and *how* they use archival materials to create new Burkean knowledge. From "archival events" and "archival provocations" to "archival heuristics" and "archival interventions," the contributors teach us how the archive has enabled them to return to Burke and reinterpret, invent, and transform our understanding.

Sandy Stelts and Jeanette Sabre, curator and collections processor of the Kenneth Burke Papers at Penn State University, respectively, open the collection by reviewing how the archive at Penn State came to be. Historian Patrick Joyce has written that "the archive which produces history is also a product of history" (36). Stelts and Sabre engagingly explore the history that produced the Kenneth Burke Papers, detailing in particular Burke's remarkably active hand in shaping the records that scholars now study. In doing so this collaborative team also underscores the importance of another archive in this history: Burke's home in Andover and the materials it still contains. By articulating the vital connection between the archives at Penn State and at Andover, the authors illuminate the practices of maintenance and use that defined Burke's home archive. Stelts and Sabre conclude by considering the unique perspective their work has granted them on the depth and range of the scholarship that the Kenneth Burke Papers has supported. In offering this reflective description, Stelts and Sabre ultimately set the foundation for rhetoricians to compose what Barbara Biesecker has termed "rhetorical histories of archives"—histories that interrogate "the situated and strategic uses to which archives have been put" (130).

Building on Stelts and Sabre's history of the Burke papers at Penn State, the subsequent contributors to the collection demonstrate and reflect on the varied roles that archival materials play in shaping Burke studies. In "Finding the Time for Burke," Ann George troubles the well-known image of Burke as a man ahead of his time, an underappreciated genius whose reception would come much later than deserved. George counters that a "relentless contextualization" of Burke through the use of archival materials forces scholars to acknowledge that he was deeply engaged in his own moment. George supports this claim by examining the archival artifacts surrounding the publication of *Permanence and Change* (1935). Reviewing Burke's correspondence, fan mail, planning notes, and nine previously unrecorded reviews of the book, George offers insight to the book's reception in its contemporary moment. This reception figures a new Burke—a man unmistakably *of* his time whom critics (and fans!) understood, disagreed with, and celebrated.

In "Burke, Mumford, and the Poetics of Technology: Marxism's Influence on Burke's Critique of Techno-logology," Ned O'Gorman and Ian Hill investigate Burke's revisions and refinements of critical inquiry as it emerged in the 1930s. Deprived of a rich range of archival resources to develop their inquiry, however, O'Gorman and Hill take up this task by fastidiously reconstructing a brief interchange between Burke and public intellectual Lewis Mumford. Mumford wrote to Burke in 1934 that the two thinkers were "converging toward the same goal" in their respective critical projects, but after this point the archives are silent. Intrigued by the possible significance of this piquant statement, O'Gorman and Hill explore this archival exchange not as definitive evidence but rather as an "archival provocation" that inspires them to probe the interanimations of Burke's and Mumford's thinking. O'Gorman and Hill come to argue that both writers were advocating a common methodological turn, one that ambitiously aimed to change the face of critical inquiry at the time. The collaborators conclude the essay by considering what Mumford and Burke's methodology might mean for scholarly criticism today, suggesting a shift in attention from an instrumental use of terms and rubrics to the identification of methodology itself as critical approach and activity.

In "Burke and Jameson: Reflections on Language, Ideology, and Criticism," Dave Tell examines a moment about which the archives hold a comparative richness: Burke's infamous exchange with Fredric Jameson. Jameson critiqued Burke's work orally at the 1977 English Institute and then again in the pages of *Critical Inquiry*. Burke's response to Jameson came, again, in *Critical Inquiry* in his essay "Methodological Repression and/or Strategies of Containment"—an essay many scholars have passed over due to its arguable incomprehensibility. Tell contends, however, that "Methodological Repression" can be deciphered by consulting what he terms the "archival event" that surrounds the publication of this piece. Extending the scope of materials that bear on this interchange between Burke and Jameson, Tell argues that Burke's correspondence has much to say about Burke's thinking as he composed this enigmatic essay as well as the primary subject of the piece itself, logology. Tell ultimately demonstrates that this "archival event" offers insight into more than the possibilities and limitations of logology; it illuminates as well the ways that Burke's logological thinking may have hindered his participation in more productive academic debate.

As Tell's work illustrates, archival materials often provide invaluable clues that clarify Burke's thoughts and theories. But archival materials can also serve, in Jordynn Jack's words, as heuristics for present-day revisions and repurposings of that scholarship. In "On the Limits of Human: Haggling with Burke's 'Definition of Man,'" Jack, like O'Gorman and Hill, considers another fleeting moment in the archive—a brief interchange between Burke and feminist scholar Barbara Bate. Jack first investigates this interchange to consider how Burke may have used Bate's scholarship to rethink and "haggle" with the gendered language he uses in his "Definition of Man." Taking this interchange as an archival heuristic and inventive example, Jack continues to haggle with Burke's definition by considering not what a feminist critique might do to the definition, but this time how the lens of disability studies might prompt further revision of this definition.

For Jack the archive serves as an opportunity for using past conversations to inform present-day imperatives; for Keith Gibson the archive is a catalyst toward rethinking our current interpretation of that past. In "Burke and the Positive Potentials of Technology: Recovering the 'Complete Literary Event,'" Gibson argues that while Burke's published materials suggest he was a skeptic of technology, a 1956 interview given to a Swedish radio station reveals that he was much less of a technological pessimist than we might believe. Carefully analyzing four successive drafts of the interview manuscript, Gibson reflects on Burke's writing process, the evolution of his thinking in that process, and his position in this interview on the interrelationships of technology and literary value. Gibson's reading reveals a Burke who, rather than pondering (and rejecting) "technology" writ large, instead contemplates the value of *individual* technologies, particularly television and radio. Burke articulates a provocative litmus test for determining the worth of these technologies: do they "round out the circle" and "restore the initial supremacy of the written word"? Gibson then considers the utility of this test by employing it in his own contemporary evaluation of technologies enmeshed in everyday, twenty-first-century life.

Archival materials are often seen as the private and personal materials of public figures. Their use value typically lies in their ability to elucidate public and published materials; how does a letter or a manuscript draft, for instance, illuminate the finished product of a particular theory or work? In "Burke in/on Public and Private: Rhetoric, Propaganda, and the 'End(s)' of Humanism," Jeff Pruchnic meditates on this dialectic between private and public in order to interrogate the ways that Burke negotiated conflicts between his private beliefs and his public role as a critic of language use. Pruchnic takes up this interrogation by analyzing the rhetorical "registers" Burke adopts both in his published writings and in his more private materials such as manuscript drafts and letters. Pruchnic's analysis, however, moves beyond Burke's ethos formation to consider how this negotiation of registers reveals much about Burke's investments in both humanism and postmodernism. Pruchnic concludes this discussion about ethical negotiation across Burke's published and archival materials by extending it into current concerns in critical theory regarding affect and ontology.

In "The Dramatism Debate, Archived: The Pentad as 'Terministic' Ontology," Michelle Smith uses the archive to intervene in a central debate regarding Burkean theory: the debate about the pentad as either epistemological or ontological in focus. Smith's analysis centers on a 1982 conference interchange between Bernard Brock, Herbert Simons, and Burke himself, where Burke surprised the panel and the audience by arguing that the pentad was an ontological rather than an epistemological tool. Smith enters this debate through her own "archival intervention," but, as she explains, intervention here does not mean prioritizing archival findings or "Truths" over critical readings of Burke's work. Rather she uses the archive to articulate a vital temporality in Burke's thinking. That is, the temporality that the archive unfolds allows for an understanding of how Burke's ideas changed over time. Smith makes use of this temporality to argue for a new reading of Burke's pentad, one wherein it becomes neither epistemology nor ontology but rather the centerpiece of a "terministic" ontology.

As discussed earlier, scholars often define archival work as a sublime or even mystical encounter. In "Notes from the Abyss: Variations on a (Mystical) Theme in Burke's Work," Jodie Nicotra delves doubly into the ethereal as she considers what Burke's archival materials have to say about his engagement with mysticism. Consulting a vast array of archival materials, including unpublished chapters of *Permanence and Change*, Nicotra traces Burke's compelling, confusing, and often contradictory ideas on mysticism. Her project, like Smith's, however, is not so much to discern the truth and extent of Burke's mystical leanings but rather to understand the intellectual ecology that infused and cultivated these ideas. The result of this ecological exploration is a dramatically heightened awareness of the rhetorical work that mysticism performed for Burke throughout his career.

In "Talk about how your language is constructed: Kenneth Burke's Vision for University-wide Dialogue," Scott Wible leverages archival materials to enter a different Burkean ecology: Burke's career as a teacher. Reinforcing the claim of Ann George's essay, Wible argues that an examination of the rich array of archival materials regarding Burke's teaching at Bennington College in particular suggests that the seemingly detached and recondite rhetorical theorist was indeed a man of his time. These materials (student papers, departmental minutes, letters to colleagues) portray Burke as a teacher who was deeply invested in education and shed light on his pedagogical career, and at Bennington College in particular. Wible's work gains even greater significance in this discussion as he explores a different relationship between Burke's archival materials and his theoretical texts. Here Wible considers how these archival materials reveal Burke translating his theoretical ideas into classroom practice. Wible examines how Burke attempted to create pedagogical renderings of the ideas he developed specifically in such texts as *Attitudes toward History, The Philosophy of Literary Form,* and "Linguistic Approaches to Problems in Education."

Reflecting on her work in Burke's archives while researching and writing *Moving Bodies: Kenneth Burke at the Edges of Language* (2009), Debra Hawhee uses her essay "Historiography by Incongruity" to offer a Burkean archival methodology that proves useful for Burke scholars in particular and for rhetoricians more generally. Hawhee challenges the notion that archives provide missing pieces to our intellectual puzzles, arguing instead that archival materials can and should also be viewed as possible "records of breakdown and failure." As a means of considering how scholars should acknowledge, address, and even embrace these breakdowns, Hawhee introduces "historiography by incongruity," an archival methodology based on two of Burke's theories: perspective by incongruity and the Beauty Clinic. In doing so Hawhee speaks to and extends the assertions of scholars such as Osborne who write of the "clinical logic at work" in the archives in which the historian "dispose[s] of facts in a particular way so as to produce a particular picture of things" (58). Furthering such claims, Hawhee contemplates the ways that historiography by incongruity might prompt scholars to reflect on the tidy archival narratives that make up their histories, calling them to be more cognizant of how the desire for archival perfection may foment the repression of (productive) breakdown and confusion.

Jack Selzer concludes the collection by reflecting on the rich intellectual and personal benefits that his extensive work in the archives has yielded. His recollections of some of his own most memorable moments tell a tale of profound challenges—and equally profound rewards—to be netted when one pursues the lure of archival scholarship.

We hope that the materials, methods, practices, and arguments that these essays explore will invigorate Burke studies with a renewed sense of openness—of possibility. Impious or otherwise, our orientation in the present is a sure influence on what we will see as we enter the archives. Of the prospects to be found there, the potential for such encounters between past and present to thus form—and trans-form—our tomorrow may be the greatest of all.

NOTES

1. Other significant volleys in these deliberations concerning the shape of the future of Burke studies include Bryan Crable's "Kenneth Burke's Continued Relevance"; Scott McLemee's "A Puzzling Figure in Literary Criticism Is Suddenly Central"; and Bernard Brock's important collection *Kenneth Burke and the 21st Century*. For the most direct argument against the possibility or necessity of a future for Burke studies, see Peter Holbrook's "What Happened to Burke?" as well as Dana Anderson's counterargument in "Burke Is Dead. Long Live Burke!"

2. Contributors to this volume also conducted archival research on Burke at the Newberry Library in Chicago, the Beinecke Rare Book and Manuscript Library at Yale University, the Van Pelt Library at the University of Pennsylvania, the Joseph Regenstein Library at the University of Chicago, the Sydney Hook papers at Stanford University's Hoover Institute, and Burke's archival holdings at the New York Public Library.

3. Left unscrutinized, it is easy to predict what altar might come to occupy the center of the Burke studies system—or, perhaps better said, what might come to preoccupy it: a self-interested preoccupation with keeping the system going, with possessing a future. Of even more concern than the narrow desire to perpetuate its own existence, the "complex interpretative network" of the Burkean system could be reduced to a much simpler kind of enterprise: homage. As valorization of the aims toward which Burke worked and wrote morphs into reverence for his efforts to achieve those aims, the altar that defines the present and promised future of Burke studies could become something even more pious: a memorial. Such sentimentalities are, after all, central to Burke's use of "piety" to describe human system building. The term reminds us that the things we build cannot help but build our own "deeply emotional" attachments to them in the process (*Permanence and Change* 69).

4. For examples of this disciplinary investment, see "Octalog: The Politics of Historiography" *Rhetoric Review* 7 (1988): 5–59; "Octalog II: The (Continuing) Politics of Historiography" *Rhetoric Review* 16.1 (1997): 22–24; "Octalog III: The Politics of Historiography in 2010." *Rhetoric Review* 30.2 (109–34); Brereton, John C. et al. "Archivists with an Attitude." *College English* 61.5 (1999): 574–93; "Feminist Historiography in Rhetoric" *Rhetoric Society Quarterly* 32.1 (2002): 7–122; Carr, Jean F., Stephen L. Carr and Lucille Schultz. *Archives of Instruction: Nineteenth-Century Rhetorics, Readers, and Composition Books in the United States.* Carbondale: Southern Illinois UP, 2005; "Forum: The Politics of Archival Research" *Rhetoric and Public Affairs* 9.1 (2006): 131–51; Kirsch, Gesa, and Liz Rohan, eds. *Beyond the Archives: Research as a Lived Process.* Carbondale: Southern Illinois UP, 2008; and Ramsey, Alexis, et al., eds. *Working in the Archives: Methods, Sources, Histories.* Carbondale: Southern Illinois UP, 2009.

5. Which may, in fact, be two ways of saying the same thing, given that attitudes are "incipient acts" (*GM* 236). For a collection that, while not archival in focus, considers

Burke from a perspective in keeping with the impiety we have outlined here, see James Chesebro, *Extensions of the Burkean System.*

WORKS CITED

Anderson, Dana. "Burke Is Dead. Long Live Burke!" *College Composition and Communication* 60.2 (2008): 441–49.

Biesecker, Barbara. "Of Historicity, Rhetoric: The Archive as Scene of Invention." *Rhetoric and Public Affairs* 9.1 (2006): 124–31.

Bizzell, Patricia. "Feminist Methods of Research in the History of Rhetoric: What Difference Do They Make?" *Rhetoric Society Quarterly* 30.4 (2000): 5–17.

Bradley, Harriet. "The Seductions of the Archive: Voices Lost and Found." *History of the Human Sciences* 12.2 (1999): 107–22.

Brock, Bernard, ed. *Kenneth Burke and the 21st Century.* Albany: State University of New York Press, 1998.

Brummett, Barry, ed. *Landmark Essays on Kenneth Burke.* Davis, Calif.: Hermagoras, 1993.

Burke, Kenneth. *A Grammar of Motives.* Berkeley: University of California Press, 1969.

———. *Permanence and Change.* 3rd ed. Berkeley: University of California Press, 1954.

———. *The Philosophy of Literary Form.* 2nd ed. Berkeley: University of California Press, 1973.

Burks, Don M. "Kenneth Burke Dies at Home in Andover." *The Kenneth Burke Society Newsletter* 9.1 (1993): 1–9.

Burton, Antoinette. "Archive Fever, Archive Stories." *Archive Stories: Facts, Fictions, and the Writing of History.* Ed. Antoinette Burton. Durham: Duke University Press, 2005.

Chesebro, James W., ed. *Extensions of the Burkean System.* Tuscaloosa: University of Alabama Press, 1993.

Connors, Robert. "Dreams and Play: Historical Method and Methodology." *Selected Essays of Robert J. Connors.* Ed. Lisa Ede and Andrea Lunsford. Boston: Bedford/St. Martin's. 2003. 221–35.

Crable, Bryan. "Kenneth Burke's Continued Relevance: Arguments toward a Better Life." *Argumentation and Advocacy* 40 (Fall 2003): 118–23.

Derrida, Jacques. *Archive Fever: A Freudian Impression.* Chicago: University of Chicago Press, 1998.

Finnegan, Cara. "What Is This a Picture Of?: Some Thoughts on Images and Archives." *Rhetoric and Public Affairs* 9 (2006): 116–23.

Freshwater, Helen. "The Allure of the Archive." *Poetics Today* 24.4 (2003): 729–58.

Glenn, Cheryl, and Jessica Enoch. "Drama in the Archives: Re-reading Materials, Rewriting History." *College Composition and Communication* 61.2 (2009): 321–42.

Gold, David. "The Accidental Archivist: Embracing Chance and Confusion in Historical Scholarship." Kirsch and Rohan. 13–19.

Henderson, Greig, and David Cratis Williams. *Unending Conversations: New Writings by and about Kenneth Burke.* Carbondale: Southern Illinois University Press, 2001.

Holbrook, Peter. "What Happened to Burke? How a Lionized American Critic, for Whom Literature Was 'Equipment for Living,' Became Lost to Posterity." *Times Literary Supplement* July 13, 2007: 11–12.

Huglen, Mark, and Clarke Rountree. "Editor's Essay: The Future of Burke Studies." *KB-Journal* 4.2 (Spring 2008).

Joyce, Patrick. "The Politics of the Liberal Archive." *History of the Human Sciences* 12.2 (1999): 35–49.

Kirsch, Gesa. "Being on Location: Serendipity, Place, and Archival Research." Kirsch and Rohan. 20–28.

Kirsch, Gesa, and Liz Rohan, eds. *Beyond the Archives: Research as a Lived Process.* Carbondale: Southern Illinois University Press, 2008.

McLemee, Scott. "A Puzzling Figure in Literary Criticism Is Suddenly Central." *Chronicle of Higher Education* Apr. 20, 2001: A26.

Morris, Charles, III. "Archival Queer." *Rhetoric and Public Affairs* 9 (Spring 2006): 141–51.

———."The Archival Turn in Rhetorical Studies, or the Archives Rhetorical (Re)Turn." *Rhetoric and Public Affairs* 9 (Spring 2006): 113–15.

Osborne, Thomas. "The Ordinariness of the Archive." *History of the Human Sciences* 12.2 (1999): 51–64.

Phelps, Christopher. "My Dream Archive." *Chronicle of Higher Education* 53.18 (2007): 1.

Rohan, Liz. "Stitching a Writing Life." Kirsch and Rohan, 147–53.

Royster, Jacqueline Jones. *Traces of a Stream: Literacy and Social Change among African American Women.* University of Pittsburgh Press, 2000.

Selzer, Jack, and Robert Wess. Introduction. *Kenneth Burke and His Circles.* Ed. Selzer and Wess. West Lafayette, Ind.: Parlor, 2008. ix–xxi.

Sharer, Wendy. "Disintegrating Bodies of Knowledge: Historical Material and Revisionary Histories of Rhetoric." *Rhetorical Bodies.* Ed. Jack Selzer and Sharon Crowley. Madison: University of Wisconsin Press, 1999. 120–42.

Simons, Herbert, and Trevor Melia, eds. *The Legacy of Kenneth Burke.* Madison: University of Wisconsin Press, 1989.

Steedman, Carolyn. *Dust: The Archive and Cultural History.* New Brunswick: Rutgers University Press, 2003.

Sutherland, Christine Mason. "Getting to Know Them: Concerning Research into Four Early Women Writers." Kirsch and Rohan. 28–36.

SANDRA STELTS *and* JEANNETTE SABRE

BURKE BY THE LETTERS

Exploring the Kenneth Burke Archives

File this, throw out that.
Alert the Secretariat
in re each claim and caveat
To better serve the Cause of Alphabet.
Throw out this, file that.

File this, throw that out,
We know beyond all doubt
how Perfect Order reconciles—

And now throw out the files.

"On Putting Things in Order,"
letter from Kenneth Burke to
Ronald Sharp, February 4, 1980

The Special Collections Library at the Pennsylvania State University Libraries houses the Kenneth Burke Papers, rich collections that include Burke's correspondence with prominent twentieth-century Americans and source materials for his major books, essays, poetry, and early fiction.[1] Since 1974 research in the Burke archives has continued to increase and contribute to our understanding of the life and works of Burke and his correspondents.

Our experience with the Burke archives derives from working with the Burke papers in our roles as curator and collection processor. As curator of rare books and manuscripts since 2000, Sandra Stelts is responsible for acquiring Burke materials, preserving them, making them accessible, conducting reference, and maintaining relations with the Kenneth Burke Literary Trust. In addition she promotes the Burke collections through exhibitions, presentations, and collaborative teaching. Since 2002 Jeannette Sabre has assisted Sandra by arranging Burke's papers in archival files and folders, describing collections in finding aids, creating the Rare Books and

Manuscripts' *Kenneth Burke Papers* Web site, and contributing to exhibitions and presentations. She also helps researchers locate relevant materials and is currently developing an item-level index for the second Burke collection.

In caring for the collections and facilitating research, we have come to appreciate the papers' complexity, and our purpose here is to orient readers to the collection with a narrative of the history and nature of the Burke archives. After providing a brief description of the Kenneth Burke Papers, we explore Burke's original archives at his home in Andover, New Jersey, the archives now at Penn State, and the archives' future potential.

BACKGROUND

With the exception of an early family letter from 1906, the papers in the Burke archives begin in 1915. Among these early papers are Burke's letters to Malcolm Cowley, his Peabody High School friend from Pittsburgh, Pennsylvania. Burke's habits of saving letters, notes, and drafts eventually created an archive that extended to his death in 1993. The continuous growth of the archives over Burke's long life almost ensures that we find them variable and changing. Moreover the sweep of their history reveals them to be archives on the move, archives traveling from Burke's home in Andover to Penn State, where the collections are preserved and publicly accessible.

In a 1969 letter from Burke to James Sibley Watson, Burke tells us that he had received at least eight offers from institutions to house his papers (KB to JSW September 11, 1969). His choice of Penn State was in part due to Henry Sams, chair of the Department of English, who had known Burke when they were colleagues at the University of Chicago from 1949 to 1950. At Sams's invitation, Burke first came to Penn State with his wife, Libbie, in 1960 and again in 1963. After another visit in 1972, Burke explained to Sams his reasons for selecting Penn State as a repository for his papers: "By all means, I'd prefer to have the things in one place. And Penn State would be ideal. There are the exceptionally happy associations I have, from the times when Libbie and I were there together. And there is the fact that Pa. is my home state. And there is the absolute confidence I have in one Aitch Sams, as regards both his goodwill and his competence. I would take it for granted without the slightest doubt that your role would be one of absolute fairness for all concerned" (KB to HS August 27, 1972). In 1974, under the directorship of Charles Mann, head of special collections, Penn State accordingly purchased the early portion of Burke's correspondence, and the collection moved from Andover to the Rare Books and Manuscripts room at Penn State. This first collection, Burke-1, dates from 1906 to 1961 and measures twelve linear feet. The earliest letter, written to "Dear Mom and Lewis" on August 8, 1906, shows Burke to be a charming letter writer even at the early age of nine. "Is Grandma there?" he writes and continues, "If she is give her a sweet kiss, and give Lewis one too, and keep one for yourself," and signs his letter, "From Master Kenneth Burke."

Thereafter the collection continues from 1915 to about 1961. Because during this time Burke did not habitually keep carbon copies of his own letters, the collection contains mostly correspondence Burke received, excepting the Burke-Cowley file, which includes some original letters by both Cowley and Burke. Additional notable correspondence in the collection includes letters from Ralph Ellison, Marianne Moore, Howard Nemerov, John Crowe Ransom, Theodore Roethke, Allen Tate, Robert Penn Warren, James Sibley Watson, and William Carlos Williams.

A second correspondence collection (Burke-2) came to Penn State after Burke's death in 1993, purchased from 2000 to 2005 from the Kenneth Burke Literary Trust, under the direction of William Joyce, head of the Special Collections Library at Penn State. This collection, Burke-2, contains Burke's remaining correspondence dating from 1950 to 1993, but largely spanning the years 1960 to 1987. At 25 linear feet it is almost double the size of the earlier Burke collection. This size is partly due to Burke's decision, sometime in the early fifties, to save copies of his own letters. Consequently researchers can reconstruct full interchanges between Burke and many of his correspondents. A few of the collection's notable correspondents include Harold Bloom, Wayne Booth, Malcolm Cowley, Denis Donoghue, Ralph Ellison, Stanley Edgar Hyman, Richard McKeon, Howard Nemerov, and James Sibley Watson.

A third collection in the Kenneth Burke Papers (Burke-3), measuring 18 linear feet, also has moved to Penn State, its purchase from the Kenneth Burke Literary Trust begun in 2008, again under the direction of William Joyce. It spans 1915 to 1969 and consists primarily of manuscripts, notes, correspondence, reviews, and annotated newspaper clippings. Highlights here include additional letters to Malcolm Cowley (1915–1929; 1931), early fiction, responses to student writing at Bennington College, and drafts of Burke's major texts, *PC, ATH, GM,* and *RM.*

While the archives at Penn State hold a great deal of Burke's correspondence, many of Burke's letters are still held in private hands, and some of these small collections also are finding their way to the Burke archives at Penn State. In 2008, Elspeth Hart and France Burke, Burke's daughters, sold to the archives Burke's letters to his first wife, Lily. The Kenneth Burke Letters to Lily Batterham Burke collection, measuring .46 cubic feet and dating from 1918 to 1933 (bulk 1919, 1922–1929), offers a unique view of Burke's life and work during the 1920s. In addition, the archives has received gifts of Burke materials from several Burke scholars, including Charles Elkins, William H. Rueckert, and Robert Wess.

The archives at Penn State certainly hold many of Burke's materials. In considering the establishment of the archive at Penn State, however, it is vital to explore and understand the rich significance of Burke's home in Andover, where Burke lived in the rural countryside among his words. There, manuscripts and notes lie tucked away, annotated books line the shelves, and one may still discern Burke's Latin phrases on his study wall. In recent summers, Burke's sons, Anthony Burke and Michael Burke, and daughter-in-law, Julie Whitaker, have graciously invited and hosted researchers to explore these materials, which in their original setting continue to evoke Burke's presence.

BURKE'S ARCHIVES AT ANDOVER

While the several purchases over time outline the different archival collections, the papers themselves offer a closer view of their role in Burke's life at his home in Andover. Indeed, they tell a story about what Burke's archives meant to him and how he managed and used them.

An illuminating moment suggesting Burke's attachment to his papers occurs after Burke decided to part with his first collection of correspondence. In a letter to Cowley, Burke recounts the appraiser's visit, writing, "Meanwhile, know that Henry Sams dug up some Librarian mazuma for an appraiser to come and inspect my epistolary hoard. This is his second day here—and unless he decides to cut corners or just sniff the rest, at his present rate of speed I compute that he should be here until about Christmas" (KB to MC October 30, 1973). Burke's "epistolary hoard," with its implications of carefully gathered, hidden wealth, seems to deserve time to appreciate. But, unexpectedly the appraiser appears to be gone by the next day, October 31, when Burke wrote to Henry Sams about the sickness and funereal feelings he experienced in going through his papers. "I realize anew," he concluded, "why I have always shied off from the notion of doing an autobiog." Burke wrote again about the experience on November 8 to Howard Nemerov, and by the time he wrote on November 17 to Charles Mann (who had also visited Burke), he had transformed his emotional reactions to the equivalence of a "sneeze" and perfected his analogy to reveal his epistolary hoard as memory, "the attic" of his mind. As he wrote, "I am glad we got to rummaging in the dusty corners of my two attics, the one upstairs, the other behind my eyes. For I found some things I wanted. You sneezed during our performance. I did my equivalent of sneezing after you both had gone" (KB to CM August 17, 1973). Burke's archives were not only storied memories, though. They were also part of a working archive. Through them for example he related to friends and colleagues, worked out ideas, communicated with editors, and negotiated teaching and speaking opportunities. These correspondence files complemented his manuscript files, which included notes, drafts, clippings, reviews, and other materials he needed at hand as he wrote his essays and books. Both kinds of files were useful to him for orienting his present-day concerns and moving them into the future. In creating this usable archive for his writing and day-to-day needs, however, he was also composing a personal and intellectual history as he lived.

Given the value of his papers to Burke and their increasing numbers as the years progressed, Burke needed ways to manage his letters and manuscripts. In both instances, Burke used titling strategies to identify papers and locate items. On his letters for example readers will notice that Burke typically wrote, in a spidery hand in the right-hand margin, the name of the person or organization under which he wanted to file the letter. He also typically dated his letters. These two practices allowed him to arrange his letters in a box covering a current time span (say from 1960 to 1963), alphabetically by the correspondents' last names, and within each correspondent's group of letters, from the latest to the earliest letter. So for example he could easily find Cowley's last letter as the first letter under "Cowley" in the box he was currently using as a file. After he began to keep copies of his own letters (often a carbon on the reverse of the received letter), he would also be able locate his interfiled response. Photocopies begin to appear in the files in place of carbons in the years after 1981, courtesy of a new Canon photocopier given to him by Mr. Raymond Posel, a grateful businessman who had read Burke in college.

In respect to his manuscripts and notes, Burke tended to group subject- and chronologically related materials together, as seen for example in his Bennington papers, arranged by academic year. Subject titles appear in Burke's handwriting on the enclosing brownish-red folders that came to Penn State. These identifying subject titles correlate to main entries in the inventory that Burke made with his son Anthony Burke, an inventory that relates the subject files by means of an overarching alpha-numerical system. Burke-3 for example extends from P.05 through R.20. When associated subjects do appear in different files, Burke's subject titles help researchers identify them in the inventory, as for example the dispersed notes and drafts having to do with *RM*.

While this system seems quite organized, Burke's letters reveal that his archive at Andover frequently shifted from order to chaos and back again. During much of Burke's life, his wife Libbie helped him keep his files under control. But after her death in 1969, Burke, left alone, ordered his own papers—notes as well as letters—in the periodic "Palace Revolution" he described to Paul Kuntz: "And since [Libbie] had been a crack private secretary before she gave that up to bear two sons, she was wonderful when it came to keeping things in ORDER (there's that word again!), whereas I tend to get surrounded by piles of books, letters, notes, until at times even the table in the kitchen is so cluttered that I am eating off one tiny corner—then, lo! there comes a Palace Revolution, I spend several days filing stuff, and then the accumulation of flotsam and jetsam and disjecta membra and detritus and Unfinished Bizz in general starts piling up again" (KB to PK February 29, 1980). The house may have become cluttered at times, but as Burke explains to Watson on two different occasions the satisfactions of ordering his papers were considerable, even sensory and approximating the divine. "Of a sud. everything seems so clear, I know exactly where to file each one of my notes. And when things are that way, Purgatory and even Hell are Paradise (and maybe that's what Dante's neat schematizing of the after-life ultimately meant)" (KB to JSW March 16, 1973). "I got my papers in order—and to have everything back in its proper file is as balm from Heaven" (KB to JSW June 9, 1974). Ultimately however Burke may not have been completely comfortable with the satisfactions of perfect order. Tellingly balm "from Heaven," and Dante's "neat schematizing of the after-life" are not associated with ordinary life in this world, and in Burke's poem, "ON PUTTING THINGS IN ORDER," we see another attitude toward the "Perfect Order" of ideally kept files:

> File this, throw that out,
> We know beyond all doubt
> how Perfect Order reconciles—
> And now throw out the files.
> (KB to Ronald Sharp February 4, 1980)

In his letter to Ronald Sharp, Burke interpreted his poem as rebelling against the "certain kind of futurity" portended by perfectly ordered indexes and files: Nothing feels better than getting something in order. So an index is a kind of killer, while at the same time it does have a certain kind of futurity, towards which my poem rebels, in hoping for a Next Phase. (KB to RS February 4, 1980)

Burke's ambiguous attitudes toward "perfect order" are evident in his filing habits, ones that practically ensured that his archives would never exemplify "perfect order." Despite his systems, Burke observed, "[M]y Filing System gets as entangled as I am" (KB to Mark Shell March 25, 1980). Burke analyzed one of their problems, their dispersed nature, when he wrote to Cheryl Plumb: I tried to locate [a certain woman's] name for you, but the business of living in a bureau drawer raises hell with one's filing system. (KB to CP August 8, 1977, filed under Inquiry)

Burke's comment about "living in a bureau drawer" likely refers to his many travels on the academic circuit after 1961 and to his habit of packing up and carrying correspondence with him. Complicating matters further, upon his return to Andover, Burke may not have always immediately filed his letters in his main files.

Additional features of his filing practices may have added to the complexity of Burke's Andover archive. For example it seems Burke often took out and set aside letters from his files, as he did temporarily with some of Matthew Josephson's letters (KB to David Shi March 18, 1976). Burke also filed letters in a number of different places, as instanced when Burke wrote to Christine Graham that composer Louis Calabro's letters were probably with his music notes rather than in the letter files (KB to CG June 8, 1977). And, Burke may have filed letters from the same person in two different locations, under both personal and organizational names: letters from Henry Rago are filed under "Rago" and under *Poetry*. Although Burke himself occasionally did note related letters on his correspondence, he recognized the problem when he wrote, "[My filing system] never was much good, since it would have needed so much cross-filing" (KB to CP August 8, 1977, filed under Inquiry).[2]

Additional dispersions occurred as the collections grew and the number of boxes and grouped materials multiplied, taking their places among unfiled "flotsam and jetsam." At Andover, even the files themselves could become landmarks, as occurred with the correspondence file by the piano where Burke hid his unsigned will and thirty-grand certificates (KB to Anthony Burke September 20, 1978 and October

3, 1978, filed under Family). Ultimately Andover itself became the file container that Burke and Anthony Burke explored, room by room, closet by closet, and hallway by hallway, to inventory the different manuscript files (telephone conversation with Sandra Stelts, 6/18/2009).

Not surprisingly even when he had filed his papers, Burke experienced some problems in locating them. Writing to Robert Zachary he notes, "I forget whether I told you (and it's simpler to say it again than to consult the files) . . ." (KB to RZ October 9, 1979). Likewise, when Paul Mariani asked to see letters from William Carlos Williams, Burke referred him to Yale and Penn State, writing, "Otherwise (worse luck!) I'd have to start digging among the archives here" (KB to PM April 14, 1977, filed under Inquiry).

Yet Burke often did find the materials he needed, and the ways he discovered them are instructive. Alert to the moment and open to discovery, Burke sometimes found what he was looking for while looking for something else. As he wrote to Geoffrey Fitzgerald, "I can't find those notes, though I may find them when I'm looking for something else" (KB to GF January 30, 1980). Tracking, too, was part of his method, as he explains in a letter to Robert Zachary: "I haven't been able to find the vast batch of notes I took in connection with the sociological gazette I mentioned. But I did come upon my copy of a letter which places the issue for me. 'Tis to Allen D. Grimshaw, editor of *The American Sociologist*. And that also puts me on the track of a letter from a guy who had seen my letter to Grimshaw" (KB to RZ February 25, 1980). Moreover, sometimes Burke made surprising discoveries in exploring his own files, as we learn when he exclaimed to Cowley in July 1974, "Wow! I just discovered among my papers a salary check for $2,300.00, which was paid me at the end of January and is marked 'void after 90 days'" (KB to MC July 1, 1974, "Next morn").

In the end, the image of Burke writing, "surrounded by piles of books, letters, notes" (KB to Paul Kuntz, February 29, 1980), suggests the working conditions under which Burke felt most comfortable most of the time. Burke's titling strategies did create good records for the future. But ironically, despite having designed his filing system for research, he was not so attentive to it that he always could find what he was looking for. In his later life as the papers multiplied, he sometimes got lost in his own files and found them just easier not to use, and when he did consult them, he had to start digging.

BURKE'S ARCHIVES AT PENN STATE

Andover, center of Burke's intellectual and social activities, still exerts an enormous influence on us and on Burke scholars, and we count ourselves fortunate to have visited Burke's home and experienced its presence as place. While exploring the house, the grounds, and other buildings in the Burke compound, one cannot help but imagine Burke in the physicality of the location. Mindful that archives removed from their physical setting can lose layers of significance,[3] we have consciously maintained a close relationship with Andover and nurtured a continuum that shapes the character of Burke's archives at Penn State and affects the range of resources researchers need to engage it.

After his early papers had moved to Penn State, Burke himself traced this continuum from Andover to University Park by visiting the archive in 1985, 1988, and 1991. One especially memorable occasion occurred in 1985 when Kenneth Burke and Malcolm Cowley spoke as part of the Year of the Pennsylvania Writer celebration. During this visit, Burke, Malcolm Cowley, and Paul Jay, editor of the Burke-Cowley correspondence, talked with Charles Mann specifically about the Burke-Cowley correspondence. Both recorded conversations are preserved in the archives. Another memorable visit occurred in 1991 at the dedication of the bust of Burke, sculpted by Virginia Burks. On that occasion Burke signed our guest book, describing his interests as "speech & motivation," and upon encountering his likeness, greeted it boisterously, "Hello, you old son of a bitch!" In 2000, the Burke archives moved from the old rare books room on the third floor of Pattee Library to its current location in the Special Collections Library in Paterno Library. The enormous sculpted head of Burke—at once impish, friendly, and demonic—moved with his collection and continues to evoke his presence near his archives.

In our archival practices we also have consciously reinforced connections with Burke's archives in Andover. We have documented Andover through photographs, and we maintain good relations with the Kenneth Burke Literary Trust. Not least in importance, we have striven to maintain the intellectual integrity of Burke's files by keeping their original conceptual order. Burke-1 and Burke-2 continue to follow Burke's filing system for his correspondence collections: chronological, alphabetical by correspondents' last names, and therein chronological. These sound practices of dating letters and identifying filing locations allowed us to make the two collections even more accessible. To this end, while keeping the original conceptual order, we arranged files by year (instead of in groups of several years), and the individual files from earliest to latest letters (rather than from latest to earliest). In processing Burke-3 we were again able to maintain original order, by refiling and describing folders in accordance with the inventory's alphanumerical order and subject descriptions.

We also connect to Burke's life at Andover through the letters themselves. Standing at the photocopier machine as we copy letters for researchers, we chuckle at Burke's wit and word play and feel connected, even after many long years, to Burke's life at Andover—to news of his houseguests, his hangovers, his daily routines, and the circadian rhythms of a vibrant intellectual life in an agrarian setting: references to planting potatoes or building a dam for example or a loving note from Libbie on the back of a letter, reminding him to take the laundry down from the line (Burke-3).

Because of the continuum, the archives now at Penn State in many ways mirror the original ones at Andover. And as papers have moved from Andover to Penn State, the Penn State archives consist of dispersed materials in different collections. Moreover, like the original collections, the ones at Penn State are often in flux. Temporarily removed, files often wait in the vault or hold room to be refiled or used by researchers. Something of Burke's own research methods also are inevitably and not surprisingly part of contemporary researchers' experiences. Like Burke, researchers "explore" the archives and—alert to the moment—follow leads and make surprising discoveries, sometimes while looking for something else. Today's researchers, though, explore without the creator's knowledge, working instead from the different perspectives of other times and communities. How then do they make their discoveries?

As many historical researchers realize, immersing oneself in archival materials is time consuming, yet invaluable in building context and focusing research topics. However most successful researchers, typically visiting the archives under time constraints, also bring background information to their search to define research questions and increase their chances of recognizing the significance of items they view.[4] Moreover Burke researchers, in particular, frequently come to the archive with knowledge of relevant dates, names, and subject terms, not only to explore particular files but also to access collections.

While Burke researchers are often skilled in finding relevant secondary resources to gain necessary background information, the usefulness of some kinds of materials may not be as immediately apparent. Calendars for example, such as those at the end of Jack Selzer's *Kenneth Burke in Greenwich Village* (1996) and Ann George and Jack Selzer's *Kenneth Burke in the 1930s* (2007), are particularly useful in identifying people and times in Burke's early life. Also helpful, especially for searching by subject or term, are the indexes at the ends of the published collections of Burke's correspondence with Malcolm Cowley (1988), William Carlos Williams (2003), and William H. Rueckert (2003). Articles on related subjects whose authors have used Burke collections may also provide leads through citations and their approaches to archival materials.[5] Other valuable resources include the searchable bibliographies of secondary resources and Burke's own writings available at the online *KB Journal.*

It might also prove useful for scholars to expand their archival research beyond the archives at Penn State to find Burke's letters in the archives of other scholars and writers. For example Burke's correspondence can be found at the Newberry Library in Chicago, the Library of Congress, the John Hay Library at Brown University, the Van Pelt Library at the University of Pennsylvania, the Beinecke Library at Yale University, the Lilly Library at Indiana University, and the archives at the Princeton University Library. Burke might be pleased that originals of his letters and documents are held at these and other repositories throughout the United States, in addition to Penn State. In his 1973 letter to Phoebe Hyman (likely in response to her inquiry), he told her not to return his letters, saying: "As to the letters: Heck, no. I doan want them. For I probably have duplicates of nearly all. And it would be best that we have all such things distributed" (KB to PH January 12, 1973). Today many of Burke's letters to Hyman reside at the Library of Congress. To identify relevant materials at these and other sites, several electronic resources exist. These include the electronic resources ArchiveGrid, ArchivesUSA (also found in Archive Finder), Repositories of Primary Resources, and Ready 'Net, Go! Archival Internet Resources. Advanced searches in WorldCat can be limited by archival materials, and Google searches can be effective by adding "papers" or "letter" to a personal name search.

Several finding aids for identifying kinds of materials and particular items in the Burke archives at Penn State are available at the Rare Books and Manuscripts' *Kenneth Burke Papers* Web site. They include a list of correspondents within the first Burke collection (1906; 1915–1961); an ongoing, item-level inventory of the second Burke collection (currently from 1950 to 1982); a historic inventory of the third Burke collection (1915–1969) created by Anthony Burke and Kenneth Burke; and a guide and annotated item-level inventory of the Letters of Kenneth Burke to Lily Batterham Burke (1918–1933; bulk 1919, 1922–1929). There is also a link to a finding aid for the Kenneth Burke Letters to William H. Rueckert (1959–1987). Researchers who come to the archives can also access the correspondents' card index to the first Burke collection. Because the collections overlap in time, researchers may need to consult finding aids for more than one collection. For example at least three collections, the first and third Burke collections and the Letters of Kenneth Burke to Lily Batterham Burke, include materials related to the 1920s. Moreover some correspondents' letters may be included in more than one collection, as instanced with the Cowley correspondence, which appears across the first, second, and third Burke collections. If these aids do not help, there is always the option of a friendly conversation with Sandra and Jeannette, or a lunch with Jack Selzer, who has been an unfailingly helpful and generous guide to visiting researchers.[6]

WIDENING CIRCLES: THE EXPANDING USEFULNESS OF THE KENNETH BURKE ARCHIVES

The Burke archives are a very broad and deep archive, a record of American cultural history in the twentieth century, reflecting the fascinating set of movements, circles, and individuals that Burke engaged. In their introduction to *Kenneth Burke and His Circles*, Selzer and Wess describe the Kenneth Burke Papers as an "intellectual biography," one that shows connections to almost every movement of the twentieth century: "Considered in their entirety, the Kenneth Burke papers constitute a rough intellectual biography of Kenneth Burke; they document the manifold intellectual associations that Burke developed and sustained from his boyhood until his death. . . . The contents provide a vehicle for understanding Burke's connections to just about every scholarly and critical and artistic (and social scientific and political) movement of substance in the twentieth century" (xii). A glance at the last ten years of our correspondence with researchers reveals much about the range of possibilities for scholarship in the rich and fertile archives. We have received inquiries from researchers whose interests were in Burke and other authors and philosophers (Shakespeare, Coleridge, and Plato for example); and in Burke and his individual correspondents (Wayne Booth, Ralph Ellison, Allen Tate, Hayden White, Scofield Thayer, John Crowe Ransom, Robert Bechtold Heilman, Harold Lasswell, Robert Cantwell, Henry Sams, Mikhail Bakhtin, Robert Penn Warren, Howard Nemerov, Harold Rosenberg, Sidney Hook, Jerome S. Bruner, Dell Hymes, Dorothy Day, Susan Sontag, Richard McKeon, Hugh Duncan, Jerome S. Bruner, Kenneth D. Benne, William Carlos Williams, Paul de Man, and Robert Coates). Researchers' interests in Burke and diverse topics also display a remarkable range: Burke and his theory of the grotesque; his impact on mid-twentieth-century American social sciences; Burke at Bennington College; Burke on race and racism, music, psychology, ecology, Christian Science, principles of psychophysiology, myth and ideology, transcendence, psychological theories, and theories of identification; Burke and political figures, nuclear testing, World War II, and the Cold War; Burke in the 1930s; and Burke and the University of Chicago, Yaddo, the Bureau of Social Hygiene, and Drew University. Ultimately the Burke archives may offer the possibility of exploring as many Burke topics as there are researchers' interests.

While the range of scholarship here seems far reaching, in the last ten years new accessions have opened new opportunities for further extending scholarship on Kenneth Burke. As researchers begin to turn their attention to the essays and reviews Burke wrote during the later part of his life, between 1966 and 1987, the large second correspondence collection offers materials for contextualizing them. Penn State's online finding aid for this collection also allows researchers to identify the verse Burke included in his letters (searchable under "poem," title, or initial words). Although the second collection includes a few typescripts, the third collection offers even more. This collection, dating from 1915 to 1969, includes a wealth of Burke writings only suggested in the historic inventory. Finally Burke's letters to his first wife, Lily Batterham Burke, shed new light on Burke's activities from 1918 to about 1929.

In addition to new accessions, technology is transforming the nature of archival work and its potential contributions to Burke scholarship. We are mindful that in this age of access to information and mass digitization of library materials, special collections libraries are focusing on making unique collections available outside of their home institutions through digitization, and we are exploring ways to scan portions of the Burke papers, beginning with his writings in Burke-3. While we wrestle with the difficulties of digitization, at the same time we actively work to make Burke's papers easy to access from Penn State. We describe the papers in finding aids and Web sites, photocopy materials, and provide reference services by e-mail and in person for researchers, classes, and conferences. We have helped the teaching faculty, both at Penn State and long-distance (at Texas Christian University for example through photocopies made available to the students of Ann George) to integrate the Burke archives into the classroom.

The Burke archives, indeed, are encouraging the development of the next generation of Burke scholars. Our practices and programs have enhanced the teaching of Burke to undergraduate and graduate students by providing students with the opportunities to work with engaging primary materials that instruct and illuminate. For example, when Jack Selzer began seriously to pursue Burke studies, he taught courses such as "Kenneth Burke in Greenwich Village" to a dozen undergraduate honors students, who studied Burke by working in the archives. At the graduate level, Selzer has also led five seminars on Burke in which Selzer encouraged and guided students toward archival research. In addition to learning about Burke, both undergraduates and graduates have gained hands-on experience and education regarding the necessary skills and intricacies of archival studies. They learn to sift through the background of Burke's various friends and professional contacts. They learn how to decipher handwriting, how to handle fragile materials safely, how to obtain rights and permissions for quotation, and how to track down resources in other collections.

Giving students the opportunity to engage in archival research produced fine results. Several of the undergraduate students who participated in the Greenwich Village course developed honors theses out of their coursework and as a consequence went on to advanced studies at other universities. Furthermore the graduate students who participated in Selzer's Burke seminars have often published articles that grew from their archival research, placing their work in top journals such as *Rhetoric Society Quarterly, Philosophy and Rhetoric, Quarterly Journal of Speech, College Composition and Communication,* and *College English.* The articles suggest the variety of topics that have emerged from archival study: there have been essays on Burke and the Bureau of Social Hygiene (Jack Selzer); Burke's engagement with progressive education (Enoch); Burke and general semantics (Nicotra); Burke and Nietzsche (Hawhee); Burke and technology (Pruchnic); Burke and sociologist Dell Hymes (Jordan); and so on.

Our active promotion of the Kenneth Burke archives is further widening the range of Burke scholarship as researchers become more aware of the archives' immense resources for understanding Burke's life and thought. In the early days of the collection, from 1974 to 1998, Charles Mann personally welcomed, initiated, and guided individual researchers through the collection in his informed and friendly way. Now we rely heavily on our Web site and our finding aids to provide more wide-ranging information about the collection to researchers, most of whom contact us by e-mail. We have made presentations on engaging with the archives at conferences (for the 2005 Kenneth Burke Society meetings at Penn State, the 2008 meetings at Villanova, and the 2009 Rhetoric Society of America [RSA] meetings at Penn State), and we have assisted Jack Selzer with a series of Burke workshops for the RSA. We have also highlighted aspects of the Burke archives in educational ex-hibitions, as instanced in the fall of 2009 exhibition "Life at Yaddo: Glimpses from Penn State," part of a celebration of Yaddo organized by the New York Public Library. Our special collections contribution to this national initiative featured dozens of letters by Burke and the New Zealand writer Janet Frame (from the Janet Frame Papers, 1925–1990), who became acquainted with each other at Yaddo in 1970.

Through internships students also have assisted in this outreach for the Burke archives, deepening their education by assisting in designing and mounting ex-hibitions. Since 2002 we have mounted four Burke-related exhibitions—two of them with the assistance of student curators, including "'She Taught Me to Blush': Marianne Moore and Kenneth Burke," with selection and text by Claire Sigrist, an undergraduate intern. "Kenneth Burke and His Circles," mounted for the 2005 Kenneth Burke Society meetings, was guest-curated by faculty, current and former graduate students, and special collections staff. Student curators have also spoken in our series of public gallery talks.

Since the first boxes of correspondence arrived at Penn State from Andover in 1974, the Burke archives has expanded and extended its potential usefulness for transforming Burke scholarship. Largely through the foresight and efforts of people who believed in the archives' value, the Burke archives have grown, become in-creasingly accessible through new technologies and teaching opportunities, and delighted new generations of Burke scholars. During the more than forty years that Penn State has been associated with Kenneth Burke, the university itself has become a center of community and conversation, bringing together our faculty, our students, and our contacts with researchers, the Burke family, and the Ken-neth Burke Literary Trust. Penn State's intellectual and financial commitment to the Burke papers—arguably our most important archival collection—includes long-term plans to acquire Burke's annotated books and additional manuscripts at An-dover. We are actively seeking endowment funds to ensure the future acquisition, processing, digitizing, preservation, and wider use of the collection. As custodians of the Burke papers, we are in a unique position to observe a secondary community of correspondence—that of the widening circle of Burke scholars and their inter-connectedness. It is our hope that through our efforts, others will become engaged in our epistolary community.

NOTES

1. The authors acknowledge the cooperation of the Kenneth Burke Literary Trust for permission to quote from Kenneth Burke's unpublished notes, drafts, and letters. Permis-sion is also granted from Rare Books and Manuscripts, the Pennsylvania State University Libraries, for quotations from unpublished notes and letters in the Kenneth Burke Pa-pers, Rare Books and Manuscripts, Special Collections Library, Pennsylvania State Uni-versity Libraries.

2. We are remedying the need for "cross-filing" in Burke-2 by creating a cross-referenced, item-level index, so researchers will be able to locate all the letters of correspondents in the collection. See Sabre and Hamburger, "A Case for Item-Level Indexing."

3. See Alexander, who develops this point as instanced in the artists' colony Yaddo. Andover, like Yaddo, was an intellectual and social center that fostered a multitude of friendships and cross-influences.

4. For a useful study of the conditions for successful historical research, see Duff.

5. See also Brummett and Young, and Huglen and Rountree. Both articles are useful for identifying contemporary approaches to Burke scholarship.

6. For the research value of consulting archivists, see Johnson and Duff.

WORKS CITED

Alexander, Ben. "'What a Setting for a Mystery': Yaddo, the Yaddo Records, and the Memory of Place." *Archival Science* 9.1–2 (2009): 87–98.

Brummett, Barry, and Anna M. Young. "Some Uses of Burke in Communication Studies." *KB Journal* 2.2 (2006).

Burke, Anthony. Personal conversation with Sandra Stelts. June 18, 2009. Telephone.

Burke, Kenneth. *Letters from Kenneth Burke to William H. Rueckert, 1959–1987*. Ed. William H. Rueckert. West Lafayette, Ind.: Parlor, 2003.

Burke, Kenneth, and Malcolm Cowley. *The Selected Correspondence of Kenneth Burke and Malcolm Cowley 1915–1981*. Ed. Paul Jay. New York: Penguin, 1988.

Burke, Kenneth, and William Carlos Williams. *The Humane Particulars: The Collected Letters of William Carlos Williams and Kenneth Burke*. Ed. James H. East. Columbia: University of South Carolina Press, 2003.

Duff, Wendy. "Accidentally Found on Purpose: Information-Seeking Behaviors of Historians in Archives." *Library Quarterly* 72.4 (2002): 472–96.

Enoch, Jessica. "Becoming Symbol-Wise: Kenneth Burke's Pedagogy of Critical Reflection." *College Composition and Communication* 56.2 (2004): 272–6.

George, Ann, and Jack Selzer. *Kenneth Burke in the 1930s*. Columbia: University of South Carolina Press, 2007.

Hawhee, Debra. "Burke and Nietzsche." *Quarterly Journal of Speech* 85 (1999): 129–45.

Huglen, Mark E., and Clarke Rountree. "Editors' Essay: The Future of Burke Studies." *KB Journal* 4:2 (2008).

Jack, Jordynn. "'The Piety of Degradation': Kenneth Burke, the Bureau of Social Hygiene, and *Permanence and Change*." *Quarterly Journal of Speech* 90.4 (2004): 446–68.

Johnson, Catherine A., and Wendy M. Duff. "Chatting Up the Archivist: Social Capital and the Archival Researcher." *American Archivist* 67 (2004): 113–29.

Jordan, Jay. "Dell Hymes, Kenneth Burke's Identification, and the Birth of Sociolinguistics." *Rhetoric Review* 24 (2005): 264–79.

The Kenneth Burke Letters to Lily Batterham Burke, 1918–1933 (bulk 1919, 1922–1929). Rare Books and Manuscripts. Special Collections Library. The Pennsylvania State University Libraries.

The Kenneth Burke Papers. Burke-1 (1906–1960, bulk 1915–1960), Burke-2 (1950–1993, bulk 1960–1987), and Burke-3 (1915–1967). Rare Books and Manuscripts. Special Collections Library. Pennsylvania State University Libraries.

Nicotra, Jodie. "Dancing Attitudes in Wartime: Kenneth Burke and General Semantics." *Rhetorical Society Quarterly* 39.4 (2009): 331–52.

Pruchnic, Jeff. " Rhetoric, Cybernetics, and the Work of the Body in Burke's Body of Work." *Rhetoric Review* 25.3 (2006): 275–96.

Sabre, Jeannette Mercer, and Susan Hamburger. "A Case for Item-Level Indexing: The Kenneth Burke Papers at the Pennsylvania State University." *Journal of Archival Organization* 6.1–2 (2008): 24–46.

Selzer, Jack. *Kenneth Burke in Greenwich Village: Conversing with the Moderns, 1915–1931.* Madison: University of Wisconsin Press, 1996.

Selzer, Jack, and Robert Wess, eds. *Kenneth Burke and His Circles.* West Lafayette, Ind.: Parlor, 2008.

ANN GEORGE

FINDING THE TIME FOR BURKE

If there is one thing rhetoric scholars have agreed on, it is that Kenneth Burke was ahead of his time. As Greg Jay observes, "It seems that the uncanny Burke is always one step ahead of his fellow critics" (169). Burke, we've been told over the last thirty years, "anticipate[d] so much of what is considered avant-garde today" (Fish 500); "anticipated . . . what have become the most stylish paradoxes in the post-structuralist armory" (Harris 455); "anticipate[d] the critique of nature and totality developed by the Frankfurt School" (Wolfe 67); "anticipate[d]" the "resolutely skeptical . . . postmodern/poststructural project" (Carmichael 144); "anticipate[d] both Thomas Kuhn and Gramsci" (Tompkins 124); "[is credited with having] anticipated . . . the 'rhetorical turn' in the human sciences" (Simons and Melia vii). Burke is a theorist "who knew too much, too soon" (Lentricchia 86), who "pointed out" language's instability "decades before today's critical theorists" (Brummett xv), and whose "notion of the symbolic act is an anticipation . . . of current notions of the primacy of language" (Jameson 508). New historicist and cultural materialist critics are his "progeny," media and cultural studies critics his "legatees" (Holbrook 11, 12). Wayne Booth demurs only slightly when commenting, "I would not want to claim that Burke foreknew *everything* that Barthes, Derrida, de Man *et cie* have shocked the academic world with, but I am sure that, if they ever get around to reading him, they will be tempted to moderate their claims to originality" (361n10).

But what do we mean when we say that Burke was ahead of his time? Certainly it is a way of acknowledging his brilliance and importance for rhetorical studies. We might wonder, though, about scholars' determination to replay this litany of Burke's propheticness, which surely says as much about us as it does about Burke. It points to a certain way of using and valuing theory, a way of doing—or not doing—history. The Burke-ahead-of-his-time theme conjures an image of Burke waiting all these years to be understood—or more pointedly to be understood by *us*. Indeed Rosalind Gabin argues that once European structuralist and Marxist theory of the 1960s "fertilized" American thought, Burke became both more acceptable and accessible, prompting her to claim, "Burke has found, finally, the rhetorical moment for his message" (198).

But surely the pressing economic and political exigencies of, say, the 1930s constituted a significant "rhetorical moment" for Burke's message. Burke at least seems to have thought so, judging by his amazing productivity (five books, countless essays and reviews) during this period. Claiming that Burke's rhetorical moment is here and now makes sense only if what we mean by rhetorical moment is a time when scholars agree with him—as if theorists' success is to be measured by their academic uptake. Such a claim also implies that Burke belongs not in "his" time, but in "our" time—or that he belongs in no time—which is to say that he belongs in every time or that he's outside of time altogether. Burke has, in our account of things, become unmoored in time—a troubling limbo for a theorist who insisted that all acts occur within specific scenes.

Finally, the depiction of Burke ahead of his time suggests how invested scholars have become in the image of Burke marginalized or misunderstood by his contemporaries, particularly in the 1930s. We see Burke "stand[ing] on the fringe" (Wolin 221) or locked in heroic struggle, a Depression-era David pitted against the Goliath of positivism, orthodoxy, and narrow estheticism. Burke, we assume, was not read or appreciated by his early contemporaries because of his unique understanding that all experience is ideologically constructed; this line of thinking often leads to the conclusion that Burke left no mark on his contemporary scene; that, rhetorically, "Burke's adaptation to his milieu was largely ineffective" (Wolin 39).[1]

Of course, in the 1930s Burke *was* dismissed, embattled, misunderstood. Sometimes. But might not the story be more complicated? As Ross Wolin has observed, with a few notable exceptions, Burke scholars have not been especially curious about how Burke's books were understood and evaluated in their immediate rhetorical moment (xii). This essay seeks to reopen the question of Burke's contemporary reception, taking *Permanence and Change* (1935) as a case in point. In doing so, it also demonstrates how archives ask us to reexamine what we "know" about Burke by reexamining how we've come to this knowledge. Archives, that is, can change *what* we study (his rhetorical strategies as well as his theory, how he wrote as well as what he wrote, his relationships with unremembered readers as well as famous friends), and they change *how* we study, enabling us to employ Burke's methodologies in our histories—to read dramatistically, to use everything. And then archives help us begin to define what "everything" means in each case. This essay capitalizes on three kinds of archival materials to provide a fuller account of Burke's interactions with his contemporaries: Burke's correspondence with friends, editors, and admirers; a newly acquired folder of unrecorded reviews of *PC;* and Burke's planning notes for the book.

These archival materials show that, contrary to Burkean lore, Burke's contemporaries typically did not perceive his work as irrelevant or inscrutable; indeed they often praised it highly. There's no doubt that Burke's 1930s work was contested, but far from signaling ineffectiveness, this controversy reflects instead his considerable cultural power. The Burke who emerges from this study, then, is not the inconsequential, out-of-step figure we've come to expect. This Burke mattered—to his time as much as to ours. Critical to my reexamination of contemporary responses to *PC* is an assumption that we will not fully understand what the reviews signify without first getting some perspective on Burke's involvement in the 1930s culture wars, so my analysis begins there.

BURKE AND THE 1930S "BATTLE OF THE BOOKS"

Scholars' image of Burke in the 1930s is typically defined by two moments. The first, a prime source of our perception of Burke as a loner, is an oft-cited line from one of Burke's letters to his best friend, Malcolm Cowley. Asked at a party why he did not support communism, Burke reported that, while he supported communism's goals, "I am not a joiner of societies" (KB to MC June 4, 1932). But as Jack Selzer and I have argued, this is a fitting description of Burke only if joining is understood as official, card-carrying membership. The record shows that Burke was part of many formal and informal political and literary circles (George and Selzer 2–3). The second of these defining moments is Burke's supposed ostracism at the First American Writers' Congress in response to his "Revolutionary Symbolism in America" speech. However, although Burke was certainly hurt by the response, evidence suggests that it was probably less harsh than has been thought (George and Selzer 12–29). In Burkean terms, then, scholars have traditionally embraced two *un*representative anecdotes, concluding "that despite great praise, Burke was largely misunderstood and misused" (Wolin xiii). Burke himself, of course, often promotes this image. He famously—and vividly—remembers the night of the Writers' Congress speech when, half asleep, he heard his name called out like "a dirty word" and imagined "that excrement was dripping from [his] tongue" ("Thirty Years Later" 507). Likewise Burke's letters repeatedly register "considerable disgruntlement or dismay" (KB to RPW February 26, 1938), even "sleep-destroying fury," over friends and critics whom he feels have misread his books (KB to WCW December 21, 1937). And Ross Wolin is certainly correct in arguing that Burke was often motivated by a determination to clarify his positions.

But this image of Burke ahead of—and hence unappreciated during—his time is, as I've suggested, based on the stories scholars have chosen to tell (or not) and how those stories are contextualized (or not). So for example while it is fair to say that Burke's Writers' Congress speech met some resistance, Burke's experience at the congress could be put into different perspective by juxtaposing it with that of Edmund Wilson, Max Eastman, and Sidney Hook, who, because they openly criticized Stalin and the Communist Party, were not even invited to attend. Burke, on the other hand, had not only been invited to speak; he had helped plan the event and, even after his provocative speech, was elected to the League of American Writers executive board. Compared to Wilson, Hook, and others, then, Burke was not marginalized; he was an insider. When scholars (myself included) discuss Burke's reception, we often similarly emphasize reviews that provoked rebuttals from Burke, and understandably so: these exchanges are tremendously interesting and revealing. But in doing so, we reinforce our image of the embattled Burke, losing sight of more positive contemporary representations. To give just one example, Granville Hicks's critical review of *Counter-Statement* gets more air time than Isidor Schneider's glowing review, which proclaims *Counter-Statement* "a work of revolutionary importance introducing . . . a new"—and much needed—"vocabulary of rhetoric" with which to talk about how texts effect readers (4).

Scholars can also gain perspective on Burke's 1930s reception by reading reviews as part of what Walter Kalaidjian calls the "super-charged ambiance" of Depression-era culture wars (161). It was, Burke remarked in 1932, "a kind of 'open season' for criticism" when a writer could "shoot arrows . . . into the air with perfect confidence that, wherever he turns, he will find them sticking in the hearts of his friends" (*Auscultation* 97). Seen in this light, the martial language of Burke's well-known rhetorical parlor, written during the 1930s, is quite telling; in this parlor, people are "engaged in a *heated* discussion": "Someone . . . *comes to your defense;* another *aligns himself against* you, to either the embarrassment or gratification of your *opponent,* depending upon the quality of your *ally's* assistance" (*PLF* 110–11; emphasis added). The Left was particularly fractured; leftists, Jay Franklin quips, "have their isms and their spasms" and "pigheadedly refuse" to collaborate (34, 33)—a sentiment echoed in Burke's memories of "sub sub-splinters of a splinter group" busily "taking things apart instead of putting them all together" (Skodnick 16; Woodcock 708).

At issue among artists and intellectuals were questions not only about what direction the country should take politically and economically, but also about how "the good life" might be defined and, more important, what kind of writing—by whom, for whom, in what genres—would bring this good life into being. These questions consumed political and critical discussions (the American Writers' Congress was designed, in large part, to address them),[2] and they were taken up by every artist at least implicitly through content and form. John Reed Clubbers shouted "Art is a class weapon," while Allen Tate scorned writers "who drape their political notions upon the arts simply because they have not the political talent to put them into action" ("Poetry and Politics" 308).

This "Battle of the Books," as Burke called it, was waged ferociously in literary essays and book reviews ("War, Response, and Contradiction" 235).[3] If we read reviews of only Burke's work, it is easy to conclude that he was being uniquely vilified. But during the 1930s culture wars, there was plenty of criticism to go around. For instance in "New Voices: The Promise of Our Youngest Writers," C. Hartley Grattan does indeed relegate Burke to membership in "the Fastidious Movement, which is attempting to make a last stand for leisure class dilettantism" (285). But Burke is in good company: Yvor Winters, Kay Boyle, John Crowe Ransom, and Robert Penn Warren round out this group. Tate criticizes Burke in "Poetry and Politics," but he criticizes I. A. Richards in the same breath. Tate also savages Midwestern poets Masters, Lindsay, and Sandburg for their "slovenly verse" and "poverty of thought" ("Poetry and Politics" 309), then turns on Robert Frost for his "average and toneless sensibility" (309). The Southern Agrarians revered T. S. Eliot, but William Carlos Williams later claimed that the publication of *The Wasteland* "wiped out [his work toward "the essence of a new art form"] as if an atom bomb had been dropped upon it" (174). So much criticism was directed at Eliot, in fact, that when Tate reviewed *Ash Wednesday,* he felt obliged to spend half his time chiding critics for dismissing Eliot's poetry because they disliked his religion (*Poetry* 105–6). Archibald Macleish's repeated reversals of fortunes marked him as "something of a lightning rod for the period's turbulent intellectual tempests" (Kalaidjian 160), and Muriel Rukeyser's poetry sparked a feud—dubbed the "Rukeyser Imbroglio"—between *Partisan Review* editors and F. O. Matthiessen (161–62).

Burke himself was "annoyed particularly" by what he saw as critics' tendency to latch onto one point and ignore the rest. "Irony: one tries to put a lot together—and the reviewers, thinking primarily of their own comfort and convenience, take it all apart, isolate one part, and play it up as a totality. Heck" (KB to WCW December 21, 1937). In his correspondence, Burke figures his disagreements, especially over Marxist criticism, as being "unseasonal" (KB to WF July 16, 1934), as using a metaphor that's "in very bad repute. . . a sea-metaphor . . . spoken to a farmer" (KB to MJ March 29, 1933) or even as speaking a different language: "Two lengvich. You spick one lengvich, ah spick nudder lengvich," he writes Cowley (KB to MC June 4, 1933). Perhaps most galling to Burke was feeling misunderstood by some of his closest friends.

Burke had long, tense exchanges over politics and poetics with Cowley and Tate as he was drafting *PC* during the summer of 1933. At one point Burke simply throws up his hands: "You are right: our points of view are so damned different that there is just nothing else to it. The points of view do not even have the translatable feature of being 'opposed.' They just lie across each other on the bias" (KB to MC June 15, 1933b). Burke sent repeated, lengthy letters to Tate, trying to persuade him that literature was rhetorical. So convinced was Burke of his rightness that he seems unable to account for a genuine disagreement except as a misunderstanding by Tate. Burke's frustration with Tate is palpable as he searches for the source of Tate's misinterpretation: "Maybe Allen read the article by Hickville Grannie [Granville Hicks]. Hickville Grannie said that I said that 'literature should make the reader go out and do some specific thing.' If Allen got his interpretation . . . from that source, then oh my God, for the same man who said that I said that literature should make people go out and do some specific thing also informed us in the same article that my esthetic system divorced literature from life" (KB to AT September 27, 1933). Stung by Tate's refusal to change his mind, Burke wrote to Cowley, "maybe if this present book [*PC*] gets published, I shall have made my stand clear enough for those things not to occur so easily any more. At least, I am making myself so painfully clear that if any intelligent man misunderstands me I can know it for a wish-fathered thought" (KB to MC July 31, 1933).[4]

But Burke was not the only one who felt misunderstood. Sidney Hook spent much of the 1930s arguing (unsuccessfully) that he, not the Communist Party, correctly interpreted Marx. Tate felt the Agrarians were consistently misrepresented—even by their close friends; he and Cowley battled intermittently for over half a decade, with Tate accusing Cowley and other leftists of "manufactur[ing] [a position] for me": "You say I advocate the feudal virtues of the Old South. I advocate nothing of the sort: you simply long ago made up your mind to something like that" (AT to MC April 26, 1936).

Into this "super-charged," politically and esthetically fractured climate came *Permanence and Change*, launched with a full-page announcement in *New Republic*'s March 27 issue. *PC*—a provocative attempt to theorize the ethical ends and rhetorical means for cultural transformation—cut to the heart of the raging debates about the need for, and goals of, social change and about the artist/rhetor's role in making this change happen. The April 1 announcement that Burke had won a Guggenheim, along with the splash made by his Writers' Congress speech, delivered exactly one month after *PC*'s release, only served to increase interest in the book. In short, this was a moment when Burke was at the top of his game, addressing the most pressing issues of the day. The question becomes, then, just what did Burke say that sparked so much interest and discussion?

BURKE'S *PERMANENCE AND CHANGE*

Like scores of early twentieth-century cultural critics, Burke railed against the materialistic, mechanistic texture of American society, and like many of them, he proposed a communal, creative life—a "poetic orientation"—as a corrective. What distinguished Burke's work then (and what it makes so useful now) was his recognition that no radical program could succeed without a rhetorically sophisticated account of why people, individually and collectively, resist change. *PC* provides such an account. In it Burke traces the process of social change through the stages of "orientation," "disorientation," and "reorientation." Part1, "On Interpretation," theorizes how culture maintains and is maintained by what he calls *piety*. All interpretation, he argues, is necessarily embedded in and thus limited by the prevailing orientation (or ideology). When an orientation is breaking down, as Burke believed was then the case, people become "dis-oriented," but their cultural ideology has become so naturalized that they cannot recognize it as either a cause of their problems or something that might be changed to solve them. It follows, Burke argues, that how people respond to the world is controlled less by their rational self-interest (the psychology behind Marxist rhetoric) than by established cultural values and "the language of common sense" (109) which constitute piety—the unquestioning devotion, not to religious faith, but to a way of being in the world.

In part 2, "Perspective by Incongruity," Burke analyzes the process of collective transformation by paralleling it to individual transformations—psychotherapy and religious conversion, both of which work, he concludes, by giving people new language for, and hence new ways to interpret, experience. That is, people gain new understanding of events by (re)naming them using unfamiliar or unexpected terms; this *perspective by incongruity* becomes the methodological centerpiece of Burke's proposal for change—a program of verbal defamiliarization designed to expose the constructed nature of experience and enable people to consider alternative perspectives.[5]

Part 3, "The Basis of Simplification," outlines the ethical grounding for Burke's proposed poetic orientation. Searching for *"one underlying motive . . . that activates all men"* (221), Burke finds constancy in "the biologic purposes of the human genus" (234); "a point of view biologically rooted," he claims, "seems to be as near to 'rock bottom' as human thought could take us" (261). Guided by the mind-body interaction he calls *metabiology*, Burke identifies action as the fundamental human purpose (a motionless body is dead), which he then links to cooperation and community (which enable action), civic participation (group action that creates a healthy state), and ultimately to poetry, broadly conceived—"our ultimate motive, the situation common to all, the creative, assertive, synthetic act" (259).

Metabiology is thus the universal ethic that transcends other shifting, partial perspectives: the good life is the creative life, and a society is sound to the extent that it fosters action as its principle value and purpose. Burke argues emphatically in *PC* that communism is the system most conducive to communal cooperation, to "an *art of living*" (66). As this outline suggests, the book has a tremendous scope. Part rhetorical theory, part social psychology, part ethics, part cultural criticism, part political tract, it would challenge any reviewer's skill. Nevertheless, the reviews of *PC* indicate that it was typically read in Burke's time with interest, sophistication, and clear understanding of its contribution to discussions of the means and ends of social change.

PERMANENCE AND CHANGE'S CONTEMPORARY RECEPTION

Central to my reexamination of *PC*'s reception is a newly discovered file of reviews collected by Burke (Folder Q11), containing nine pieces that, to my knowledge, are not listed in Burke bibliographies—increasing the number of known reviews from twelve to twenty-one.[6] It's immediately clear then that *PC* was reviewed more often and more widely than scholars have previously realized. Sixteen reviews appeared in publications with national circulation or big-name contributors, including four newfound reviews by Lionel Abel (*Modern Monthly*), John Chamberlain (*New York Times*), Herbert Lamm (*Mosaic*), and Philip Wheelwright (*New Democracy*). Reviews appeared in the expected places—*New York Times Book Review, Nation, New Masses*— but also in publications as diverse as *American Review, Quarterly Journal of Speech, Poetry,* and *American Journal of Sociology*.[7] That the book found a wide audience is also indicated by the fact that reviews were carried by *Midwestern Observer*, based in Chicago; *Reader's News* out of Hollywood;[8] and two college papers (*Daily Cardinal* from the University of Wisconsin[9] and *Northwest Viking* from Washington State Normal

School). In addition R. P. Blackmur's "A Critic's Job of Work" (1935), although not technically a review, discusses the book at length; hence, I include it in my discussion of *PC*'s reception but not in the review tally.[10]

It is perhaps surprising, given our image of the hostility or indifference of Burke's contemporaries, that the response to *PC* was predominantly positive (overwhelmingly so in the newly found reviews): some reviews are mixed, but seven of the sixteen major reviews praise the book, some extravagantly, while only three flat-out pan it (those by Abel, Ernest Bates, Joseph Wood Krutch).[11] Edgar Johnson, writing in the *Saturday Review of Literature* for instance, applauds *PC* as "one of the important books of our day" ("Society"), and Blackmur praises the "sheer remarkableness of [Burke's] speculations" (392).[12] Many reviewers explicitly admire the range and power of Burke's analysis; *brilliant* is the word that keeps popping up: Burke uses his resources with "brilliance, virtuosity, grace" (Eliot 114); the book is "brilliant" and "illuminating" (Hazlitt), "studded with brilliant definitions" (Chamberlain), and "brilliant in detail, constantly exhilarating" (Warren 201). Even a reviewer as hostile as Bates, writing for the *New York Herald Tribune,* notes the book's "amazing intellectual fecundity."

Readers today, used to joke about Burke's dense style and nonlinear argumentation, might be surprised to find that although some reviewers note the difficulty of the prose or what one reviewer calls his "godlike disregard for the pedantries of logical classification" (Bates), fewer than one-third make more than a passing comment about this difficulty, and two of those (Krutch and Hazlitt) proceed to give accurate accounts of the book.[13] In fact, a number of critics remark upon Burke's "rationally organized language" (Rosenberg 348) and approach. Wilson Waylett, writing for the *Northwest Viking,* describes Burke's style as "pellucid" and "smooth flowing."[14] The *South Atlantic Quarterly* reviewer, Charles Glicksberg, an English professor at Brooklyn College, even calls Burke's style "logical, compact, almost wearisome in its insistence on defining terms and clarifying meanings," which, he says, renders the book too hard for the general public but which makes Burke "the critic's critic par excellence" (74).[15] In fact Glicksberg asserts: "There are few critics writing at the present time who are exerting a more pronounced, though subterranean, influence than Kenneth Burke. If in the future American criticism moves in the direction of increased clarity, precision, and understanding, it will be due in no small measure to the important contributions made by this comparatively young critic" (75).

Current scholars might also expect Burke's politics to be a flashpoint, but despite the book's explicit advocacy of communism, reviewers were more alarmed, as I will show, by Burke's perceived relativism than by his politics; only two (Bates and Glicksberg) raise serious objections to Burke's "militant Marxist gospel" (Glicksberg 78).[16] Both the *Nation* and *New York Times* reviewers (Krutch and Hazlitt, respectively) find Burke's arguments for communism not so much wrongheaded as odd or, in Hazlitt's case, "irrelevant": Burke's alignment of communism with poetry (not, as expected, with science) would, they claim, baffle readers. But if reviewers do not talk much about Burke's politics, what do they talk about? Two topics: methodology and epistemology.

PERSPECTIVES ON *PC*'S METHODOLOGY

The reviewers most interested in large-scale workings of society, the Marxists and social scientists, dominate the discussion of methodology. Their responses are mirror opposites—the Marxists approving Burke's ends but not his means and the social scientists approving his means but almost indifferent to his ends. Because Depression-era leftist intellectuals regarded Marxism primarily as a method of social analysis, Marxist reviewers were keenly interested in, but extremely wary of, any method of sociological criticism launched, as Burke's was, under a communist banner. John Chamberlain's prediction that "Marxists of the world-bound variety will not like Mr. Burke for his constant redefinition of terms" or for his rejection of the materialist dialectic proved to be accurate: the Marxist reviewers criticize Burke's method for not being sociological enough (something the sociologists never do, which may be of interest in itself).[17] *New Masses* reviewer Norbert Guterman for instance, while pleased that Burke advocates communism "in most noble and eloquent language," disapproves of Burke's "having taken insufficient account" of orthodox Marxist analysis.[18] Abel, in *Modern Monthly*, is even more disturbed that "with all the advantages of the immense instrument of Marxian social analysis at his disposal," Burke instead employs "a curious method of his own" (187)—namely perspective by incongruity.[19]

The social scientists, on the other hand, have only praise for Burke's "apparatus for socio-economic criticism" (Lee). Not intent on measuring Burke's Marxist orthodoxy or the waywardness of his critical theory, the social scientists want to use Burke's methodology not so much to remake society as to understand it, particularly as Louis Wirth notes, to understand "the role of symbols in social life, especially in creating and maintaining loyalties, integrating groups and cultures, facilitating and hindering rationality" (485). Hence Northwestern University professor Irving Lee, writing in *Quarterly Journal of Speech*, praises the book for "establish[ing] . . . a 'unitary' critical perspective by means of which to analyze the disorders in our social structure"—a tool by which "anyone is able to subject not only discourse, but all social achievement to criticism." And in light of Burke's claim that perspective by incongruity is "the essence of the whole business" (qtd. in Skodnick 10), his ideal reader may be the sociologist T. D. Eliot, who actually experienced the book as a series of perspectives by incongruity: "What will you get from [the book]? . . . probably a set of mental explosions of the sort which break down old combinations without sense of loss, since the explosions themselves synthesize one's previous mental content in new and more dynamic configurations" (115).[20] Eliot continues: "[Burke] is able to apply with great effectiveness the very techniques he proposes: the stimulus got by the slight distortions of meaning which occur when concepts are juxtaposed in more or less incongruous perspectives. *Species of ideas are to be deliberately and experimentally cross-bred, profitable mutations selected, and the cultural stock improved.* This is *poetry* in the original Greek sense of the verb; viz., creation" (115). This comment also indicates that Eliot registered Burke's argument for action/creation as the fundamental human purpose.

The Marxists and social scientists, however, were not the only critics to identify perspective by incongruity as the methodological heart of the book. Johnson admires this "technique" that enables Burke to reveal the dominant ideology as just that—an ideology ("Society"). Similarly Glicksberg argues that perspective by incongruity is a singularly valuable critical tool that "is wielded like a surgical knife cutting away diseased or superfluous tissue" and "punctur[ing] the pretensions of many a vested critical system" (76, 74). Whether reviewers read Burke's methodology as an incisive critical tool or a suspicious deviation from Marxist analysis, however, it is clear that they understand Burke, that they seriously engage his work, and that many agree with it. That is, their responses do not support current assumptions that Burke was consistently misread, embattled, or marginalized.

BURKE: EPISTEMOLOGICAL SKEPTIC OR FOUNDATIONALIST?

The second—and most contested—issue was one that has often dogged Burke: to what extent is he a relativist—or, in the terms of 1930s readers, a skeptic? While some reviewers see Burke's purpose as establishing a "new [system] of values" based on metabiology (Waylett), half of them read *PC*—disapprovingly—as an expression of Burke's "radical skepticism" (Krutch 453), as a denial of any objective ground, including science, from which to understand and evaluate experience. Thus Austin Warren, whose review is ironically entitled "The Sceptic's Progress," laments Burke's shift from *Counter-Statement*'s productive questioning to *PC*'s fruitless claim that "anything *may* be true" (204; emphasis in original).[21] The Marxist Abel objects to the political quietism he sees as the inevitable consequence of Burke's relativism: "If every type of human thought is a type of perspective by incongruity, . . . how after all, can it be objected to?" (189). The most virulent attack on Burke's perceived relativism, however, came from the *Herald Tribune*'s Ernest Bates. Bates opens by remarking that initially *PC* seems to provide exhilarating, albeit dizzying, "mental intoxication." "On a reperusal, however," Bates continues, readers "will discover an underlying philosophy of a most devastating character"—a "nihilistic metaphysics." Bates positively sneers at Burke's argument that there are no ideologically free zones: "'The universe,' he tells us, 'would appear to be something like a cheese: it can be sliced in an infinite number of ways.' . . . Since there is, at worst, to be expected only some slight recalcitrance of nature to a few of our more outlandish ideas, why not will to believe what we most desire to believe?" By the end, Bates's sarcasm has turned to contempt: "It is a brilliant essay of ratiocination in behalf of irrationalism. It is, in the last analysis, another self-contradictory expression of . . . modern madness."

That Burke had anticipated such resistance to his "cheese slicing" is indicated by a passage from the *Plowshare* version of part 1, in which he defends his method against critics who may "fail to understand the purpose of suspended judgment. Suspended judgment is absolutely worthless except insofar as it eventually assists in the formation of judgments ("On Interpretation" 18). Because ideologies appear natural, the only way to puncture them, Burke argues, is "by bringing ourselves to question the obvious" (19). Burke's instincts were sound—his "suspended judgment," read as absolute relativism, was the biggest sticking point for those who wrote negative reviews.[22]

But if Bates saw only the suspension and not the formation of judgments, an equal number of reviewers read *PC* (correctly, I'd argue) as theorizing a universal ethics built upon the basic human motive to create. Blackmur observes that Burke "uses literature . . . as a . . . home for a philosophy or psychology of moral possibility" (392). These reviewers not only discuss Burke's call for a poetic orientation but also follow the more difficult—and more important—step in which he identifies metabiology as the basis for judging cultural health and hence directing social change. Glicksberg for instance sees Burke's goal as the "development of a norm based on . . . a universal biologic constant" (79), and Wheelwright claims that Burke's "poetic metaphor gives rise to an ethics based not on rules nor on authority, but on the socio-biological genius of man" (195). Such sophisticated readings suggest that it is an oversimplification to say, as Burke lore has it, that few of Burke's contemporaries understood his work.

In keeping with this traditional view, for instance, Wolin argues that *PC* "was by and large misunderstood" (86), noting reviewers' resistance to Burke's dismantling of scientific neutrality. And there is certainly evidence to support that claim. Hazlitt for one concedes that perspectives are often ideological but maintains that "to argue . . . that because we cannot entirely rid ourselves of metaphorical and poetic interpretations . . . we must . . . prefer them to 'scientific' interpretations, seems like contending that because we cannot entirely rid ourselves of prejudice we should deliberately embrace it." Warren is more blunt: human progress, he claims, depends upon "the denuded language of reasoning" (210); "to doubt Reason is [nothing less than] intellectual suicide" (213).

And yet Krutch, bristling at Burke's skepticism, nonetheless understands Burke's purpose as teaching readers "to think in a different way about the nature and functions of the perspective itself" and so realize "that no [perspective] is true or false in an absolute sense" (454). Glicksberg, who rates Burke's attempt "to overthrow the Goliath of science" as "the least convincing" part of the book (78), similarly provides this masterful encapsulation of *PC:* "In an age of disintegrating faith, when all of man's knowledge and belief is undergoing a searching re-examination, he has taken upon himself the enormously difficult task of tearing down the whole cumbersome critical structure and building anew on a firmer and more lasting foundation" (75). As with the critical debate on Burke's methodology, then, these passages suggest it is not so much that Glicksberg and others do not get Burke's point as that they do not buy it. We need to take care lest our postmodern sensibilities blind us to the perceptiveness of earlier readers.[23]

In fact we can learn a lot from their perceptiveness—and even, I'd argue, from their questions and criticisms. Studying how and why they reach their conclusions helps us hone current thought and question our assumptions. I'm particularly struck for instance by Glicksberg, who as I've indicated articulates Burke's methodology and argument so clearly and fully. What then do we make of the fact that he nevertheless concludes that *PC* is "the breviary of skepticism" (84)? For me, Glicksberg's reading foregrounds the huge, abrupt shift in Burke's argument from the postmodern epistemology (interpretation as necessarily ideological, perspective by incongruity) of parts 1 and 2 to the foundational ethics (metabiology) of part 3. Indeed Krutch's criticism of *PC* hinges precisely on his sense that Burke's argument for a universal ethic is undermined by his initial, "profoundly skeptical" argument that all interpretations are partial. Krutch maintains that "it is doubtful whether the transition from such skepticism to affirmation can possibly be made without a long leap across a chasm which no intellectualizing can bridge" (454). Considering that the 1935 text contained no introductory headnotes to sections, it is understandable that some readers did not make the jump.

What was Burke up to here? This is no longer a rhetorical question, for among Burke's papers is a folder (P9.5a) of notes for *PC*, complete with rhetorical strategizing. These notes indicate that this chasm was actually part of the plan: "One can use this formula [perspective by incongruity] . . . in such a way as to leave the field of 'logic,' 'judgment,' 'taste' a glorious wreck. . . . Why all this? Simply that, if one could, by a ranging back and forth, really get the whole field of so-called 'orientation' into a total muddle, would one not have the scene all set for the salvational uncorking of his 'way out'? Would one not then be fallen-upon-the-neck-of, by his distraught reader, if he now released his Biological Ought [metabiology]?" ("Outline Material" n.p.). Burke imagined "[reader's] eyes . . . filled with tears of gratitude" for being so rescued ("Outline Material" n.p.). Judging from the reviews however, he succeeded so well at creating the ideological muddle that instead of gratefully embracing Burke's poetic orientation, his "distraught readers" concluded that no such permanent perspective could exist (and then perhaps felt a bit testy at Burke's having pulled the epistemological rug out from beneath them). In that sense reviewers who complained about Burke's relativism may have been quite sensitive to his rhetorical emphasis or philosophical bent; indeed Burke wrote to Cowley while drafting *PC*, "I believe in the necessary triumph of skepticism" (KB to MC June 15, 1933b). So we might say that contemporary reviewers, who have been represented as misreading, often emphasize what we now value most in *PC*—analysis of the ideological nature of language and interpretation. The chief difference between us and them is that we agree with Burke and many critics then did not.

In fact there is considerable symmetry between 1930s reviewers' claims about Burke's relativism and claims by our own contemporary scholars. Rueckert for example is sympathetic to Warren's 1936 reading of *PC* as an argument for skepticism, claiming that a "transient skepticism" runs throughout Burke's early work—"a form of openness" (60) so clearly evident in dramatism's emphasis on ambiguity and "suspended judgment" of dialectical transformation. Likewise Warren's claim that Burke's "*dialectic of motivation* lands him at no terminus of conviction" (205) initially suggests that he's missed Burke's explicit choice of metabiology as a universal ethics and creation as the quintessential human motive. A more generous reading, however, might see Warren's comment as recognizing the same tension in *PC*'s model of historical change noted by Robert Wess and by George and Selzer: on the one hand, Burke posits an "opened ended" history in which every orientation, inevitably incomplete, is replaced by a new one—a history, that is, "without a telos" (Wess 68); on the other hand, Burke's claim that "the *ultimate* metaphor for discussing the universe and man's relations to it *must* be the poetic or dramatic metaphor" suggests that Burke sees the poetic orientation as complete and permanent (*PC* 263; emphasis added). Put into conversation with archival materials, contemporary reviewers' responses to *PC* enlarge and sharpen our understanding of Burke.

Finally, any attempt to reevaluate Burke's position among his contemporaries is incomplete, I'd argue, without taking into account an unexpected, undervalued kind of archival evidence: fan mail.[24] A Chicago branch manager of the fashionable Kroch's Bookstores wrote to say that sales were brisk and suggested that, with a color dust jacket, *PC* could be a bestseller (Joseph Kreloff to *New Republic* May 25, 1935). Philanthropist Ethel S. Dummer congratulated *New Republic* editors on "the brilliant formulations of Kenneth Burke," expressing her "delight" in the book and ordering extra copies for friends, one of whom was future reviewer T. D. Eliot.[25] I find particularly compelling evidence that "ordinary" people read and appreciated his work. *PC* was sold in Macy's (Mebane to KB May 14, 1935); *New Republic* readers bought it via an order form accompanying an ad for the book (Mebane to KB March 29, 1935). Leif Larson of Fair View, Montana, reported feasting on the book; Abe Mechlowitz, representing Brooklyn College's chapter of the National Student League, invited Burke to lecture on the recommendation of members who'd read *PC*;[26] Billy Justema made his thirtieth birthday the occasion to write Burke (also Eliot, Pound, Wallace Stevens, and Edmund Wilson) that he'd found Burke's work indispensible during the last decade and a half (BJ to KB December 7, 1935). We do not know, of course, what these readers made of the book, but their letters *do* matter. That we likely find their existence surprising indicates how completely we've internalized the image of an inscrutable, ignored Burke. They demonstrate too that Burke had a larger, more varied audience than we typically assume—that we'll underestimate Burke's impact if we examine only published reviews by professional critics.

A TIME FOR BURKE

That Burke *felt* misunderstood is fairly certain. That he actually *was* misunderstood is much less so. Casting Burke as the heroic underdog makes an attractive story, to be sure, but our attachment to the unappreciated, out-of-sync Burke in the face of evidence to the contrary raises questions about our historical practice—about our slowness in consulting the records of personal and intellectual relationships that Burke himself so assiduously preserved. So I propose a little perspective (by incongruity) to suggest how we might acknowledge Burke as exceptional (a brilliant, invaluable theorist, for his time and ours) but not necessarily an exception (not part of his time).

Perspective one: Gauging a writer's position among contemporaries requires a nuanced appreciation of the critical climate. Today effusive blurbs are the mark of a book's success. Reviews from the 1930s signified differently—incongruously. As Kalaidjian explains, "In the divisive milieu of the Great Depression, the sign of a [text's] cultural power lay not in its widespread acclaim . . . but instead in the critical conflict it provoked. . . . What signals cultural power in the 1930s is a work's localized and contentious interpretive productivity" (160–61). By these standards, *PC* was indeed powerful: the fan letters and conflicting reviews demonstrate that readers deemed the book worth writing about and fighting over. Convincing or not, *PC* was effective—that is, it created effects. As Colleen Reilly and Douglas Eyman note, "To be cited—even as a negative or oppositional example—means that an . . . author['s] . . . work *matters,* in every sense of the word: It is . . . part of the conversation, and it is visible and needs to be acknowledged as belonging to the foundation for building new ideas" (355). In Burke's words, "The ways of influence are devious"; texts work on audiences in complex ways (KB to MC June 2, 1932, unsent). Burke actively participated in 1930s conversations, and Selzer and I have examined how his work grew out of those discussions. But if we take seriously our theories about rhetoric as epistemic and knowledge as socially constructed, it is fair to push that claim further: Burke's work was not only *created by* the 1930s; Burke's work *created* the 1930s. Archives provide opportunities to trace Burke's "devious" influence even as they remind us how partial accounts of that influence will necessarily be, dependent as they are on what materials others have deemed worthy of preservation and what we deem worthy of study. Burke's impact on his time—so much wider than just his critical reception—is literally incalculable, but it is also unquestionable.

Perspective two: Responding to a comment that Burke had habits of mind that bucked trends, Steven Mailloux once remarked that Burke would not have had those habits if he had not been so immersed in cultural trends. That is, there is no separating habits of mind from culture: even Burke's seeming contrariness—or the particular forms that contrariness took—is a sign of his belonging to his time. As one 1930s reader claims, "[PC] is very much a book for our own time, and Kenneth Burke was the man to write it" (Rev.). If we take Burke seriously, we will acknowledge the necessary dialectic between intrinsic and extrinsic, between agent and scene, the theorist never completely apart from—ahead of—his time. The archives, prompting relentless contextualization, keep us grounded in a particular time and place even as they urge us to keep reconfiguring those rhetorical moments.

Ultimately Burke himself helps explain this paradox of a theorist who seems both in his time and ahead of it. It's in *PC*, after all, that he theorizes "language and thought [as] a socialized product" (20). In what sounds like self-description, Burke explains the coexistence of the old and new: "We learn to single out certain relationships in accordance with the particular linguistic texture into which we are born, though we may privately manipulate this linguistic texture to formulate still other relationships. When we do so, we invent new terms, or apply our old vocabulary in new ways, attempting to socialize our position by so manipulating the linguistic equipment of our group *that our particular additions or alterations can be shown to fit into the old texture*" (36; emphasis added). Burke's additions and alterations, his new terms and relationships (ahead of his time) nevertheless fit the old texture into which he was born (in his time). We can take the full measure of one only in light of the other. To do otherwise would be decidedly un-Burkean.

NOTES

1. Representing Burke ahead of his time also betrays simplistic assumptions that criticism between the wars consisted largely of lockstep thinking when only Burke marched to the beat of his own drum. However Burke was only one of many independent, highly sophisticated critics, who wrote (as, for instance, Van Wyck Brooks, William Carlos Williams, and Lewis Mumford did) postmodern ethics, revisionist histories, or analyzed the cultural construction of subjectivity; in *The Public and Its Problems,* John Dewey even analyzes symbols and ideology in ways strikingly similar to (and earlier than) Burke's. The ways we think of Burke as ahead of his time might be the very ways that clearly mark him as deeply immersed in it.

2. Among the two hundred participants at the congress were John Dos Passos, Meridel Le Sueur, Tillie Olsen, Langston Hughes, Theodore Dreiser, Richard Wright, André Gide, and Ford Madox Ford. A few weeks earlier, Agrarians and future New Critics, including Allen Tate, Robert Penn Warren, and Cleanth Brooks, had met at the Baton Rouge Conference on Literature and Reading in the South and Southwest to discuss similar issues.

3. This article was itself Burke's intervention in a "battle" in the *New Republic* between Malcolm Cowley and Archibald Macleish over representations of war in a poetry collection.

4. For a detailed account of Burke's relationship with Tate, see George and Selzer.

5. In more familiar terms, perspective by incongruity can be understood as a way to reframe a debate, to analyze and shift terministic screens.

6. I have included two reviews of "On Interpretation," a slightly longer version of part 1 of *PC* published in the journal *Plowshare* in February 1934. Folder Q11 is part of the Burke-3 accession in the Kenneth Burke Papers at Penn State. We can only speculate

about why these reviews did not surface earlier. Reviews in local publications and those in short-lived larger publications (such as *New Democracy*) would quickly disappear from view. The absence of Chamberlain's *New York Times* review is harder to explain, but possibly earlier scholars assumed that the *Times* and the *Times Book Review* would not both run reviews.

7. To Burke's disappointment, the *New Republic* ran no review, probably due to a policy forbidding the magazine to carry reviews of books published by its own press (KB to Cowley October 27, 1934). *American Review* had a self-proclaimed fascist publisher; oddly, the 1935 index is dominated by Agrarian issues and contributors such as Tate, John Crowe Ransom, Robert Penn Warren, Cleanth Brooks, and Donald Davidson. Austin Warren, of Wellek and Warren fame, wrote the *AR* review. Burke, who began reviewing for *Poetry* in late 1934, asked editor Morton Zabel to commission a review of *PC*: "It is essentially a work on social psychology, or ethics, but its concern with such subjects as meaning, symbolism, ritual, perspective, and its plea for a philosophy having *homo poeticus* as the key concept, might make it a candidate for treatment in your magazine" (KB to MZ November 3, 1934). Zabel selected Harold Rosenberg, who had reviewed *Counter-Statement*, rather critically, but whom Burke had warmed to after the Writers' Congress (Skodnick 16). Burke thanked Zabel "for entrusting the book to a man whose keenness is considerable" (KB to MZ May 1, 1935).

8. An Edgar Johnson review of "On Interpretation" sent to Burke by his editor Daniel Mebane (DM to KB December 19, 1935).

9. The folder contains only a typed excerpt from the *Daily Cardinal* review—probably one of several Burke was compiling for an ad to announce the book's second printing (KB to Daniel Mebane April 24, 1936). It also contains a retyped copy of a complete but unidentified review.

10. As coeditor of the esthetically conservative *Hound and Horn* magazine, Blackmur had published chapters of what eventually became *Towards a Better Life;* Burke and Blackmur had known and respected each other since the late 1920s.

11. Selzer and I argue that the known reviews indicate that *PC* was well received (but see Wolin for a counterreading). Since eight of the nine new reviews are also positive, the percentage of favorable reviews increases dramatically.

12. Johnson was a novelist, an English professor at City College, and later a celebrated biographer of Dickens and Scott. An acquaintance of Burke's, he also lectured at the New School for Social Research.

13. Krutch, an editor at the *Nation,* had originally assigned the *PC* review to Abel, but not having read the book himself, Krutch, in an extraordinary move, sent Abel's review to Burke, asking for a "frank" opinion (JWK to KB January 25, 1935). Burke drafted a "frank" reply on the back of Krutch's letter: "I think it's lousy." Krutch asked Abel to "try again" (JWK to KB January 30, 1935), but when he still wasn't satisfied, Krutch wrote the review himself, leaving Abel to publish his piece in *Modern Monthly.* Krutch later wrote Burke that he didn't think his review "is terribly good, but at least I think it more understandable than Abel's" (JWK to KB April 2, 1935). Burke agreed with the first part—he

immediately penned a rebuttal only to be told that the *Nation* printed author's replies only in cases of "demonstrable errors of fact" (JWK to KB April 16, 1935). Henry Hazlitt, an economist and libertarian philosopher, wrote numerous books and contributed to such publications as *New York Times* and *Wall Street Journal*.

14. Waylett sent his review to *New Republic* editors (WW to *New Republic* May 25, 1935), who then forwarded it to Burke.

15. *SAQ*, published by Duke University Press, describes itself as offering "bold analyses of the current intellectual scene, both nationally and worldwide, dele *cultural, intellectual*" ("*South Atlantic Quarterly*" n. pag.).

16. Cowley, however, calls Burke's Communism "mild" (MC to Matthew Josephson February 1, 1934).

17. Chamberlain was, with Burke, a regular in New York City leftist literary circles. The two corresponded, and Chamberlain occasionally spent weekends at Burke's house in Andover.

18. Though not an official Communist Party organ, the *New Masses,* with its emphasis on radical proletarian literature, was associated with party orthodoxy and, in Burke's mind, simplistic criticism.

19. *Modern Monthly* was edited by the dissident Marxist V. F. Calverton and took an anti-Stalinist stance.

20. Louis Wirth was a University of Chicago social scientist and coeditor of the *American Journal of Sociology.* Eliot, whose review appears in *American Sociological Review,* was another Chicago school sociologist who befriended Burke during his summer of 1938 teaching stint at the University of Chicago; Lee, then a graduate student at Chicago, also met Burke that summer.

21. Two years earlier, Warren had written a long, sympathetic article about *Counter-Statement* and *Towards a Better Life* for the *Sewanee Review;* that article established a relationship of mutual interest and respect between the two.

22. Blackmur however admires Burke for this very reason, insisting that any approach is "provisional and tentative and highly selective. . . . No observation . . . ever tells the whole story" (378).

23. This is not to say however that no misreading went on. It did of course. Most puzzling is Rosenberg's *Poetry* review, which launches a seemingly irrelevant critique of modernist poetry and which, as Wolin notes, "turns Burke inside out" (89), somehow concluding that not communism but science "promotes coöperation and thus turns society towards conditions favorable to poetry" (348).

24. Sales figures should also be accounted for in such a reevaluation. For a book of its type published in the middle of the Depression, *PC* sold quite well: 250 copies in the first five days, over 1,300 within six months; by April 1936 the book had gone into a second printing with sales hitting 1,800 by that August (DM to KB February 19, 1935; April 29, 1936; October 21, 1936).

25. In 1908 Dummer founded the Chicago School of Civics and Philanthropy, later the University of Chicago School of Social Service Administration.

26. Burke's correspondence files are littered with invitations to speak.

WORKS CITED

Unless otherwise noted, correspondence comes from the Kenneth Burke Papers, 1906–1960, Accession 1974-0202R, Rare Books and Manuscripts, Special Collections Library, University Libraries, Pennsylvania State University.

REVIEWS OF PERMANENCE AND CHANGE

Abel, Lionel. Rev. of *Permanence and Change,* by Kenneth Burke. *Modern Monthly* n.d., 187–89. Folder Q11.

Bates, Ernest Sutherland. "A Spendthrift with Ideas." Rev. of *Permanence and Change,* by Kenneth Burke. *New York Herald Tribune Books* May 12, 1935: 8.

Chamberlain, John. "Books of the Times." Rev. of *Permanence and Change,* by Kenneth Burke. *New York Times* Feb. 15, 1935: 17. Folder Q11.

Eliot, T. D. Rev. of *Permanence and Change,* by Kenneth Burke. *American Sociological Review* 2.1 (1937): 114–15.

Glicksberg, Charles I. "Kenneth Burke: The Critic's Critic." Rev. of *Permanence and Change,* by Kenneth Burke. *South Atlantic Quarterly* 36 (1937): 74–84.

Guterman, Norman. "Analysis of Communication." Rev. of *Permanence and Change,* by Kenneth Burke. *New Masses* Apr. 16, 1935: 23.

Hazlitt, Henry. "Kenneth Burke's Metaphysics." Rev. of *Permanence and Change,* by Kenneth Burke. *New York Times Book Review* May 5, 1935: 19.

Johnson, Edgar. "The Artist and the World." Rev. of "On Interpretation," by Kenneth Burke. *New Republic* Sept. 5, 1934: 109–10.

———. "One Man Literary Show." Rev. of "On Interpretation," by Kenneth Burke. *Reader's News* n.d. N. pag. Folder Q11.

———. "Society and the Poetic Method." Rev. of *Permanence and Change,* by Kenneth Burke. *Saturday Review of Literature* Oct. 26, 1935: 22.

Krutch, Joseph Wood. "Marx as Metaphor." Rev. of *Permanence and Change,* by Kenneth Burke. *Nation* Apr. 17, 1935: 453–54.

Lamm, Herbert. "Burke." Rev. of *Permanence and Change,* by Kenneth Burke. *Mosaic* Spring 1935: 33–34. Folder Q11.

Lee, Irving J. Rev. of *Permanence and Change,* by Kenneth Burke. *Quarterly Journal of Speech* 25.4 (1939): 688.

Rev. of *Permanence and Change,* by Kenneth Burke. n.p., n.d. N.pag. TS. Folder Q11.

Rosenberg, Harold. "Meaning and Communication." Rev. of *Permanence and Change,* by Kenneth Burke. *Poetry* Mar. 1936: 347–49.

Sillen, Samuel. Rev. of *Permanence and Change,* by Kenneth Burke. *Daily Cardinal.* n.d. N.pag. TS. Folder Q11.

Warren, Austin. "The Sceptic's Progress." Rev. of *Permanence and Change,* by Kenneth Burke. *American Review* 6.2 (1936): 193–213.

Waylett, Wilson. "Reorientation." Rev. of *Permanence and Change,* by Kenneth Burke. *Northwest Viking.* n.d. N.pag. Folder Q11.

W.H. Rev. of *Permanence and Change,* by Kenneth Burke. *Midwestern Observer* May 1935: 3. Folder Q11.

Wheelwright, Philip. Rev. of *Permanence and Change,* by Kenneth Burke. *New Democracy* Feb. 15, 1936: 194–95. Folder Q11.

Wirth, Louis. Rev. of *Permanence and Change,* by Kenneth Burke. *American Journal of Sociology* 43.3 (1937): 483–86.

OTHER PRIMARY AND SECONDARY SOURCES

Blackmur, R. P. "A Critic's Job of Work." 1935. Rpt. in *Language as Gesture: Essays in Poetry.* New York: Harcourt, 1952. 372–99.

Booth, Wayne C. *Critical Understanding: The Powers and Limits of Pluralism.* Chicago: University of Chicago Press, 1979.

Brummett, Barry. Introduction. *Landmark Essays on Kenneth Burke.* Davis: Hermagoras, 1993. xi–xix.

Burke, Kenneth. *Auscultation, Creation, and Revision: The Rout of the Esthetes, or, Literature, Marxism, and Beyond.* In *Extensions of the Burkeian System.* Ed. James W. Chesebro. Tuscaloosa: University of Alabama Press, 1993. 43–172.

———. Letters to Malcolm Cowley. June 2, 1932 (unsent); June 4, 1932 (sent); June 4, 1933; July 31, 1933; Oct. 27, 1934. June 15, 1933b (unsent) TLS. Burke-3 collection, Folder P9.5a.

———. Letter to Waldo Frank. July 16, 1934. TLS. Waldo Frank Papers. Van Pelt Library, University of Pennsylvania, Philadelphia.

———. Letter to Matthew Josephson. Mar. 19,1933. TLS. Matthew Josephson Papers. Beinecke Rare Book and Manuscript Library, Yale University, New Haven.

———. Letter to Daniel Mebane. Apr. 24, 1936. TLS.

———. Letter to Allen Tate. Sept. 27, 1933. TLS.

———. Letter to Robert Penn Warren. Feb. 26, 1938. TLS. *Southern Review* Papers. Beinecke Rare Book and Manuscript Library, Yale University, New Haven.

———. Letter to William Carlos Williams. Dec. 21, 1937. TLS. Beinecke Rare Book and Manuscript Library, Yale University, New Haven.

———. Letters to Morton Zabel. Nov. 3, 1934; May 1, 1935. TLS. Morton Dauwen Zabel Papers. Joseph Regenstein Library, University of Chicago.

———. "On Interpretation." *Plowshare: A Literary Periodical of One-Man Exhibits* 10.1 (Feb. 1934): 3–79.

———. "Outline Material." Burke-3, folder P9.5a.

———. *Permanence and Change: An Anatomy of Purpose.* 1935. Berkeley: University of California Press, 1984.

———. *The Philosophy of Literary Form: Studies in Symbolic Action.* 1941. Berkeley: University of California Press, 1973.

———. "War, Response, and Contradiction." Rpt. in *The Philosophy of Literary Form: Studies in Symbolic Action.* 1941. Berkeley: University of California Press, 1973. 234–57.

Carmichael, Thomas. "Screening Symbolicity: Kenneth Burke and Contemporary Theory." *Unending Conversations: New Writings by and about Kenneth Burke.* Ed. Greig

Henderson and David Cratis Williams. Carbondale: Southern Illinois University Press, 2001. 143–53.

Cowley, Malcolm. Letter to Matthew Josephson. Feb. 1, 1934. TLS. Matthew Josephson Papers. Beinecke Rare Book and Manuscript Library, Yale University, New Haven.

Dewey, John. *The Public and Its Problems.* New York: Holt, 1927.

Dummer, Ethel S. Letter to *New Republic.* Aug. 10, 1935. TLS.

Fish, Stanley. *Doing What Comes Naturally: Change, Rhetoric, and the Practice of Theory in Literary and Legal Studies.* Durham: Duke University Press, 1989.

Franklin, Jay. "What's Wrong with Our Radicals?" *Vanity Fair* Apr. 1935: 33–34.

Gabin, Rosalind J. "Entitling Kenneth Burke." *Rhetoric Review* 5.2 (1987): 196–210.

George, Ann, and Jack Selzer. *Kenneth Burke in the 1930s.* Columbia: University of South Carolina Press, 2007.

Grattan, C. Hartley. "New Voices: The Promise of Our Youngest Writers." *Forum* Nov. 1932: 284–88.

Harris, Wendell V. "The Critics Who Made Us: Kenneth Burke." *Sewanee Review* 96.3 (1988): 452–63.

Holbrook, Peter. "What Happened to Burke?" *Times Literary Supplement* July 13, 2007: 11–12.

Jameson, Fredric. "The Symbolic Inference; Or, Kenneth Burke and Ideological Analysis." *Critical Inquiry* 4.3 (1978): 507–23.

Jay, Gregory S. "Burke Re-Marx." *Pre/Text* 6.3–4 (1985): 169–75.

Justema, Billy. Letter to Kenneth Burke. Dec. 7, 1935. ALS.

Kalaidjian, Walter. *American Culture between the Wars: Revisionary Modernism and Postmodern Critique.* New York: Columbia University Press, 1993.

Kreloff, Joseph. Letter to *New Republic.* May 15, 1935. TLS.

Krutch, Joseph Wood. Letters to Kenneth Burke. Jan. 25, 1935; Jan. 30, 1935; Apr. 2, 1935; Apr. 16, 1935. TLS.

Larson, Leif. Letter to *New Republic.* Apr. 4, 1935. TLS.

Lentricchia, Frank. *Criticism and Social Change.* Chicago: University of Chicago Press, 1983.

Mailloux, Steven. Penn State Conference on Rhetoric and Composition/Triennial Conference of the Kenneth Burke Society. State College. July 12, 2005. Roundtable Discussion.

Mebane, Daniel. Letters to Kenneth Burke. Feb. 19, 1935; Mar. 29, 1935; May 14, 1935; Dec. 19, 1935; Apr. 29, 1936; Oct. 21, 1936. TLS.

Mechlowitz, Abe. Letter to Kenneth Burke. Mar. 6, 1935. ALS.

Reilly, Colleen A., and Douglas Eyman. "Multifaceted Methods for Multimodal Texts: Alternate Approaches to Citation Analysis for Electronic Sources." *Digital Writing Research: Technologies, Methodologies, and Ethical Issues.* Ed. Heidi A. McKee and Danielle Nicole DeVoss. Cresskill: Hampton, 2007. 353–76.

Rueckert, William H., ed. *Critical Responses to Kenneth Burke, 1924–1966.* Minneapolis: University of Minnesota Press, 1969.

Schneider, Isidor. "A New View of Rhetoric." Rev. of *Counter-Statement,* by Kenneth Burke. *New York Herald Tribune Books* Dec. 31, 1931: 4.

Selzer, Jack. *Kenneth Burke in Greenwich Village: Conversing with the Moderns, 1915–1931.* Madison: University of Wisconsin Press, 1996.

Simons, Herbert W., and Trevor Melia. Preface. *The Legacy of Kenneth Burke.* Madison: University of Wisconsin Press, 1989. vii–ix.

Skodnick, Roy. "CounterGridlock: An Interview with Kenneth Burke." *All Area* 2 (1983): 4–32.

"South Atlantic Quarterly." Duke University Press, n.d.

Tate, Allen. Letter to Malcolm Cowley. Apr. 26, 1936. TLS. Malcolm Cowley Papers. Newberry Library, Chicago.

———. *The Poetry Reviews of Allen Tate.* Ed. Ashley Brown and Frances Neel Cheney. Baton Rouge: Louisiana State University Press, 1983.

"Thirty Years Later: Memories of the First American Writers' Congress." *American Scholar* 35.3 (1966): 495–516.

Tompkins, Phillip K. "On Hegemony—'He Gave It No Name'—and Critical Structuralism in the Work of Kenneth Burke." *Quarterly Journal of Speech* 71.1 (1985): 119–31.

Waylett, Wilson. Letter to Kenneth Burke. May 25, 1935. TLS.

Wess, Robert. *Kenneth Burke: Rhetoric, Subjectivity, Postmodernism.* Cambridge: Cambridge University Press, 1996.

Williams, William Carlos. *The Autobiography of William Carlos Williams.* New York: Random House, 1948.

Wolfe, Cary. "Nature as Critical Concept: Kenneth Burke, the Frankfurt School, and 'Metabiology.'" *Cultural Critique* 18 (1991): 65–96.

Wolin, Ross. *The Rhetorical Imagination of Kenneth Burke.* Columbia: University of South Carolina Press, 2001.

Woodcock, John. "An Interview with Kenneth Burke." *Sewanee Review* 85.4 (1977): 704–18.

NED O'GORMAN *and* IAN E. J. HILL

BURKE, MUMFORD, AND THE POETICS OF TECHNOLOGY

Marxism's Influence on Burke's Critique of Techno-logology

In 1934 Kenneth Burke's *Plowshare* essay "On Interpretation" landed on the desk of the influential public intellectual and *New Yorker* critic Lewis Mumford. A month later another Burke article, "My Approach to Communism," arrived on Mumford's desk. Mumford read through both pieces with some interest, noting an affinity between Burke's mediations on interpretation, technology, and communism and themes of his own work, particularly his just-published *Technics and Civilization*. That fall the full manuscript of Burke's forthcoming *PC* confirmed Mumford's impressions, so he picked up his pen, pulled out a piece of paper, and began to write:

> Dear Burke,
> Your essay in *The Plowshare* had whetted my appetite for your present manuscript: and I am reading the latter with pleasure and admiration, so far unmixed with dissidence. . . . Ever since I read your essay defining your attitude toward Communism last spring I have felt that our respective ideas, marching from different directions, were converging toward the same goal. (LM to KB October 11, 1934, courtesy of the estate of Lewis and Sophia Mumford; quoted with the permission of Rare Books and Manuscripts, Special Collections Library, Pennsylvania State University Libraries)

Mumford's enthusiasm persisted into the next year. When *PC* came off the presses in 1935, he went to work to promote it. As C. A. Pierce of Harcourt Brace wrote Burke, "Mumford, as you probably know, is very keen about the book." A month later, on March 13, Pierce wrote Burke again, "It is very swell to hear that the new book is going so well, and I will continue to do all that I can to talk to people about it. Lewis Mumford tells me that Lee Simonson is completely sold on it, and is one of your best press agents" (CAP to KB March 13, 1935). Mumford spent 1935 talking up *PC* and Burke, even writing the Guggenheim Foundation to support Burke's fellowship application to write *ATH*.

The Burke archives make this much clear about the relationship between Lewis Mumford and Kenneth Burke. Unfortunately however, unlike a number of other significant intellectual relationships in Burke's career, little else is documented. Indeed, among the challenges of Burke's archives are the texts that have left unfinished stories, texts that can be addressed only by moving out of the archive to other texts, contexts, and ultimately interpretive argument. Such arguments, in turn, have implications for how we direct and transform the future of Burkean scholarship.

In our study of the mid-1930s intellectual relationship between Burke and Mumford, we approach the archive as a provocation. What, we ask, was the "same goal" with regard to communism that Mumford shared with Burke? While we know that they walked in the same broad New York intellectual circles in the 1920s and 1930s, we also recognize that the two critics were quite different: Mumford was established by the 1930s among an elite and prominent circle of public intellectuals, and Burke was struggling to maintain a life in which to write his eclectic tomes on interpretation, history, and language. Nevertheless they felt a shared sense of not just intellectual but political aspiration in the mid-1930s. Burke felt this sense so strongly that in the mid-1950s he reported to Malcolm Cowley that the publication of his *Book of Moments: Poems 1915–1954* put him in the frame of being "Thirty-minded" (1930s), and thus he wanted to send the poems to two compatriots from the period, Edmund Wilson and Mumford (KB to MC March 16, 1955).

In this essay we work from a provocation offered by the Burke archives to argue that what Mumford found in Burke in 1934–35, and Burke in Mumford, was a common *methodological turn*. The 1930s, the decade of Depression, presented critics with a crisis in the history of capitalism, a crisis in the history of communism, and a crisis in the history of technology. Taken together these crises had a dramatic impact on the critical and political outlooks of many contemporaneous intellectuals. Burke and Mumford, however, responded to these crises not with a renewed vision of social order per se, but with a new, shared approach to critical inquiry itself.

In the 1920s and into the 1930s a central question asked by the American Left was *how* to instrumentalize a radical social and political vision. This was, to use the language of Mumford, a "utopian" question. But in the mid-1930s Burke and Mumford turned from this question to ask instead, What are the characteristics of "instrumentalization" itself? What are the characteristics of the basic materials of human life—organisms, tools, and words—that might be instrumentalized within a political project? These, to use Mumford's terminology again, were "eutopian" (*eutopos*) questions, questions about the "good" (*eu*) of places, objects, and discursive and material arrangements (*topoi*). This methodological turn, we argue, comprises the "same goal" toward which Burke and Mumford marched in the 1930s.

We present our argument in three sections, beginning with the crises that constituted the exigency for Burke's and Mumford's common methodological turn, particularly the crises of technology and communism. We then look at their new methodological turn through the lenses of Burke's "dialectical biologism" and

Mumford's "organic ideology." In the third section we explore how Burke and Mumford worked to translate this methodological turn into more pragmatic forms of social and political action, emphasizing the divergent courses they pursued, for better and worse. In conclusion we consider how the methodological turn we see in Burke and Mumford in the 1930s has consequences not only for the past but also for the future of Burke studies, provoking us to envision "Burkean criticism" as deriving not from specialized terms and rubrics but from a basic attitude toward seeing the world.

YOUNG AMERICANS: BURKE, MUMFORD, AND THE CRISES OF *HOW*

When Mumford took up Burke's "On Interpretation" in the winter of 1934, New York, besides suffering from record cold temperatures, was witnessing record unemployment, mass poverty, and a massive upheaval, rooted in an unprecedented crisis in the social imagination. The effects of this social upheaval on the Left, however, were surprising: for while it had been self-evident to socialists and communists that industrial capitalism was a dire system, a conclusion validated by the Depression, the massive economic crisis ended up biting the Marxists, communists, and radicals just as hard as it bit the industrialists and capitalists. Far from settling and solidifying the social program of the Left, the Depression splintered it, as shown by the many competing concepts of capitalism, communism, and technology that circulated in the 1930s.

Burke and Mumford did not just witness this splintering; they felt its wounds in both their personal and professional lives. Burke (in)famously became a center of controversy at the First American Writers Congress in 1935. As Ann George and Jack Selzer have suggested, the incident was riddled with contradictions: Burke garnered wrath for suggesting that "the people" be substituted for "the worker" in communist symbolism, yet the congress was itself called to broaden the appeal of the radical Left. Burke's suggestion there was thus consistent with the declared aim of the congress. For Mumford the splintering was as much internal to his thought as external: on the one hand, he admired that the communists "mean business," but on the other he could not tolerate their "war-psychology" (qtd. in Blake 281–82).

At the heart of the splintering of the American Left stood a question about how to integrate politics, technology, and culture in order to correct the social crises of the 1930s. The question was anticipated in public form in a scathing comment on Mumford's work in the *New Masses* in 1927. In this socialist periodical Genevieve Taggard accused Mumford of being "false and literary" in his appraisal of industrial technology. "The Machine Age has one meaning," she argued, contra Mumford. " It need neither to be rejected or aestheticized—it can be accepted as a very interesting and enormously clever way of trying to do some of the work that has to be done" (qtd. in Blake 280). Ironically, even as Taggard lambasted him for a "false" appraisal of the machine, Mumford was integral to raising the question in the first place. The critical triad of politics, technology, and culture had gained purchase in New York in the 1920s in significant part through the efforts of a group of intellectuals and critics Casey Nelson Blake has called the "Young Americans," of which Mumford was part and with whom Burke often corresponded.

The Young Americans were—like so many in and around Greenwich Village in the 1910s and 1920s—radical critics of capitalism and industrialism. Their number included Randolph Bourne, Van Wyck Brooks, Waldo Frank, and Mumford, but their influence and circles incorporated many more Greenwich Village critics, from Dorothy Day to Burke. The Young Americans helped define the common topics and questions of a generation of the American Left. Arguably their public and intellectual project began in November 1916, amidst the fire of World War I, in a bold new journal out of Greenwich Village, *The Seven Arts*. Edited by James Oppenheim and Waldo Frank, the publication promised to be "an expression of our American arts which shall be fundamentally an expression of our American life" (Oppenheim 52–53). Its intellectual scope was profound, featuring writers like John Dewey, John Reed, Robert Frost, Amy Lowell, Paul Rosenfeld, and Brooks, pledging as part of its platform to put American art, literature, philosophy, and criticism to work on behalf of the American national community. "*The Seven Arts*," the magazine declared, "is not a magazine for artists, but an expression of artists for the community" (53).

Their particular interest in American culture as a means of political reform, even revolution, set the Young Americans apart from more conventional socialist and communist radicals in the period. They drew on distinct traditions of cultural politics, taken from the English radicalism of John Ruskin and William Morris and a Left version of civic republicanism. As Blake writes, "What marked both of these traditions off from conventional progressivism—whether of the liberal or Marxist variety—was their relative inattention to the public sphere as an arena of conflict and their subordination of questions of class or rights to an ideal of community" (3). They thus subordinated political questions to larger cultural questions. These larger cultural questions meant that they sought an acute awareness of the "symbolic" with respect to both language and technology. The Young Americans influenced a generation of intellectuals among the American Left to frame what were ultimately political questions in terms of art, artifacts, and culture.

Their political critiques extended to the fundamental questions of "the human spirit." As Frank noted, "We were all sworn foes of Capitalism not because we knew it would not work, but because we judged it, even in success, to be lethal to the human spirit" (qtd. in Blake 4). Their vision of human unity, in turn, centered in what Mumford called "basic communism," which for Mumford included not a strict reorganization of industrial society (for example the collective ownership of land), but a strong biological sense of society as an organism made up of animate and inanimate objects. In its ideal culmination such a society would not orient itself toward Darwinian survival or political power but toward what Mumford, in a deceptively simple formulation we will unpack below, referred to as *life*.

The project of the Young Americans had several problems, owing to widespread disagreement about what visions of communism and technology looked like and how they could benefit life. As Blake notes, it appealed to an ideal of community life that "rested on a conception of total unanimity on one single vision of the good, as revealed to the public through its prophetic vanguard" (Blake 291). But its "spiritual" quality also made the vision appear fuzzy—too unclear and vulnerable to accusations of contradiction. Finally the Young Americans disagreed as much as they agreed on how to better American society; but because of their reticence to envision the public sphere as an arena of conflict they did little to vocalize and explore their own conceptual disagreements. Nevertheless Mumford, more than any of the other Young Americans, did try to offer their basic program a concrete direction, and he worked more than any of his compatriots with organizations and institutions to build and protect the rudiments of basic communism.

These rudiments find striking echoes in Kenneth Burke's work of the 1930s. Looking at what Burke had to say then about communism—controversial then and since—the characteristic features of Mumford's thought are pervasive and most apparent in the final pages of the 1935 edition of *PC*.[1] It is no wonder that Mumford read the manuscript of *PC* with delight, and became an outspoken champion of the work. Burke articulated an "art" of communism biologically grounded, organically oriented, and targeted at the machine age—all themes Mumford had been developing since his 1922 *The Story of Utopias*. Burke wrote, "Communism is a cooperative rationalization, or perspective, which fulfills the requirements suggested by the poetic metaphor. It is fundamentally humanistic, as poetry is. Its ethics is referable to the socio-biological genius of man (the economic conquest of the machine being conceived within such a frame). Its underlying concept of vocation is radical—for it does not permit our sense of duty to arise simply from the contingencies which our ways of production and distribution force upon us, but offers a point of view from which these contingencies themselves may be criticized" (*PC* 344–45). Beyond the organic, biological, and technological thematic affinities with Mumford's thought, this passage pointed toward their converging goal of envisioning communism not as an ideal political state but as a "point of view," a means of altering human society by recasting how to see. Thus both Mumford and Burke approached communism in terms of *poesis*—the ancient, Renaissance, and counter-Enlightenment notion of "making" that melds "production" with "perspective."

Implicit in this approach to communism was a sense that one of the biggest problems posed by the crises of the 1930s entailed the instrumentalization of people, tools, and words as primary *means* toward larger political and economic transformations. A central question before the Left was thus *how* to instrumentalize a social vision, a question made more difficult to answer given the scarcity of attention paid by many of the Young Americans to the technical designs of the instruments themselves. The culturally oriented Left assumed that "culture" encompassed an end as well as a means of social and political transformation; but the literary and cultural sensibilities of the New York Left tended to render the artifacts of culture instrumental, as primarily means toward an imagined end. Thus critics like Frank envisioned literature as a means toward social renewal, and critics like Taggard thought that industrial technology could be appropriated by the masses without any fundamental alteration of the material itself. But for Mumford and Burke in the 1930s literature seemed to point to the conundrums of a more basic human condition, and industrialism would always be a poor and destructive material order, one that needed desperate realignment and remaking in accordance with a biologically oriented human ecology. Consequently they both proposed methodological turns, ones that would give due heed to the intricate relationship between human society and the poetic power of technology and language.

METHODOLOGICAL TURNS: DIALECTICAL BIOLOGISM AND ORGANIC IDEOLOGY

Given the paucity of correspondence between Burke and Mumford, understanding what Mumford meant when he wrote that they were "converging toward the same goals" presents an interpretive challenge. Focusing on this provocative sentence of Mumford's, we argue that their conviviality was methodological in nature. They both responded to the political, technological, and social problems raised in their intellectual circles by reengaging methods of inquiry. Instead of focusing on political strategizing, Burke and Mumford turned to "method," framing it as an open perspectival term rather than a strict instrumental term. And to approach the question of method, they turned to the basic materials of life—organisms, tools, and words. Thus in "technology" or in "communism" Burke and Mumford saw ways of looking rather than new social vistas. They saw points of view rather than mere instruments; they saw verbs rather than nouns. This particular kind of methodological turn was theorized in Mumford's *Technics and Civilization* as "organic ideology" and in Burke's *PC* as "dialectical biologism." Both concepts rested upon a conception of the multifaceted relationships between organisms and their "made" and "natural" environments, and both thus imply a reinterpretation of an organism's behavior.

By appealing to "organic ideology" Mumford did not mean "ideology" in a negative sense. The term for him denoted a scheme of ideas and outlooks that was materially and linguistically conditioned, having had in this sense a neutral tenor. And yet his affirmation of "organic ideology" did have a sharp critical edge, since he pitted it against what he labeled "mechanical ideology." The latter, as he argued in *Technics and Civilization,* formed the impetus of Western industrialization in what he called, in his historicist schema, the "neotechnic phase" of technological development. Mechanical ideology was for him both a perspective and a power system, holding all modes of life accountable to order and predictability, fostering the voracious expansion of industrialism, and tempting humanity toward self-destructive consumption and control (364–65). Mumford connected this false faith in technology to a more diffuse false faith in science as the codification of the pure, unalterable, and permanent laws of nature (368). This ideal "mechanical world-picture," he suggested, was in fact inconsistent with the historical progression of science and technology, with its changing doctrines, shifting interests and knowledges, and regular innovations. Mumford thus presented "organic ideology" as a counter-statement.

Burke presented "dialectical biologism" in *PC* as a kind of counter-statement as well, the avant-garde of "systems of verbalization" (229). Specifically he presented dialectical biologism as a conceptual counter to a form of historicism that would present a "given *historical* texture . . . as the underlying basis of a universal causal series" (228). Dialectical biologism asserted instead a fundamental biological basis for history and in doing so also sought to synthesize antecedent theories of human historical development, namely "materialism, idealism, and dialectical materialism" (229). Following Marx, mind and matter, body and soul, and means of production and human aspirations are envisioned as interactive, but in dialectical biologism Burke added a new, nonhistorical ground to Marx's approach: "our organic equipment" (228). Biology was for Burke "non-historic," but this "permanence" was not at all an argument for a static conception of humanity; rather it was the basis of change.

Indeed both Mumford and Burke set out to ride the fine line between permanence and change, at once positing some stable ground from which to make judgments about the course of human societies, and arguing for the relativity of perspectives, orientations, and outlooks. They each sought a paradoxical critical method that was both historicist and counterrelativist. New points of view, they argued, form the basis of new ways of being, but human being was at the same time seen as relatively continuous. Consequently both thinkers encouraged the careful consideration of the complex, intricate dynamics of permanence and change.

Mumford thus could not easily separate *how* people see from *what* they see. "Once the organic image takes the place of the mechanical one," he argued, "one may confidently predict a slowing down of the tempo of research, the tempo of mechanical invention, and the tempo of social change, since a coherent and integrated advance must take place more slowly than a one-sided advance" (*Technics and Civilization* 372). He advocated this sort of "slowing down" as a means toward realizing an organic image. Over and again he asked, "How far does this or that instrument further the biological purposes or the ideal ends of life" (318)? Such slowed-down and visualized habits of critical inquiry, he argued, would lead to a historical condition in which "the machine is no longer the paragon of progress and the final expression of our desires: it is merely a series of instruments, which we will use in so far as they are serviceable to life at large, and which we will curtail where they infringe upon it or exist purely to support the adventitious structure of capitalism" (365). Thus *Technics* and its 1938 follow-up study, *The Culture of Cities*, which focused on urban spaces in Western history, together constituted a thousand-page survey of the social impact of *things* in Europe, America, and elsewhere: wheels, walls, tools, buildings, engines, glass, clocks, avenues, wagons, locomotives, towers, landscapes, novels, newspapers, radios, assembly lines, and so on. By looking at these objects from the perspective of organic ideology, Mumford introduced a way of seeing them which underscored that *how* society looks through and at its objects constitutes *what* it sees.

By exposing the complex overlapping domains of technology, society, and symbolism, Mumford also problematized and "complicated" social change. He argued that all our really primary data are social and vital. One begins with life; and one knows life, not as a fact in the raw, but only as one is conscious of human society and uses the tools and instruments society has developed through history—words, symbols, grammar, logic, in short the whole technique of communication and funded experience (*Technics and Civilization* 370).

These data then lead to the problem of social change: "the problem is equally one of altering the nature and the rhythm of the machine to fit the actual needs of the community" (367). To solve the problem, Mumford called for *complication* as a means of transformative social action: "we have begun to complicate the mechanical," he argued, "in order to make it more organic: therefore more effective, more harmonious with our living environment" (367). Mumford thus moved between simplicity and complexity. A technico-political order, he argued, must focus on maintaining the simple human biological necessities in as holistic a manner as possible, all the while communicating the necessity of constant adaptation. Furthermore Mumford blurred the line between organism and environment, the human subject and history. "Organic ideology," he hoped, would result in a basic communism that rested on a "dynamic equilibrium" seen at moments in Western history, such as in medieval Catholic towns and Calvinist cultures in Holland and America. The gesture was not nostalgic; the goal was not to return to the past. Rather it was, in Brooks's famous formulation, to create a "useable past," one drawn from well beyond the borders of America ("On Creating a Usable Past").

Like Mumford, Burke proposed in *PC* a methodological revision of ways of looking at and using organisms, tools, and words, condensed in his notion of "dialectical biologism." And as much as *Technics and Civilization* represented Mumford's reaction against "mechanical ideology," Burke's *PC* was a reaction against a master "occupational psychosis," the "technological psychosis," presented as a general "pro-technological attitude" that justified behavioral psychology, waste, war, and industrial greed (46, 49). Like Mumford, Burke proposed a type of dialectic based on the interaction between life and machine, organism and environment. And yet Burke maintained a pragmatic, skeptical, and linguistic perspective that would mitigate against any technocratic momentum that such a project might gain. Thus while sharing a basic methodological goal with Mumford, Burke also introduced friction to any smooth realization of the goal.

In his afterword to the 1984 edition of *PC* Burke noted that he had sought in the 1930s to reimagine the concept of dialectic in a more integrated and complex fashion than that endorsed by some of his contemporaries. Paraphrasing Marx's famous revision of Hegelian idealism, he wrote in the afterword, "In the Hegelian 'ideology' ideas come, as it were, 'from the top down,' whereas the Marxist dialectic derives them 'from the bottom up.' I end by stoutly maintaining that both derivations exemplify the 'genetic fallacy,' and regardless of how our aptitude for 'symbolicity' came to be a part of our physiological structure, once it began to develop it manifested a nature of its own" (304).

To inject the primacy of human biology into dialectical philosophy, Burke proposed envisioning a philosophy of technology grounded in human biology, but even more a philosophy of political *technê* rooted in the primacy of perception.[2] In the final pages of the 1935 edition of *PC*, Burke expressed his hope that communism would provide a political means to enact dialectical biologism, writing, "Under capitalism, man must accommodate his efforts to the genius of machinery—under Communism he may accommodate machinery to the genius of his fundamental needs as an active and communicating organism" (344–45). And yet communism appeared here and elsewhere in Burke's writing of the 1930s as an orientation more than a political system. Burke viewed communism as a more pragmatic perspective from which to realize the factualness of dialectical biologism, more pragmatic than any other political orientation with which he could align his method.

As readers of this volume likely know, the thrust of Burke's work was methodological in character. But reading Burke alongside Mumford helps us to see the extent to which this methodological emphasis was inherently social and political in character. Both thinkers were pushing beyond "politics as usual" and assumed (mis)conceptions of politics. Both pushed to the background ideal political visions, foregrounding instead ways of looking at the "stuff" of life that people assumed were mere means of instrumentalizing political visions, whether tools, words, or even other organisms. The introduction of the biological into the dialectical served as a way of reimagining the instrumental—and thus the methodological—as *for* something, namely *life*. Instruments and methods appear as expressions of the more basic "equipment for life" or "equipment for living."[3] This equipment—organic, artificial, material, linguistic—provides a teleology by virtue of biology and thus provides as well the possibilities of critical assessment, judgment, action, and change. In Burke and Mumford we find a rapprochement of language, body, spirit, and machine to aid humanity in inventing a better life.

TOWARD EUTOPICS

As much as Burke's dialectical biologism and Mumford's organic ideology converged toward the same methodological goal, aiming at reenvisioning "method," the two critics' careers diverged in significant ways that tell us much about the possibilities of their common methodological turn. While Mumford delved deeper into technology and urban society, Burke delved deeper into terminologies and literature. Whereas the technological order came to represent for Mumford more and more of a socio-technical problem, it represented for Burke more and more a problem of an even more pervasive *technê*, language. Mumford summoned architects, city planners, and engineers; Burke summoned philosophy and rhetoric. Both remained preoccupied with the symbolic character of things-in-the-world, however; both recognized, in Burke's words, that "these household Things [indeed, any Things] are also Spirits" (*Rhetoric of Motives* 296). Mumford, drawing on the emphasis of the Young Americans and the social purposes of art, presented a picture of humans as fashioners, makers, and producers of technologies that communicate, and thus he offered a conception of humans as technology-fabricating animals—*homo faber*.[4] Burke's even broader conception of humans as communicants as well as technology fabricators in turn offered a rich perspective on the worlds of symbol-using animals.[5]

Thus in divergent ways the two writers worked toward what Mumford would call "eutopias," rather than *u*topias. The distinction, one Mumford had drawn in 1922's *The Story of Utopias* between realistic "good places" and abstract perfect places that do not exist, signaled an important commitment to pragmatism on the part of both thinkers (303–5). For Mumford this pragmatism served as an important qualification to his historicism—for example as seen in his argument in *Technics and Civilization* and *The Culture of Cities* that the history of the West was progressing toward a "biotechnic age" (*Technics* 353–56). Mumford did not think the biotechnic phase inevitable. He did not cast himself as a prophet of historical progression, and he could envision relapses into other orders. But he held out hope that the contradictions of industrial capitalism, especially their Victorian repression of life, would result in the creation of biotechnic good places.

By 1938's *The Culture of Cities* Mumford articulated his eutopic political vision as "basic communism," which included standard Marxist proposals like collective ownership of land and other means of production, but he extended his vision in line with organic ideology. In tandem with his organicism, basic communism was an ethic as much as a politics, central to a eutopian "re-orientation" of human society. It was "basic" because it was nonpartisan and nonreductive, requiring a kind of "catholic" orientation toward the human and natural worlds. Its "basic-ness" was also integral to its egalitarian, collectivist outlook. And thus it was a form of "communism," rooted in *collectivist* assumptions, ranging from the Aristotelian and civic republican conviction that " society as a whole fortunately tends to act more wisely than its individual members" (*Culture* 300), to the recognition that the organism is not an atom, as it is ultimately impossible to separate the biological "thing" from its environment. Mumford's call for a new age of biotechnics, where machines were subservient to *life*, entailed a radical paradigm shift in which Mumford asserted the social primacy of life, cooperation, community, and environment. For Mumford the biotechnic eutopia would be one in which there would be no society-wide trained incapacities, where the "psychosis" of a people (as Burke would term it) would be to think in terms of complex integration as well as holism. It would be, in our words, an "ecological communism" grounded in human biological necessity rather than unattainable party politics.

The eutopic spirit too possessed Burke's work as he casted his suggestions for alternate social orders in a skeptical frame. If, as both Burke and Mumford both held, organicism disrupted straightforward systems of *vis a tergo* causality, a capacity to consider complex relationships became essential. However, with statements such as "one school's reason is another school's rationalization," *PC*—which Austin Warren in a 1936 review framed as "The Sceptic's Progress"—risked coming across as an argument for hyperrelativism. In fact Burke's "criticism of criticism" drew attention to the myriad ways perspectives can be formed, worldviews can be justified, and motives can take shape but did not make a case for radical epistemological subjectivism (*PC* 13). Rather in diagnosing his age he argued that a component of the technological psychosis was "our emphasis upon intellectual tolerance" connected to an "individualism" seen in the "departmentalism" of knowledge "restricted to small groups" (47). Burke implied that if one went beyond a critical frame to a poetic and productive frame, then one needed to address questions of value in a way that could transcend such individualism and departmentalism, precisely the point of Burke's "metabiology" in *PC* (48, 232–36). In this second movement skepticism entailed a kind of "realistic" tolerance for complexity integral to the organic outlook that would form the basis of his pragmatic eutopic vision, which he initially called "Communism." "So far as I can see, the only coherent and organized movement making for the subjection of the technological genius to humane ends is that of Communism, by whatever name it may finally prevail. For though Communism is generally put forward on a purely technological basis, in accordance with the strategy of recommendation advisable in a scientific ear, we must realize the highly humanistic or poetic nature of its fundamental criteria" (*PC* 93). Communism, Burke argued, was a philosophy that took "human needs as its point of reference" and thus could function as a "corrective to the technological rationalization" (94). Communism was a philosophy of *life* before the departmentalization of the machine, and metabiology was an ethical project of action before the interminable and destructive ideology of technological progress.

Nevertheless, such pragmatism presented challenges to these two eutopic thinkers. Mumford's qualified historicism pushed him into technocratic projects and collaborations with powerful elites. He worked with the influential Regional Planning Association, cheered on aspects of FDR's New Deal, and later became one of the most vocal American intellectuals supporting U.S. intervention in Europe to push back fascism (he saw fascist politics as the natural consequence of the machine age). These activities entailed a subtle but important movement away from attention to language and literature and toward the transformative capacities of material power. At the same time, perhaps, Burke's resolute attention to language and literature kept him from the sort of collaborative, public projects that made Mumford a more significant and influential figure in American life and thought than Burke. Indeed Burke was sensitive to the accusation that his emphasis on language would keep his approach from "real-world" consequence. Thus he defended himself in his 1936 contribution to "What Is Americanism: A Symposium on Marxism and the American Tradition": "The philosophy of capitalism can only be combated by *another* philosophy. I always use the example of the dust storms in the West. 'What?' I murmur. 'You say philosophy doesn't matter? Then just look at the dust storms. They are absolute evidence of the ways in which a bad philosophy can actually have an effect upon the weather. They show how, if you don't get things straight, you may even ruin the climate of a whole continent. A *bad* philosophy can thus endanger vast populations. Whereupon, all the greater need to have a *good* philosophy.' Yours for the *good* philosophy, the philosophy of communism" (11; emphasis in original). Nevertheless by stressing "good philosophy" over Mumford's eutopic "good places" Burke suggested that language, which is always subject to *change*, was the prime mover of social transformation, even as he argued for an "underlying purpose"—biological and permanent—to ground a new universalism (*PC* 232–36). In this way his methodological turn was an ambitious attempt to synthesize permanence and change, the universal and the particular, toward the eutopic project conceived with "good philosophy" (234).

But it is nevertheless arguable that Burke stretched the concept of "method" so far as to make it pragmatically inconsequential: "Man is methodical, even methodological. To sprawl under a tree at noontime, besotted with food, wine, and relaxation after labor, as with the harvesters in Breughel's painting—should we call this rational, irrational, or simply method? As we say of philanderers, man "has a way with him" (234).

Such a notion of method, while freeing the concept from its entrapment within technological psychosis, could do little more than offer a critique of the limited perspective of the regnant age, and perhaps suggest a preference for an agrarian, romantic style of life. With even "metabolism" being a "method" for Burke, he casted doubt upon the political ramifications of method while casting technology and programmatic communism as recalcitrant but negotiable (234). Mumford, on the other hand, seems to have found in ecosystems, topographies, and material artifacts the primary restraining forces against practical political action.

In fact Mumford—who went on to a voluminous career, leaving a legacy as one of the most important, if not the most important, American critic of architecture, urban planning, and technology in the twentieth century—continued to carry the burden of "basic communism" into the 1970s, so much so that in 1970's *The Myth of the Machine: The Pentagon of Power,* he chastised, in its name, the welfare state for its complicity with "the machine" and its dehumanization of the worker (326). In 1970 Mumford could still call for the radical reorientation of society, though his call became increasingly inaudible in Cold War culture. Burke in contrast dropped communism. Communism, by whatever name, would soon after the 1935 edition of *PC* be evacuated from his texts. Thus William H. Rueckert writes, "*Permanence and Change* is a book of beginnings, an exploratory work in which Burke tries to get his bearings as a social critic and to define his own orientation. Having rejected Communism, Burke commits himself to the poetry of action he describes so eloquently at the end of *Permanence and Change*" (67). Yet it is hard to discern political or social radicalism in his later criticism—perplexity, concern, and outrage, perhaps, but not radicalism. The critic got the better of the communist, and language the better of the organism.

CONCLUSION: BURKE'S PROVOCATIONS

In a 1947 letter to his poet-friend William Carlos Williams, Burke expounded his "idea of teaching philosophy": "Get key terms, then speculate as to the various ways they may be manipulated. This along with noting the particular way in which the given writer manipulates them. This method (a) enables one to call the plays, (b) enables one to see the limitations of a given use, (c) enables one to see how other terms shd. be spawned and spun (or are spawned and spun)" (qtd. in East 120). In this essay we have examined some of the key terms discussed by Burke, Mumford, and their contemporaries in the 1930s (capitalism, communism, technology, and utopia). We have then considered how Mumford and Burke spun and manipulated these terms as they searched for ways to solve the American crises they witnessed. But we have even more looked at the attention Burke and Mumford brought to the acts of spinning and turning themselves through examining their common methodological turn.

However, their shared methodological turn and the methodologies they generated—organic ideology and dialectical biologism—should be viewed critically. As Burke joked in another letter to Williams a year later, "The great trick in our racket [criticism] is that you can use anything, if you merely learn to shift among 'therefore,' 'and,' and 'however'" (qtd. in East 138). Thus as critics Burke and Mumford provoke us to interpret not only culture but also the character and possibilities of criticism itself. At best dialectical biologism and organic ideology need their terms spun and their "therefores" manipulated to suit the ever-changing biological necessities of life as they become constrained by new iterations of politics and technology. At worst however all this spinning and turning can distract us from ever focusing on the issues critical to life. Both organic ideology and dialectical biologism insist on constant revision of how to look at the instrumentalization of political plans, the methods employed, and the communication of the results, all according to the dynamic political interplay of organisms, tools, and words. But both methodologies open up the possibility of merely spinning our heads.

The correspondence between Mumford and Burke thus provoked us to examine not only their conceptual and methodological affinities, but in turn our critical approaches, which have not been incidental to Burkean scholarship. One of the principal reasons so many literary and rhetorical critics have taken up Burke resides in his methodological turn. But this essay suggests that critics influenced by Burke should not grasp onto his various methods of analysis as static templates for critical use. Instead they should be seen as inroads into both the vital potentials and real perils of a methodological turn. Burke and Mumford both took method seriously, and not as mere means of instrumentalization, but as an activity and approach integral to human life in all of its biological, organic, and social dimensions. Burkean criticism should not consist of a specialized set of terms and rubrics. Instead it should incorporate Burke's attitude toward the world that demands our constant attention to the simple tools of life. At the same time, Burke suggested that one of the pitfalls of the technological psychosis (one in this essay we suggest that Burke did not fully avoid) was dissociating tools and methods from questions of social value. Criticizing his methodological turn thus has its own complex challenges.

This essay began with a provocation offered by the Burke archive. It has culminated with a provocation offered by Burke's career as a student of method. We began with an unfinished story and worked toward a bigger story about the challenges of criticism. The archives thus represent a collection of provocations, but also the starting place for thinking through the questions endemic to our work as teachers, scholars, students, and critics.

NOTES

1. Seventy years after the publication of *PC* it still creates controversy, especially concerning the book's (and its author's) relationship to Marxism and communism. Burke's Marxisms seem to be many, and a survey of the critical literature produces a broad continuum of Burkean Marxisms in *PC*. Don Burks argues that Burke's communism in *PC* is "largely his own creation, a personal ideal," a one-of-a-kind (219). Burks agrees with Armin Paul Frank that it is an "idealistic, tentative kind" of Marxism (Burks 220 and A. P. Frank 84). Philip Wander similarly characterizes Burke's Marxism during the 1930s, the decade of *PC*, as experimental. He writes, "About Marx, Marxism, and the American Communist Party during the 1930s, Burke hedged, vacillated, wavered, sent arguments this way and that, danced metaphors, and tried out perspectives" (208). James Arnt Aune traces out "three different Burkes—the pragmatic Marxist, the premature neoconservative critic of Marxism, and, finally, Burke the unrepentant 'left liberal'" (235). Gregory Jay writes that *PC* and *Attitudes toward History* are "distillations of Marx" but with a "*Burkean twist*," that is, an emphasis on the rhetorical (170, 171). Ross Wolin portrays a Burke who must approach Marxism and communism "on his own terms" (79). Taking Burke's 1935 Writer's Congress speech as an exemplum, Frank Lentricchia portrays Burke as a renegade among the 1930s radicals, an American ilk of Gramsci, pushing academic criticism through political thresholds. In sum, these scholars understand Burke's Marxism in *PC* as a tentative, idealistic, and, perhaps most of all, idiosyncratic.

It is true that Burke's own revisions and excisions of his Marxism have further muddled analysis of it. Concern about potential repercussions deriving from his Marxist tendencies led to his infamous "omissions" of overt communistic statements from later editions of *PC* that Edward Schiappa and Mary F. Keener examined in 1991, as well as the rationalizations about the omissions he added to the book's 1953 prologue and 1983's afterword, "In Retrospective Prospect." Although these omissions and appendages may have helped keep *PC* a "live" work among critics, or although, as Burke explains it, they may have "helped bring the text back to its original nature" (*PC* xlix), they did not seem to help make the nature of Burke's Marxism in *PC* any clearer.

Rather than concluding that Burke's Marxism in the 1930s was idiosyncratic, we think it better to characterize his approach as a departure from and a critique of orthodox Marxism in favor of the established "organic" form of communism familiar to the Young Americans.

2. For an overview of Burke's rhetorical philosophy of technology, see Ian Hill's "'The Human Barnyard' and Kenneth Burke's Philosophy of Technology."

3. Mumford hinted at this terminology in *Technics* (365), but in 1966's *The Myth of the Machine: Technics and Human Development* Mumford wrote, "Tool-technics, in fact, is but a fragment of biotechnics: man's total equipment for life" (7). Burke introduced his similar terminology in *Counter-Statement* (183). Also see *PC* (271).

4. See, for example, Mumford's later work in *Art and Technics*.

5. See Burke's "Definition of Man."

WORKS CITED

Aune, James Arnt. "Burke's Palimpsest: Rereading *PC*." *Communication Studies* 42.3 (1991): 234–37.

Blake, Casey Nelson. *Beloved Community: The Cultural Criticism of Randolphe Bourne, Van Wyck Brooks, Waldo Frank, and Lewis Mumford.* Chapel Hill: University of North Carolina Press, 1990.

Brooks, Van Wyck. "On Creating a Usable Past" *Dial* Apr. 1918: 337–41.

Burke, Kenneth. *Attitudes toward History,* 3rd ed. Berkeley: University of California Press, 1984.

———. *Counter-Statement.* Berkeley: University of California Press, 1968.

———. "Definition of Man." *Language as Symbolic Action: Essays on Life, Literature, and Method.* Berkeley: University of California Press, 1966. 3–24.

———. "My Approach to Communism." *New Masses* Mar. 20, 1934: 16–20.

———. "On Interpretation." *Plowshare* Feb. 10, 1934: 3–79.

———. *Permanence and Change: An Anatomy of Purpose.* New York: New Republic, 1935.

———. *Permanence and Change: An Anatomy of Purpose,* 3rd ed. Berkeley: University of California Press, 1984.

———. *A Rhetoric of Motives.* Berkeley: University of California Press, 1969.

———. "What Is Americanism? A Symposium on Marxism and the American Tradition." *Partisan Review and Anvil* 3.3 (Apr. 1936): 9–11.

Burks, Don M. "Kenneth Burke: The Agro-Bohemian 'Marxoid.'" *Communication Studies* 42.3 (1991): 219–33.

East, James H., ed. *The Humane Particulars: The Collected Letters of William Carlos Williams and Kenneth Burke.* Columbia: University of South Carolina Press, 2003.

Frank, Armin Paul. *Kenneth Burke.* New York: Twayne Publishers, 1969.

Frank, Waldo. *Our America*. New York: Boni and Liveright, 1919.

George, Ann, and Jack Selzer. "What Happened at the First American Writers' Congress? Kenneth Burke's 'Revolutionary Symbolism in America.'" *Rhetoric Society Quarterly* 33.2 (Spring 2003): 47–66.

Hill, Ian. "'The Human Barnyard' and Kenneth Burke's Philosophy of Technology." *KB Journal* 5.2 (2009).

Jay, Gregory. "Burke Re-Marx." *Pre/Text* 6.3–4 (1985): 169–75.

Jay, Paul, ed. *The Selected Correspondence of Kenneth Burke and Malcolm Cowley, 1915–1981*. New York: Viking, 1988.

Kenneth Burke Papers. Patee and Paterno Library. Pennsylvania State University.

Lentricchia, Frank. *Criticism and Social Change*. Chicago: University of Chicago Press, 1983.

Mumford, Lewis. *Art and Technics*. New York: Columbia University Press, 2000.

———. *The Culture of Cities*. 1938. New York: Harcourt Brace Jovanovich, 1966.

———. *The Myth of the Machine: The Pentagon of Power*. New York: Harcourt Brace Jovanovich, 1970.

———. *The Myth of the Machine: Technics and Human Development*. New York: Harcourt, Brace, and World, 1967.

———. *The Story of Utopias*. New York: Boni and Liveright, 1922.

———. *Technics and Civilization*. New York: Harcourt Brace, 1963.

Oppenheim, James, et al. Editorial Statement. *The Seven Arts* 1 (Nov. 1916): 52–56.

Rueckert, William H. *Encounters with Kenneth Burke*. Urbana: University of Illinois Press, 1994.

Schiappa, Edward, and Mary F. Keener. "The 'Lost' Passages of *Permanence and Change*." *Communication Studies* 42.3 (1991): 191–98.

Wander, Philip C. "At the Ideological Front." *Communication Studies* 42.3 (1991): 199–217.

Warren, Austin. "The Sceptic's Progress." 1936. *Critical Responses to Kenneth Burke, 1924–1966*. Ed. William H. Rueckert. Minneapolis: University of Minnesota Press, 1969. 51–60.

Wolin, Ross. *The Rhetorical Imagination of Kenneth Burke*. Columbia: University of South Carolina Press, 2001.

DAVE TELL

BURKE AND JAMESON

Reflections on Language, Ideology, and Criticism

In September 1977 the English Institute dedicated its annual meeting to the work of Kenneth Burke. From Burke's perspective the entire institute was a disaster: some of the keynote speakers failed to send him advance notices of their comments; the chairman of the institute, Hayden White, allowed so much time for comments from the floor that Burke was left with no time to deliver the responses he had stayed up for all but three of the previous forty-five hours preparing; the hall in which the meetings were held was such "a disgrace to even the *word* 'acoustics'" that, even with his new hearing aid, Burke could understand little of these protracted comments from the floor (he complained that Yale's Geoffrey Hartmann "fell into a prolonged meditative trance, not one word of which I heard"); and although White had arranged for Burke to give a final plenary talk, they realized at the last moment that the meeting room had been reserved only until five-thirty and there would be no time for the plenary. In a moment of restraint Burke confided to his friend Bill Rueckert that "it just worked out that things dint work out right." With less restraint he admitted, "I nearly blew my top, I felt so tense" (KB to WR September 21, 1977). And with still less restraint he confessed to Sibley Watson that the institute put him on the "edge of a stroke," that the very movements of his body seemed unnaturally slow, and that he thought "this was it" (KB to SW September 19, 1977).

All the logistical problems however were so many minor inconveniences compared to the one thing that pushed Burke to the "edge of a stroke": Fredric Jameson's keynote address. As Burke confided to his friend Mary Milam, Jameson's critique was one of the most devastating he had ever endured: "I've been in this business for half a century, and naturally have taken many bumps—but never before have I been so deeply cut as that. I consulted a lawyer, but he wanted too much to defend me" (KB to MM June 29, 1978). Burke had gotten so upset because Jameson used his keynote to ask whether Burke's project could be "reread or rewritten as a model for contemporary ideological analysis" ("Symbolic Inference" 71). Coming from Jameson, this was no ivory tower inquiry; six years earlier Jameson had written in

Marxism and Form that ideological analysis was "the most urgent task of a genuinely dialectical criticism." Without it, he argued, criticism "consists in separating reality into airtight compartments, carefully distinguishing the political from the economic, the legal from the political, the sociological from the historical, so that the full implications of any given problem can never come into view" (354, 368). Such criticism, Jameson wrote in 1981, is "worse than error": it "maims our existence as individual subjects and paralyzes our thinking about time and change just as surely as it alienates us from our speech itself" (*Political Unconscious* 20). In asking whether or not Burke could be "rewritten" as a model for ideological analysis, then, Jameson was going for the jugular. He was asking whether Burke's work would paralyze thinking or if it could be taken as a model of ideological criticism that could "spring us outside our own hardened ideas into a new and more vivid apprehension of reality itself" (*Marxism* 372).

Jameson's judgment was negative. Although "it would seem" that Burke's conception of symbolic action would function as a "powerful incitement to the study of a text's mode of activity in the general cultural and social world beyond it," in actual fact it "provides aid and comfort to those who want to limit our work to texts whose autonomy has been carefully secured in advance." In other words Jameson concluded that Burke's system undermined ideological criticism by "comforting" those who would critique a text without reference to its "social ground." Further Jameson argued that Burke's dramatism was marred by three "strategies of containment," a phrase he popularized in *The Political Unconscious* to describe the mechanisms whereby nonideological critics preserve the "illusion that their readings are somehow complete and self-sufficient" ("Symbolic Inference" 83, 73; *Political Unconscious* 10). Jameson's talk finished just before five o'clock in the afternoon; Hayden White directed the audience to refreshments outside the hall; and, with the meeting room suddenly unavailable, Burke got no chance to respond.

Yet Burke would get his chance. After *Critical Inquiry* published Jameson's keynote address in spring 1978 under the title "The Symbolic Inference; or, Kenneth Burke and Ideological Analysis," Sheldon Sacks, editor of *Critical Inquiry*, gave Burke the opportunity to respond. The result was a much-overlooked essay in the Burkean corpus: "Methodological Repression and/or Strategies of Containment" (MRSC). Burke grew to dislike the essay intensely, and for good reasons. It is a rambling, disjointed, and tragic response to Jameson, the argument of which can be quickly summarized. Burke argued that he too understood ideology, and he spent a dozen pages citing passages in his own books as proof. He then briefly and enigmatically suggested that his own logology was superior to Jameson's ideological criticism. By the time the essay went to print, however, Burke himself regretted the vast majority of what he had written. And generations of Burke scholars have been no kinder, ignoring the theoretical contributions of the essay almost entirely. The regret of Burke and the oversight of Burkeans are both however easily explained. The essay is simply not very good. It captures neither the stunning emotional capital that Burke invested in the Jameson affair, nor the central, methodological issue that Burke believed lay at the root of the disagreement.

For these purposes, we must turn not to "Methodological Repression" but to the vast correspondence that surrounds it. Although no record substantiates that Burke ever corresponded with Jameson, he corresponded with virtually everyone *about* Jameson. In letters to Wayne Booth, J. Hillis Miller, Hayden White, Christian Susini, William Rueckert, Bob Zachary, and Malcolm Cowley—to mention only the most prominent names—Burke explained his regrets vis-à-vis the institute and his complaints vis-à-vis Jameson. Fortunately the Kenneth Burke Papers at Pennsylvania State University provide access to these forgotten contours of the Burke/Jameson debate. They reveal facets of the debate we could never appreciate with sole recourse to the published record. They register just how deeply Burke was impacted by his brief encounter with Fredric Jameson. Beyond clarifying the points of the debate, they also lay bare the pathos and pride of Kenneth Burke—a scholar "deeply cut" (perhaps too deeply cut) by a cutting critique of his work. For these reasons I believe Burke's encounter with Jameson is best understood as an *archival event*. Although traces of this encounter surface in the *Critical Inquiry* exchange, both the tone and substance of the exchange are preserved only in the archives. Read properly then the archive brings to us a Burke/Jameson encounter that exists only nominally in the printed record.

In his correspondence Burke insisted that the closing pages of MRSC contained, if only in germ, a fundamental distinction between Jameson's Marxist criticism and his own logological approach. What "it berls [sic] down to," he wrote Booth, is "a distinction between a historicist approach to human nature in terms of ideology, and my methodological approach in terms of Logology" (KB to WB June 24, 1978). To take the rambling incoherence of "Methodological Repression" and "boil it down" to this simple distinction was no easy task. To do so Burke repeatedly provided his interlocutors with a set of concrete protocols for reading MRSC: ignore these pages, privilege these paragraphs, and contextualize it in terms of these essays.

In this essay I foreground Burke's reading of his own response to Jameson. I argue that by reading MRSC in the context of a correspondence constantly commenting upon it, we gain much more than simply a better understanding of the Burke/Jameson debate. We gain also a lesson in critical temperament. As Burke's "boiled-down" summary suggests, the points of the debate focused on the nature of language, the role of ideology, and above all questions of critical methodology. To Jameson's charge, enumerated above, that Burke's critical method could not account for the role of ideology, Burke countered that Jameson's "ideological analysis" was flawed by its inability to account for the nature of language. Thus we have two critics reflecting on criticism, each advocating his own method for selfish purposes: Burke advocating logology because only logology could account for what interested him (the nature of language); Jameson advocating ideological analysis because only it could account for what interested him (ideology). The debate so cast might be dismissed as mere academic posturing: Burke criticizing Jameson for not being Burke and vice versa. Such a dismissal would be a mistake, for the very texture of the debate reveals a position that neither of its participants articulated: the necessity of methodological pluralism. Burke made a fantastic case for the merits of logology, but as he did so he inadvertently made an equally strong case for the merits of ideological criticism. Otherwise put, I argue that in the very act of demonstrating the virtues of logology, Burke also set in bold relief the limitations of logology, and in so doing he provided a valuable reminder to all of us about the dangers of deifying any methodological system. Burke argued for logology and Jameson for ideological criticism, but the debate itself demonstrates the importance of an open critical temperament. Such at least is the argument I advance.

The argument proceeds in three sections. First I focus on the first three-quarters of MRSC, the largest section of the essay and the section that Burke begged his interlocutors to ignore. I will attend not so much to the essay itself but to the after-the-fact justifications and rationalizations by which Burke explained this unfortunate section to his correspondents. From these rationalizations emerges a key norm of academic debate, a norm to which Burke holds Jameson and to which I will later hold Burke. In the second section I attend to the final quarter of "Methodological Repression," or more precisely to Burke's repeated insistence that his interlocutors do so. When this final section of MRSC is so framed, the virtues of logology are displayed prominently. Finally, in the third section, I judge Burke's response to Jameson in terms of the critical standards to which Burke held Jameson and which he advocated as universal norms for critical debate. Here the limitations of logology and the necessity of ideological criticism emerge.

METHODOLOGICAL REPRESSION AND THE NORMS OF ACADEMIC DEBATE

MRSC is a disjointed, poorly organized essay. Indeed except for the last two pages, the essay's only principle of organization appears to be parataxis. That is, the essay reads as little more than an index of Burkean references to ideology, listed somewhat chronologically, but without developing any substantive argument. This much was by design. Burke's first and most enduring objection to Jameson was one of "methodological repression": Jameson attacked Burke's work as being insufficiently ideological while not once citing Burke's work on ideology. It was this oversight that Burke wrote to correct. "I have no intention of arguing with him," he told his friend Wayne Booth (who also happened to be Jameson's former teacher); "I simply want to note where I did what he says I didn't do. I can't understand how he could be so misinformed, if he read me at all" (KB to WB May 4, 1978).

Burke was infuriated by Jameson's failure to extend him the basic courtesy of citing appropriate passages, and this anger is well recorded in the correspondence. "What a pissant job Jameson's pretentious piece is," Burke wrote to Booth (KB to WB June 24, 1978). To Howard Nemerov, he called Jameson a "competent shit"

(KB to HN April 15, 1978). To Malcolm Cowley, he wrote, "I have finished an absurd waste of time and energy in commenting on an essay anent my Sickly Selph
by Fredric Jameson" (KB to MC June 27, 1978). And a full year after the institute,
he again wrote Hayden White and asked him to "explain to me by what canons
of competence [Jameson] makes [ideology] the very basis of our disagreement yet
quoted not a single sentence of what I say explicitly on the subject" (KB to HW
August 11, 1978).

Jameson's failure to cite Burke's work on ideology was, to Burke's mind, in-
excusable; it became one of the foremost themes of his Jameson-centered correspondence. To Sheldon Sacks he wrote, "But there enters our Champion, Jameson,
who ruled out (by sheer Quietus) every single sentence I wrote on the subject of
ideology" (KB to SS June 10, 1978). To the French Burke scholar Christian Susini, he
wrote: "I have written a response [to Jameson]. But it's too long, 23 typewritten pp.
And the first half is a damned nuisance, since I had to waste my time reviewing my
references to the term 'ideology' (in *Counter-Statement* and *Rhetoric of Motives*). He
is so prompt at 'rereading' and 'rewriting,' the reader gets no chance to know what
was *actually written*. . . . I demand at least that he say how I have used the term, and
exactly how, as judged from his point of view, my treatment was inadequate" (KB
to CS July 18, 1978). Burke complained similarly to J. Hillis Miller that the "first
half of the Response was necessarily wasted undoing Jameson's omissions" (KB to
JHM September 7, 1978). It was precisely because Jameson never quoted a single
sentence that Burke felt compelled to use the majority of MRSC as little more than
an index to his references to ideology.

By the time he submitted his response to *Critical Inquiry*, Burke felt keenly that
he had indeed wasted his time replying to Jameson—so much so that he suggested
to the editor, Sheldon Sacks, that the first eighteen pages of the twenty-three-page
manuscript might be reduced to "a paragraph summarizing the references to the
astounding omissions" (KB to SS July 17, 1978). Sacks resisted Burke's suggestion
and on August 3, 1978, wrote Burke with the news that the piece was "interesting
in toto": "I don't think any cutting or salvaging operation is necessary or advisable"
(SS to KB August 3, 1978). Thus all twenty-three pages of MRSC went to print, the
first three-quarters of which, Burke confided to William Rueckert, was "but a waste
of time" (KB to WR September 15, 1979).

The sense that the first half of the article was indeed a "waste of time" is heightened when we realize that Burke may well have been chasing a straw person.
Jameson was clear about the object of his critique: he was interrogating Burke's
"conception of literature as a symbolic act" ("Symbolic Inference" 83). To engage
the substance of Jameson's arguments, Burke should have sought recourse in his notions of symbolic action, the pentad, and dramatism more generally. For Jameson
was not attacking Burke on ideology, he was suggesting that Burke's critical method
was ill suited for ideological criticism. Instead of engaging this critique however
Burke was distracted by a tangential comment near the end of Jameson's piece in

which he claimed that Burke's work was tainted by a "reluctance to pronounce the word ideology itself" ("Symbolic Inference" 87). Thus instead of defending the social value of his critical method—an argument for which his own works provided ample support (as Frank Lentricchia and Stephen Bygrave would show in the coming years), he responded by indexing his pronunciations of ideology.

It is perhaps for these reasons that, despite a general interest in the theoretical intersections of Burke and Jameson, very little attention has been paid to MRSC, the one text in which Burke addressed Jameson directly. The most sustained analysis of Burke's relationship to Jameson belongs to Robert Wess, who was himself so provoked by Jameson's English Institute address that he immediately drafted his own response for *Critical Inquiry* (RW to KB December 7, 1982). Although the untimely death of Sheldon Sacks and the disruption this caused at *Critical Inquiry* prevented this response from being published, Wess persevered. In *Kenneth Burke: Rhetoric, Subjectivity, Postmodernism* he suggested that Burke's account of rhetoric could redress the insufficiencies of Jameson's treatment of narrative in *The Political Unconscious* (see RW to KB February 14, 1982). But even here MRSC is scarcely mentioned; it is as if Burke's own response to Jameson is of marginal importance in crafting a Burkean response to Jameson. Perhaps most telling on this score is the work of Lentricchia and Bygrave, for insofar as both of these scholars read Burke as an ideological critic of the first order, both of them may be read as providing a rather direct answer to Jameson (Bygrave 3; Lentricchia 38, 87). Lentricchia himself suggested as much, noting, "I did not write the book in order to answer Fredric Jameson's critique of Burke, but I suppose that's one way of reading what I've done" (qtd. in Bygrave 14). In light of this it is all the more remarkable that neither Lentricchia nor Bygrave draws heavily on Burke's response to Jameson.[1] In sum Burke's account of methodological repression has itself been repressed. The fact that so many scholars are sensitive to the theoretical promise of reading Burke and Jameson together and yet, almost to a person, find little assistance in Burke's published response is telling: it suggests that MRSC did indeed miss the key issues, that it is in fact little more than a glorified Burkean index, and that the real substance of the exchange lies elsewhere. Perhaps Burke himself sensed this. After all, he not only gave Sacks the freedom to delete the vast majority of his response, he also characterized the same majority as a "nuisance." For my purposes, the value of this "wasted" effort lies here: as Burke sought to rationalize the essay, he explained to anyone who would listen that Jameson's omissions meant, "I had to waste my time." From this imperative emerges the foremost norm of academic debate: Burke believed that intellectuals should engage each other's work carefully and thoughtfully. Burke returned repeatedly to Jameson's purported failure on this score because it helped him rationalize and justify a large portion of his essay which, he assures us, was otherwise a nuisance and waste of time. A simple norm to be sure—and its very simplicity seemed to make Jameson's infraction and Burke's reaction all the more severe. But as we will see, this is a critical norm that Burke himself would find difficult to practice.

CRITICISM AND THE NATURE OF LANGUAGE: THE VIRTUES OF LOGOLOGY

Burke's gradual disenchantment with the first half of his response is matched only by his growing enthusiasm for its final pages. Although Burke confided to Sacks that the first fourteen pages were a "damned nuisance" necessitated by Jameson's "faulty reporting," he maintained that the remainder of the essay was quite important: "The second half is what I enjoyed doing, pticly [*sic*] from the bottom of p. 18. I fondly dream of our salvaging at least that much" (KB to SS July 10, 1978). He shared similar thoughts with many of his interlocutors. He entreated J. Hillis Miller to attend to the final pages of his essay with care: "The first half of the Response was necessarily wasted in undoing Jameson's omissions. But please for Gawsake do look at things from the bottom of p. 18 to the end" (KB to JHM September 7, 1978). After the manuscript was printed in *Critical Inquiry* Burke was even more specific, asking Miller to attend to pages 414 through 416 (KB to JHM January 13, 1979). To Rueckert he wrote, "But please do read the paragraphs I have marked on pp. 414–416. As you probably know, that's what I'm building around now" (KB to WR January 15, 1979). With Booth he is more specific still, directing him to begin reading at the second paragraph on page 414 (KB to WB January 16, 1979).

As Burke amplified and explained these closing pages of his argument, he suggested that the decisive flaws of Jameson's "ideological criticism" stemmed from his Marxist perspective. Indeed in both MRSC and the letters that surround it, the only relevant factor seems to be that Jameson, "one of the Hermeneutics Boys now at Yale," "has Marxist slant" (KB to Malcolm Cowley June 27, 1978). Burke's conflation of Jameson and Marxism writ large will be the subject of section 3. Here I wish only to stress that if we grant Burke this conflation, the virtues of logology will readily appear. To Burke's mind the singular achievement of logology—and what it decisively separated it from ideological criticism—was its capacity to account for the nature of language.

Burke argued that the fundamental flaw of ideological criticism inhered in Marxism's structural tendency to commit what he called a "genetic fallacy." This fallacy involved treating discourse as a function of its social ground rather than, as Burke's logology would have it, a force that is irreducible to the circumstances of its origin. As Burke developed this argument, he insisted on something that is only alluded to in MRSC. He argued that a fundamental, methodological distinction separates Marxist criticism from logological criticism. "The ideological approach," he explained to Booth, "focuses on the fact that human consciousness is modified by its material environment; the logological approach stresses that the mere fact of discussion tells us something about the type of animal we are: the type that uses language" (KB to WB June 24, 1978). Rather than focus on the extent to which symbolic action is a function of time and place, as "Jameson's o'erstress upon the 'historicist' aspect of 'ideology'" goads Burke to do, Burkean criticism begins with the sheer existence of symbolic action, suggesting that the presence of such action distinguishes humans from the realm of nonsymbolic motion (KB to Bob Zachary

June 28, 1978). As he put it in *Critical Inquiry,* logology begins not "with the class struggle," but rather "with the 'prime' logological . . . question, 'What is it to be the typically symbol-using animal'" (MRSC 415).

As students of *LSA* or *RR* know well, for Burke the question of what it means to be a symbol-using animal leads directly to his familiar distinction between action and motion—"A duality of realm [that] is implicit in our definition of man as the symbol-using animal" (*RR* 16; see also *LSA* 53). In other words Burke believed that defining "man" [*sic*] as a "symbol-using animal" implied that any theory of "man" must account for two "realms" of experience: that of motion and that of action. Although Burke never mentions the action/motion dichotomy in MRSC, he returns to it consistently in the correspondence. Thus he wrote Booth: "I'm spoiling for haggles about what I take to be the central issue [between myself and Jameson]; namely: my statement of the case as summed up in my Motion/Action routine. . . . I want to see everything discussed in connection with that tie-up" (KB to WB September 18, 1978). In fact to several of his interlocutors, Burke insisted that his reply to Jameson be understood in the context of three essays: his recently published *Critical Inquiry* piece, titled "(Nonsymbolic) Motion/(Symbolic) Action"; its sequel in the *Kenyon Review,* "Theology and Logology"; and a never-published essay titled "Nature, Symbolism, Counter-Nature," which, he wrote Booth, "brings to fulfillment the sumjick in my Response [to Jameson]" (KB to Wayne Booth January 16, 1979; see also KB to Howard Nemerov April 15, 1978; KB to D. Donoghue June 15, 1979). In each of these essays Burke stressed that logology as a critical method starts from the nature of language as such, from a fundamental distinction between nonsymbolic motion and symbolic action. Given the consistency of Burke's admonitions, it behooves us to reread the closing pages of MRSC, this time in the context of the action/motion dichotomy and the essays Burke suggested.

"(Nonsymbolic) Motion/(Symbolic) Action" and "Theology and Logology" are very similar essays. Both begin by positing a "basic polarity" between nonsymbolic motion and symbolic action ("(Nonsymbolic)" 809). As Burke put it in the *Kenyon Review,* "logology must insist categorically upon a polar distinction between verbal and nonverbal behavior" ("Theology" 184). From this distinction both essays argue that, since infants are born speechless into the realm of motion and pass into the realm of action only with the acquisition of language ("Theology" 152–53; "(Nonsymbolic)" 814; MRSC 415), the "immediate context" of language is "the realm of nonsymbolic motion" ("Theology" 156). Both essays quote Jeremy Bentham to make the point: "To every word that has an immaterial import there belongs, or at least did belong, a material one" ("(Nonsymbolic)" 812; see also "Theology" 158). In the "(Nonsymbolic) Motion" essay, Burke added a quotation from Ralph Waldo Emerson's "Nature," which he claimed was making the same point "tender-mindedly" that Bentham made "matter-of-factly": "Every word which is used to express a moral or intellectual fact, if traced to its root, is found to be borrowed from some material appearance" ("(Nonsymbolic)" 810–11; see also *LSA* 46–47).

In other words Burke uses Bentham and Emerson to make a point that is, to his mind, fundamental. Because the "immediate context" of language is the realm of motion, he believed that language was originally "physicalist"; each word denoted a particular object; each word was a "proper name" ("(Nonsymbolic)" 813). From its "physicalist" origin, language expanded tropologically, borrowing words-for-things for abstract concepts. Burke writes, "Terms that have a quite literal meaning as applied to physical conditions can be adapted figuratively to subject matter that does not admit of such usage" ("Theology" 158). The most famous example of such tropological expansion is the movement of the word "tree" from its supposed origin as the proper name for a particular tree, to a general name designating an entire species of plant life. Such transformations, Burke argued, capture the very nature of language: "To meet the minimum conditions of what is meant here by 'symbolic action' all that is necessary is the inability of words to 'stay put,' as when even a proper name like 'Caesar,' referring to one particular person in history, gives birth to such words as 'Kaiser' and 'Czar'" ("(Nonsymbolic)" 813).

This insight is surely one of the underappreciated constants of Burke's work. Across a wide variety of texts and decades, Burke argued that language was fundamentally tropological. That is to say, it develops metaphorically, turning words-for-things into words-for-concepts. As early as 1941, he wrote in "Four Master Tropes," "Language develops by metaphorical extension, in borrowing words from the realm of the corporeal, visible, tangible and applying them by analogy to the realm of the incorporeal, invisible, intangible; then in the course of time, the original corporeal reference is forgotten, and only the incorporeal, metaphorical extension survives" (*GM* 506).

In 1945, in *GM,* Burke quoted Bentham to the same effect as above (162), and five years later, in *RM,* he described Bentham's mode of "rhetorical analysis" in similar terms: "Scrutinizing the most abstract of legalistic terms, asking himself just what it meant to please and pass judgment in terms of 'legal fictions,' he proposed a methodic search for 'archetypes'"—the concrete images that "underly the use of abstractions" (90). In 1961 Burke opened the *RR* with the same point, writing, "The words for the 'supernatural' realm are necessarily borrowed [analogically] from the realm of our everyday experiences" (7). And in 1962, in the well-known essay titled "What Are the Signs of What," Burke argued, "No matter how firm may be one's conviction that his terminology for the supernatural refers somehow to a real order of existence, there is the obvious fact that he necessarily borrows his terms from the terms prevailing in . . . worldly orders. At the very start, therefore, he must concede: . . . His statements are but metaphorical, analogical, mere makeshifts for talking figuratively about a supposed superhuman realm that, no matter how real it may be, cannot be adequately discussed in human terms" (*LSA* 376). Indeed it is precisely because the language of theology conspicuously lacks concrete referents that Burke believes it provides such a profound model for logology. That is, theology forcibly reminds us that symbolic action is indebted for its terminology to the realm of nonsymbolic motion. As he put it in "Four Master Tropes," "If you trail language back far enough, you will find that all our terms for 'spiritual' states were metonymic in origin" (*GM* 506). By the time of his debate with Jameson, Burke was convinced that tropology—the refusal of words to "stay put," the capacity of language to move towards abstraction—was the "very essence of language" ("Theology" 158). In sum the two essays that Burke insisted contextualize his response to Jameson foregrounded a critique of language that Burke had advanced for nearly forty years.

What bearing has all this on Burke's feud with Jameson? The "point I make by putting Bentham and Emerson together," Burke explained to Booth, is that "except when Marxism is attacking the enemy, it is soaked in naïve verbal realism." "But will your champion [Jameson] see that?" (KB to WB September 18, 1978). To Burke's mind, "naïve verbal realism" was the result of forgetting the action/motion distinction, and here he indicts Marxism on just this score. For context it may help to briefly return to a 1952 essay in which Burke described "naïve verbal realism" and its connections to Marxism: "There is a brand of naïve verbal realism, always ready to permeate any terminology. For instance whereas there is nothing in Marxist 'dialectical materialism' as such to require that the concept of negativity be interpreted literally, as though some situations in nature actually *said* 'no' to others, the linguistic usage itself can be confused with a state of nature" (*LSA* 421). In this account "naïve verbal realism" is connected directly to Burke's long-standing interest in the movement of symbols away from the physicalist realm of nonsymbolic motion—here called the "state of nature." Naïve verbal realism then is the consequence of forgetting the lesson that Burke drew from Bentham and Emerson—the consequence of forgetting that words for immaterial concepts "are but metaphorical, analogical, mere makeshifts for talking figuratively" (*LSA* 376).

The "simplest instance" of the verbal realism of Marxism, Burke wrote Booth, is its reliance on the word "class." "Class" is a conspicuous example of what Burke, following Bentham, called a "fiction," a term with no concrete referent. Its fictive status means it is "a purely linguistic invention unknown to the world of sheer wordless motion" ("Theology" 158, 167). The reliance of Marxism on a "fiction," and, what is more important, its failure to recognize it as a fiction, reveals the contradictions of Marxist analysis that Burke believed logology could remedy. In the same letter to Booth, Burke wrote, "Marxism says that superstructure is a mere reflection of the substructure" (KB to WB September 18, 1978). Its reliance on fictions however undercuts this claim. For how could "class," a term with no substructural referent, "reflect" anything but the nature of language itself? The virtuosity of its applications notwithstanding then, Burke believed that the premises of Marxist criticism were deeply flawed. In emphasizing the situatedness of all discourse in time and place, Marxism blinded the critic to the fact that the realm of symbolic action cannot be fully explained with recourse to Jameson's mantra: "Always historicize!" (*Political Unconscious* 9). It blinded the critic, in other words, to the fact that, from Burke's perspective, to historicize "class" is precisely to miss its power, a power that derives not from the vagaries of time and place but rather from the "essence of language."

And this takes us to the heart of Burke's critique of Jameson. Marxist criticism, he claimed, cannot account for the nature of language, the autonomous action of symbols. By beginning with the "class struggle" and treating symbolic action as "derivative," Marxist analysis, Burke claimed, is deflected from considering the realm of symbolic action as "an originating force in its own right" (MRSC 414). And indeed another definition of "naïve verbal realism" makes exactly this point: it is the refusal "to realize the full extent of the role played by symbolicity in [man's] notions of reality" (*LSA* 5). Pace Marxism, Burke argues, logology holds that symbols are not "merely 'derived,'" they are "positively creative of material conditions. In this sense, a theory of 'consciousness' as historically conditioned would not be accurate enough" (MRSC 414).

In his correspondence regarding MRSC, Burke consistently foregrounded precisely this claim. To Booth he wrote, "Here is the issue [with Jameson], I beg you: Is it permissible to talk about the nature of *symbolic action in general*? And though ye Dramatismus agrees with Marxismus that language is grounded in non-linguistic nature, I'd hold that once developed, language has innovative powers of its own. . . . Marxism says that the superstructure is a mere reflection of the substructure, except where distorted by class conflict. I'd call that a variant of the genetic fallacy"(KB to WB September 18, 1978).

By treating the realm of symbolic action as a "mere reflection of the substructure," Marxism consigns the realm of symbolic action to a "derivative" status. So consigned, symbolic action thus cannot be recognized as "an originating force in its own right." Thus like Darwinism and Hegelianism before it, Marxism "invites a kind of 'genetic fallacy' whereby overstress upon the *origins* of some manifestation can deflect attention from what it *is*, regardless of what it came from" (MRSC 415, 414, 415).

One month after he wrote Booth, Burke sent a similar letter to Christian Susini. "Jameson," Burke complained, "doesn't have a properly *logologically realistic* view of nomenclature as a realm in its own right." Logology, he continued, "attacks *head-on* the Marxist notion that 'ideas' are to be seen as but 'reflections' of a 'material 'substructure.' Regardless of where they come from . . . *they have a nature of their own*—and Realism as I conceive of it proceeds from there. I'd class it but an example of the 'genetic fallacy' to talk of their possible *origin* when we should be concerned with the *functioning nature, however they arose*"(KB to CS October 25, 1978).

To Bob Zachary, Burke explained that although his response to Jameson was an "absurd waste of time and effort," "the guy brought up a couple of points that I wanted to say things about." In particular he noted Jameson "helped sharpen my point about both Darwinism and Marxism: Both of such nomenclatures so play up the distinction btw. natural and supernatural that they don't give proper placement to the realm of 'symbolic action' as a dimension in its own right" (KB to BZ June 28, 1978). This refrain became Burke's mantra. In a separate letter to Booth, Burke complained that Jameson's historicism "slighted the role of 'symbolic action' as an intermediate realm with powers of its own." "Ever on the alert for evidences of the 'genetic fallacy,'" Burke continued, "Logology also lays great stress upon the fact that, whatever such aptitude for 'symbol-using' behavior developed *out of*, it is what it is" (KB to Wayne Booth June 24, 1978).

As Burke saw things then, one fundamental, methodological fact separated his approach to criticism from Jameson's. Jameson was distracted by the material origins of language; his historicism obligated him to explain discourse with primary recourse to its "social ground," and in Burke's eyes this obligation slighted the realm of symbolic action. Logology, on the other hand, maintains a profound indifference to the origins of language. Whatever the circumstances of its development, Burke held that language must be taken simply as a "given"—it "is what it is" (*LSA* 44). Not that logology is ignorant of the virtues of historicism; Burke was well aware that historical-political factors had a profound impact on language, and he told Booth with some exasperation that his "scene-act ratio" was designed to account for "precisely that" (KB to WB September 18, 1978). But the scene could never exhaust the act. Thus he began his *Critical Inquiry* response by claiming, "I can't go as far as I think I should if I share with Jameson what I take to be his overinvestment in the term 'ideology'" (MRSC 401).

While both Jameson's historicism and Burke's scene-act ratio could speculate regarding the social ground of a discourse, only logology could account for what Burke called the "originary," "innovative," and "creative" powers of symbolic action. This is the promise of logology: it accounts for the power latent in the nature of language itself. Apart from the contingencies of its context, the politics of its deployment, and the circumstances of its development, logology pushes the critic to account for the force of language in its own right. In Burke's terms, logology thus pushes us "to realize the full extent of the role played by symbolicity in [man's] notions of reality."

CRITICISM AND IDEOLOGY: THE INSUFFICIENCY OF LOGOLOGY

It must be immediately acknowledged that such claims required Burke to engage in "methodological repression" more severe than that of which Jameson was guilty. Indeed as Burke turns from indexing his pronunciations of ideology to distinguishing logology and Marxism, Jameson himself all but disappears from Burke's text and is replaced by Marxism writ large. Worse still, he is replaced by a *vulgar* Marxism, a Marxism in which, as Burke put it, "the superstructure is a mere reflection of the substructure." Not only was such a Marxism-as-economic-determinism a straw person by the 1970s, and not only was it a version of Marxism that Burke himself had rejected as early as *CS* (79–81), it was a version of Marxism that Jameson himself had done much to argue against. Granted, Jameson's most sustained critique of vulgar Marxism would not come until the long opening essay of *The Political Uncon-scious* in 1981, but the critique was certainly present in *Marxism and Form,* and even more disconcerting, it was explicitly thematized in his 1977 address to the English Institute, the very text against which Burke was responding. For a thinker such as Burke, so sensitive to "methodological repression," it is deeply disappointing that he would substitute for the subtleties of Jameson's argument an already discredited form of Marxism.

In *Marxism and Form* Jameson argued, "The work of art or the cultural fact cer-tainly reflects something," but "the [Marxist] model proposed allows for a fairly wide range of possibilities in the mode of reflection itself." Distancing himself from the determinism Burke would later condemn, Jameson concluded that a "passive conception of the way in which 'reflection' takes place" must be replaced by "a rela-tively active one where the ingenuity and creative power of the writer or ideologue are more strongly insisted on" (*Marxism* 381–82). Thus as early as 1971 Jameson too attacked "head on" the idea that a work of art was but a reflection of its social ground. The work of art certainly reflected its social ground—this much Jameson's Marxism committed him to—but the nature of this "reflection" was anything but straightforward. It was a reflection not at odds with the ingenuity, creativity, or agency of the speaker. The "best dialectical analyses," he wrote, "show not so much that external social reality *causes* a particular type of thought, as that it imposes basic inner limitations upon it" (*Marxism* 345). Given that this perspective differs not at all from Burke's 1931 formulation, in which he argued that although ideas may "'reflect' a situation," they can "hardly" be said to be "caused" by a situation (*CS* 80), it is difficult to understand how Burke could complain about Jameson's Marxism so loudly.

Had Jameson said nothing more on the subject, however, Burke's complaints might still have found a point of purchase. For although Jameson clearly distances himself from uncomplicated assumptions regarding the textual reflection of an eco-nomic base, he does so to rescue the agent from economic determinism. That is to say, while the speaker emerges from *Marxism and Form* as an "originating force" in her own right, it is less clear that the realm of symbolic action is so liberated. How-ever there is a key passage in the English Institute keynote, a passage that Jameson copied nearly verbatim into *The Political Unconscious,* in which he argues, in almost Burkean terms, for the autonomy of the symbolic ("Symbolic Inference" 73–74; *Political Unconscious* 81–82).

In "The Symbolic Inference" Jameson described ideological analysis as "the re-writing of a particular narrative trait or seme as a function of its social, historical, or political context." Although this may seem like precisely the vulgar Marxism Burke decried, Jameson *immediately* qualified his definition, arguing that it would be "futile, if not regressive" to posit the "ontological priority of the context over the text itself." Rather Jameson argued that the "social, historical, or political context" against which the text is to be read must be understood as intrinsic to the text it-self: "The symbolic act therefore begins by producing its own context in the same moment of emergence in which it steps back over against it." In other words, pace Burke, Jameson's ideological criticism never reads a text as a "mere reflection" of its social ground. Quite the opposite: the text "produces" the social ground against which it reacts. Jameson concludes that "the literary or aesthetic gesture thus al-ways stands in some active relationship to the real" ("Symbolic Inference" 73–74). This claim, I take it, is virtually synonymous with Burke's claim that "language has innovative powers of its own," as well as his exhortation that the critic appreciate "the full extent of the role played by symbolicity in notions of reality." Holding fast to the "active relationship" between the symbolic and the real, Jameson argued, prevents his critical method from deteriorating into "vulgar materialism" ("Sym-bolic Inference" 75).

Jameson's arguments against interpreting a text as a "mere reflection" of its social ground were not hidden in the subtleties of his argument. In both *Marxism and Form* and his address at the English Institute, Jameson argued openly, albeit in his own terms, that the symbolic was, as Burke claimed, an "originating force in its own right." That Burke could complain so loudly for so long to so many people about Jameson's "quietus," and at the same time tell so many people that the issue between himself and Jameson hinged on logology's capacity to liberate the sym-bolic from the so-called genetic fallacy implicit in Jameson's system, suggests a bit of Burkean hypocrisy. When Burke argues that Jameson does not "explicitly con-front" the issue of the derivative-versus-formative status of ideas, he reveals only that he had not read Jameson's charge with any care (MRSC 415). Jameson could have justifiably responded with the same complaint Burke once leveled at him: "I can't understand how he could be so misinformed, if he read me at all." Thus the argument made in the closing pages of MRSC, especially as this argument is read through Burke's letters to Booth, Susini, and Zachary, required a quietus more se-vere than Jameson's. For Jameson was guilty only of not quoting Burke's work on ideology—a body of work only tangentially related to his own focus on Burke's criti-cal system—while Burke was guilty of simply ignoring Jameson's explicit argument against "vulgar materialism."

This evasion of Jameson's texts is what I had in mind when I claimed that, in his exchange with Jameson, Burke demonstrated the limitations of logology at the very moment he sought to articulate its virtues. He claimed his critical system was "ever on the alert for evidences of the 'genetic fallacy'" but did not seem to recog-nize the same fallacious reasoning in his own reply, for the only way to characterize Jameson's historicist criticism as baldly as does Burke is to read Jameson's system in terms of its origin. That is, Burke knew that Jameson had a "Marxist slant," and that apparently was all he needed to know. It is as if it was enough to know that the charges against him originated in Marxism to dismiss them as misguided. And this is just as much methodological repression as it is a genetic fallacy; the two charges that Burke so vigorously applied to Jameson turn out to be equally—if not more—applicable to himself.

Beyond being merely disappointing, the hypocrisy of Burke's response foregrounds the insufficiency of logology. For it is abundantly clear that Burke's reply to Jameson is driven not by the principles of his own logological system but by the need to justify his own work vis-à-vis Jameson's English Institute attack. Burke's response is political and polemical; it is ideological in Jameson's sense of the term, conspicuously and inescapably a product of its "social ground." In one sense, this is hardly a critique of Burke's response, for from Jameson's perspective (and mine), every text is ideological and thus "it is hard to see why saying so should be construed as a blanket repudiation" ("Ideology and Symbolic Action" 419). In another sense however the ideological character of Burke's response does indeed foreground the limitations of his system, for he described his system in expressly nonideological terms. As he confided to Booth, "Logology is not historicist, because it is claiming to make statements about human-nature-in-general" (KB to WB June 24, 1978). The ideological character of Burke's response displays the difficulty, if not the impossibility, of making "statements about human-nature-in-general." Thus it is not surprising that Jameson responded to Burke's response by arguing against those "intellectual positions" that operate under the "pretence" that their "ideas exist in the eternal and have no practical function in the first place" ("Ideology and Symbolic Action" 420). For all of logology's efforts to bracket the realm of historicity, Burke's own response reveals the sheer tenacity of the "social ground"—it will simply not be bracketed.

It must be acknowledged that there is no evidence that Burke envisioned his reply to Jameson as an example of logological criticism. Perhaps then it is unjust to interpret the hypocrisy of his response as evidence of logology's insufficiency. Were no other evidence available, such a reading would be tantamount to critiquing Burke's response for not measuring up to something it never aspired to be. There is, however, further evidence. While Burke may not have envisioned his response as an example of logology, he was, as we saw earlier, quite explicit about the methodological requirements of an academic exchange such as this. He told Booth that "sheer *reporting*" was "Obligation No. 1 in a gazette such as CI" (KB to WB June 24, 1978). Six months later he told Booth that such reporting should be the very foundation of intellectual debate: "I do decidedly go along with the idea that your gazette [*Critical Inquiry*] should welcome haggles of all sorts, though preferably in terms of what the guy actually said, as vs. all the new twists whereby e'en a *Marxist*, of all species, doan attack you by quoting undeniably verbatim and smacking you down accordingly, but make it up as he goes along" (KB to WB January 29, 1979). For all the moral superiority evinced in this passage, it is imperative to remember that at the precise time Burke was writing these lines, he was writing, distributing, and widely commenting on his rejoinder to Jameson. That rejoinder, as I have shown, defaulted on what Burke took to be the polemicist's number one responsibility: accurate reporting. The substance of his response functioned, sans reportage of any kind, by assimilating Jameson to vulgar Marxism, a Marxism that Jameson himself had disowned consistently and explicitly for at least seven years.

The sheer fact that at the same historical moment Burke could complain with such vehemence against Jameson's quietus and so blatantly betray his own principles speaks to the tenacity of ideology itself: a text simply cannot be divorced from what Jameson called its "social, historical, or political context." At a moment when Burke was thinking (and writing) explicitly about the norms of academic debate, the sheer force of the political context surrounding this particular debate so captivated his attention that he disregarded the norms he was in the very process of articulating. The rhetorical force of Burke's response can thus not be explained with recourse to the notion of symbolic action or the originary force of the symbolic. This is, I believe, a powerful argument for Jameson's version of ideological criticism, for texts such as MRSC will remain opaque to any method, such as logology, designed to elucidate symbolic action. To understand MRSC, in other words, Burke's meditations on the originary, creative, tropological force of language will not be helpful. More helpful than these would be Jameson's "social ground": the fact that Burke had been slighted, that this slight was very public, and that he was denied an opportunity to respond. It is only as we understand these external variables—variables that would remain invisible to logology but plain to ideological criticism—that we will begin to understand MRSC.

CONCLUSION

MRSC is in many ways a tragic text. It is has been largely ignored by scholars otherwise invested in the intersections of Burke and Jameson; Burke himself immediately regretted the vast majority of the essay; and its final pages—the only pages that Burke himself championed—violated the very principle that motivated the first fourteen. For these reasons it is all the more important that we remember the Burke/Jameson affair as an *archival event,* rather than filtering our memory of it through the unfeeling, disorganized pages of MRSC. Seen as an archival event, the episode is no more satisfying—the disappointment of cold, disorganized pages is replaced by the disappointment of heated, yet hypocritical arguments—but the archive allows us to turn these disappointments to our edification. For when the MRSC is placed in the context of the correspondence that surrounded it, when we give back to Burke the voice that justified, rationalized, and explained the essay years after Jameson provoked it, we find that it does indeed have much to teach us. Within this context it provides insight into Burke's critical system of logology, reminding us that Burke designed logology as a critical system uniquely attuned to symbolic action. This is no small attainment. Symbolic action may no longer be under siege from the Marxist threat that Burke perceived (if indeed it ever was), but there is no doubt that today's critical methods—from genre analysis, to new historicism, to the rhetorical situation, to critical rhetoric, to psychoanalysis, and even to dramatism—threaten to obscure that which logology clarifies: the originary force of language itself. Moreover when MRSC is read in light of the correspondence, even the tragic nature of the essay becomes instructive: it casts in bold relief the outer limits of logology.

My emphasis on the limits of logology or the hypocrisy of Burke should not suggest that Jameson won the debate of 1977. Indeed it is misleading to think of the exchange between Burke and Jameson as a "debate" at all. There was no winner here. To the extent my reading holds, the exchange demonstrates both the necessity and inadequacy of logology. It is necessary because it enables the critic to account for symbolic action; it is insufficient because the powers of language never tell the whole story. The exchange thus reminds us that the insights of every critical system must be discounted by the insights of every other system. As Wayne Booth put it, the Burkean passage to certainty requires "deliberate interference with perfection by enforcing on every terministic screen an ironic reminder of other truths according to which it should be discounted" (114). This of course is a very Burkean point, a point he had preached since at least the middle section of *PC;* a point that the political context of the English Institute may have briefly occluded, but a point that can be—and now has been—revealed by ideological criticism.

NOTE

1. Similarly neither David Blakesley nor Thomas Carmichael, both of whom restage the Burke/Jameson debate, attends to the essay in any detail. Carmichael passes quickly to LASA to find substantive material with which to engage Jameson, and Blakesley, while he leans on it heavily in his creative effort to stage a conversation between himself, Jameson, and Burke, provides no interpretation of the essay or its place in the debate. Christine Oravec also does not mention the essay in her account of the debate.

WORKS CITED

Blakesley, David. "So What's Rhetorical about Criticism? A Subjective Dialogue Featuring Kenneth Burke and Fredric Jameson." *Textuality and Subjectivity: Essays on Language and Being.* Ed. Eitel Timm, Kenneth Mendoza, and Dale Gowen. Columbia: Camden, 1991.

Booth, Wayne C. *Critical Understanding.* Chicago: University of Chicago Press, 1979.

Burke, Kenneth. *Counter-Statement.* Berkeley: University of California Press, 1968.

———. *A Grammar of Motives.* Berkeley: University of California Press, 1969.

———. *Language as Symbolic Action: Essays on Life, Literature, and Method.* Berkeley: University of California Press, 1966.

———. "Methodological Repression and/or Strategies of Containment." *Critical Inquiry* 5.2 (1978): 401–16.

———. "(Nonsymbolic) Motion/(Symbolic) Action." *Critical Inquiry* 4.4 (1978): 809–38.

———. *A Rhetoric of Motives.* Berkeley: University of California Press, 1969.

———. *The Rhetoric of Religion: Studies in Logology.* Berkeley: University of California Press, 1970.

——. "Theology and Logology." *Kenyon Review* 1.1 (1979): 151–85.

Bygrave, Stephen. *Kenneth Burke: Rhetoric and Ideology.* London: Routledge, 1993.

Carmichael, Thomas. "Postmodernism, Symbolicity, and the Rhetoric of the Hyperreal: Kenneth Burke, Fredric Jameson, and Jean Baudrillard." *Text and Performance Quarterly* 11 (1991): 319–24.

Jameson, Fredric R. "Ideology and Symbolic Action." *Critical Inquiry* 5 (Winter, 1978): 417–22.

——. *Marxism and Form: Twentieth-Century Theories of Dialectical Literature.* Princeton: Princeton University Press, 1971.

——. *The Political Unconscious: Narrative as a Socially Symbolic Act.* Ithaca: Cornell University Press, 1981.

——. "The Symbolic Inference; or, Kenneth Burke and Ideological Analysis." *Representing Kenneth Burke.* Ed. Hayden V. White. Baltimore: Johns Hopkins University Press, 1982. 68–91.

Lentricchia, Frank. *Criticism and Social Change.* Chicago: University of Chicago Press, 1983.

Oravec, Christine. "Kenneth Burke's Concept of Association and the Complexity of Identity." *The Legacy of Kenneth Burke.* Ed. Herbert Simons and Trevor Melia. Madison: University of Wisconsin Press, 1989. 174–95.

Wess, Robert. *Kenneth Burke: Rhetoric, Subjectivity, Postmodernism.* Cambridge: Cambridge University Press, 1996.

JORDYNN JACK

ON THE LIMITS OF HUMAN

Haggling with Burke's "Definition of Man"

In 1975 a young graduate student at the University of Oregon named Barbara Bate wrote to Kenneth Burke to request a meeting at the Western Speech Communication conference in Seattle. At the time Bate was beginning her dissertation, which investigated how male and female faculty responded to gender-neutral language, and how women in particular have been affected by the use of generic masculine language (BB to KB November 19, 1975). Bate, now author of the textbook *Communication and the Sexes,* recalls that she indeed met with Burke at the conference, an event she describes as "a special moment for me at the time" (e-mail to the author, August 8, 2009). Bate later forwarded Burke a copy of an essay she had published, "Generic Man, Invisible Woman: Language, Thought, and Social Change" (BB to KB December 26, 1975). The article drew upon Burke's theories to establish the importance of gender-neutral language, but it also questioned the use of "man" as a universal term. Burke, like most writers of his generation, relied on the generic "man" throughout his work.

Since she never heard back from Burke, Bate assumed her article had little impact on him or his thought. However, archival evidence shows that Bate's article actually inspired Burke to consider his own use of gendered language, particularly in his "definition of man." For Bate masculine language excluded women and led to psychological effects, such as a failure to identify with the language in question. In response to this critique, Burke revised the first half of the famous opening clause, "man is the symbol-using animal," changing man to human.

Using this archival moment as a heuristic, this essay considers how we might continue to haggle over the "definition of man" by thinking through the second part of its famous first clause. What does it mean to define humans as "the symbol-using animal?" Bate's encounter with Burke prompted him to expand the definition to encompass those who had previously been marginalized by masculine language. It has prompted me to consider how that definition fails to include those who may be marginalized by ableist language. In this essay I first examine the evolution of Burke's definition of man and its reception among rhetoric scholars. Then I outline in more detail the exchange between Bate and Burke and consider how it may have prompted Burke to revise his definition by using the term "human" instead of "man." Building on this exchange, I move on to speculate about how the term "human" might itself be expanded, especially if its definition excludes individuals with disabilities. I examine in particular how Kenneth Burke's "definition of man" might be modified based on an analysis of nonverbal, embodied communicative strategies used by autistic individuals. As an archival heuristic, Burke's encounter with Bate can open up new lines of inquiry that extend Burke's thought forward, stretching the definition further to encompass humans who communicate differently.

BURKE'S DEFINITION OF MAN

Burke's "definition of man" was an ongoing project, a set of propositions he reworked and revised in order to arrive at, in his words, a definition that would "sum things up" ("Definition of Man" 491), providing all the properties so that "the thing defined can be as though derived from the definition" (491). When first published in *RR* (1961), Burke's definition included the following clauses:

Man is
1. The symbol-using animal
2. Inventor of the negative
3. Separated from his natural condition by instruments of his own making
4. And goaded by the spirit of hierarchy. (40)

Later, in his *Hudson Review* article ("Definition," 1963/1964) and in LSA (1966), Burke amended the definition as follows:

Man is
the symbol-using (symbol-making, symbol-misusing) animal
inventor of the negative (or moralized by the negative)
separated from his natural condition by instruments of his own making
goaded by the spirit of hierarchy (or moved by the sense of order)
and rotten with perfection. (*LSA* 16)

In a 1976 article, "Colloquy I: The Party Line," Burke suggested adding an additional clause to the definition: "acquiring foreknowledge of death" (65).

Given this series of changes, it seems that Burke was still actively examining the implications of his definition when in November 1975 Bate wrote Burke to say that she would be attending the Western Speech Communication conference, and that she was "eager to talk with you about some ideas I have derived from your writings" (BB to KB November 19, 1975). In particular she notes she was beginning her dissertation project, in which she planned to interview men and women about the use of female-inclusive language: "I'm interested in the ways our perception and evaluations have been affected by the use of 'generic man,' and whether male-female divisiveness can be tied in with our uses of these old or new symbols" (BB to KB November 19, 1975)

While Bate remembers little about her meeting with Burke today, her letter to Burke from December 26 informs us that the two had chatted about some poems Burke shared, one of which Bate mistook as having been authored by Theodore Roethke. In the margin of the letter, Burke corrected: "not Roethke's—it was a burlesque I did of him" (KB to BB December 26, 1975).

The archival record here provides some interesting clues but does not indicate which poems the two discussed. However using this encounter as an heuristic helps to identify some possibilities. Most likely Burke would have shared poems with Bate that related to the generic "Woman." Some digging into Burke's oeuvre suggests a few possibilities. In 1950 Burke had written in a review that Roethke's poems figure "Woman in the Absolute," personifying "flowers and fishes" as female, rather than "personalizing" or "*individualizing* . . . human relations" with actual women ("Vegetal Radicalism" 107–8). In 1952 Burke had also published a poem in *The Hopkins Review* titled "Post-Roethkean Translations," which might be one of the poems he showed Bate. In this poem Burke burlesques Roethke's poetic tendency to rely on simple, sensory-laden images and kennings (such as "flower-dump" or "chicken-yard"). Burke's parody is full of such kennings, one of which is "Womb-man," a kenning that epitomizes Roethke's simplified images of "Woman in the Absolute" (7). Perhaps then Bate and Burke discussed the figure of "generic Woman" as it appears in poetry—a tendency Burke had himself noted earlier.

Another possibility might be Burke's 1972 poem, "Ms. Universe," which appears in *Late Poems—1968–1983*. The poem ends with these lines: "All is but Woman / and deviations from Woman / and deviations from/those deviations" (70). Yet the title, with its feminist "Ms." seems designed to poke fun at the women's liberation movement and its own tendency (similar to Roethke's) to essentialize Woman (an insight that shows some prescience indeed). Indeed in a letter to William Rueckert of May 25, 1972, Burke sends along a draft of the poem, with the comment: "I patched up my 'Ms. Universe' bleat a bit. But I guess I must accept it (though not without embitterment) that the Women's Lib. Movement frowns on such clowning" (*Letters* 188).

These poems show Burke engaging with feminist concerns about language in ways that do not appear in his theoretical works. While the archive does not tell us in this case what exactly happened between Bate and Burke, it does open up new questions and lines of inquiry. Following the leads in this encounter—Burke's mention of a "burlesque" of Roethke—led me to search for elements of engagement with feminism in his poetry, a source I might not have consulted otherwise.

Despite Burke's own skepticism about the women's movement, Burke apparently did mention to Bate that he was "interested to know what [she] thought about language as it treats and affects men and women" (BB to KB December 26, 1975).

Accordingly Bate sent Burke an article she had published on this topic in *University of Michigan Papers in Women's Studies*. In the article, "Generic Man, Invisible Woman: Language, Thought, and Social Change," Bate argues that the use of the term "man" as a generic term "place[s] women at a disadvantage for understanding themselves as persons and for determining their actions in current social circumstances," and that accordingly "it is appropriate to seek alternatives within the existing language which might alleviate confusion and encourage the full development of all persons" (83). To make this argument Bate draws on Burke's theories to show how language patterns "are intertwined with modes of thinking" (83). In particular Bate writes that Burke "asserts that much of what people regard as 'reality' is built up as they engage in processes of symbol-making and symbol-using" (83). Thus gendered language colors our perceptions of the world, which "places women at a disadvantage for understanding themselves and deciding their actions" (84). Bate underscores the ways that gendered language "directs attention toward some things and away from others" (83). Clearly she has in mind Burke's concept of terministic screens, which, in his words, refers to the fact that "any nomenclature directs the attention into some channels rather than others" (*LSA* 45).

In her analysis Bate explains how a "generic man" nomenclature directs readers' attention towards the masculine even when it ostensibly refers to both masculine and feminine objects. She highlights the ambiguities inherent in the use of "generic man" by pointing to the following three examples:

Socrates is a man
All men are created equal
Caution: Men at Work

Bate notes that these examples demonstrate "the ambiguities and contradictions involved when females in particular try to interpret and respond to 'generic man' language" ("Generic Man"84), since they may find themselves unsure whether such nomenclature refers to the masculine or to the universal. In the first example it is unclear whether we are to notice Socrates' humanness or his maleness. Those readers who can fill in the classical syllogism will recognize the reference to the class of "men" (or humans), but there is nothing in the sentence itself that clarifies this meaning. Bate's key insight here is that male and female readers might bring different "terministic screens" to such sentences. While male readers might have no problem with such a sentence, female readers might have to translate the sentence, mentally, in order to understand that it is the generic meaning, not the gender-specific one, that is being referenced.

Bate similarly notes that female readers might confront the historical as well as syntactical meanings of generic man. The phrase, "All men are created equal," is sometimes taken to mean "all persons," but historically it excluded not only women, but also slaves and non-property-owners. Thus in some cases, Bate concludes, the term "men" is "not only gender-specific, but race- and class-specific"

("Generic Man" 85). Finally, from a social perspective, the accuracy of the generic man is a function of social conditions. "Men at work" makes sense in a sociohistorical context in which women seldom performed manual labor, but less sense in an environment where occupational patterns have shifted.

While Bate did not explicitly critique Burke's own use of "generic man," it appears that Bate's paper served as a heuristic for Burke, as an invitation to consider the implications of his own word choices. Burke underlined sections of the paper and made notes in the margins. One note reads, "'father-mother god'—PLF omitted the reference to gender" (83).[1] Burke is presumably here referring to his tendency to overlook gender in some aspect of *PLF*, which deals with symbolic action in poetry. One possibility is that Burke was thinking of the three levels of symbolic action he outlines: the "bodily or biological" level (36), the "personal, intimate, familiar, familistic" level, and the "abstract level" (37). Of the second of these levels, Burke notes that "both a father and a state may be 'authorities,'" (37).[2] Burke typically refers to this second level, the familistic level, in terms of father-son relationships, referring for instance to "symbolic parricide" (41) as a key transformational element in poetry. The poet in question is implicitly male, a "medicine man," who may seek to kill the father or commune with the mother (an act Burke sees as representative of narcissism or "communion with the self"), but not vice versa (64, 42). For Burke, readers "participate" in the poem, experiencing the situation of the author, "though with a difference," since the writer's and reader's situations are not identical (90). If Bate is right in that female and male readers' situations differ, then this should be taken into account in Burke's theory. For instance a female reader might be conflicted when reading a tale of a male protagonist's parricidal quest: is she meant to identify with the male character's quest as a universal human impulse, or as a uniquely *male* struggle based on a father-son relationship? For male readers such a conflict will not exist, much as phrases such as "Men at work" may pose no conceptual challenge to those who are always included in the generic term.

On another page, Burke emphasized the terms "male" and "man" embedded in the words "hu*man*," "wo*man*," and "fe*male*" (90).[3] Burke, always ready to see the irony in word choices, rightly notices here that even the alternatives Bate poses are derivations from the masculine terms "man" or "male." Along these lines, the archive also includes a draft of a note to Bate, dated January 11, 1976, which Bate never received and which presumably remained unsent. The note opens as follows: "Many thanks for your convincing words anent 'generic' and 'invisible.' Your point is well taken. Recalling my title, 'Definition of Man,' I feel so contrite I have vowed to go a step further by ruling out 'humanity,' 'woman,' and 'female.' Or do converts always carry things to excess? (At least, I hope that the faults of my title aren't also reflected in the clauses of my definition!)" (KB to BB January 11, 1976). It is perhaps not surprising that Burke was interested in how the generic man is embedded in words—even in the words Bate offers as alternatives, such as "human." As Burke himself suggested, humans are "inventor[s] of the negative"; humans possess the ability to distinguish that which is from that which is not, as well as between the hortatory "thou shalt" and "thou shalt not." The very terms we use to specify the *female* (or *woman*), as Burke's notes suggest, contain within them the irony that women are both "man" and "not man." They embody the paradox of substance, which for Burke is exemplified when a word "used to designate what a thing *is*, derives from a word designating something that a thing *is not*" (*GM* 23).

However, Burke's notes indicate that he was more skeptical of the idea that a feminist perspective might change the propositions in his "definition of man." Another page of notes begins as follows: "If you ever care to examine my Definition of [generic] man for traces of male chauvinism, please let me know right smack between the ears" (Notes 1). The remainder of the note is tantalizing, yet unfortunately it is frustratingly inscrutable (even in relation to Burke's typically inscrutable penmanship). While a complete translation has been impossible, it includes phrases such as "MAN IN AUTHORITY," "Nature & Culture," "bear a child," "unless you discover some essential differences between a man and a woman," and "social differences." One might surmise that Burke was thinking through biological and social differences between men and women, including how those might shape his "Definition of [generic] man."

Despite his uncertainty about the clauses of his definition, Burke did begin to use the term "human" instead of "man" sometime after his encounter with Bate in 1975. In the years following he published several essays dealing with the implications of his definition, including "(Nonsymbolic) Motion/(Symbolic) Action" (1978), "Methodological Repression and/or Strategies of Containment" (1978), and "Theology and Logology" (1979). Burke's 1974 response to Wayne Booth, "Dancing with Tears in My Eyes," refers to a "definition of man" (23, 27), as does "Colloquy I" (published in 1976 but presumably written earlier). But Burke's 1978 piece "(Nonsymbolic) Motion/(Symbolic) Action" refers to the "human organism" as "the only typically symbol-using animal existing on earth" (810). "Methodological Repression" (1978) similarly refers to "human history," "human individuals," and the "human body" (404), while "Theology and Logology" (1979) discusses "human relations" and "human sense" (153, 156). Even later Burke seems to have moved away from the term "human" as well, preferring alternatives such as "bodies that learn language" ("Dramatism as Ontology" 28) or "wordy animals" ("Dramatism and Logology" 90).

Indeed as late as 1987 Burke stated in an interview that he was "still clarifying" his "work on human symbol-using" (Rountree et al. 12). In *College Composition and Communication* Burke revised his definition once more, resulting in this, his last version: "Being bodies that learn language thereby becoming wordlings humans are the symbol-making, symbol-using, symbol-misusing animal inventor of the negative separated from our natural condition by instruments of our own making goaded by the spirit of hierarchy acquiring foreknowledge of death and rotten with perfection" (qtd. in Coe 332–33).

Thus Burke began to avoid the implied "man" altogether. However Burke himself also tinkered with the propositions in the definition itself (although not based on Bate's feminist intervention).

It is not surprising that feminist scholars have since continued to question the "generic man" *and* woman. In 1992 Celeste Condit argued that scholars must go beyond the "dualistic stage" that recognizes only two genders; instead we should extend our focus to "a broad 'humanity' and to 'human beings,' discovering ways to speak that emphasize human plurality" (351). In other words, our use of the terms "men and women" (or "ladies and gentleman" or "male and female") also carry with them assumptions that we might now find problematic. Such phrases reinforce a binary gender system, one that we now know to be reductive, given the range of genders we recognize. Instead Condit offers this version: "People are players with symbols inventors of the negative and the possibility of morality grown from their natural condition by tools of their collective making trapped between hierarchy and equality (moved constantly to reorder) neither rotten nor perfect, but now and again lunging down both paths" (352). In an era where human rights occupy great exigence, Condit's "haggle" offers relevance. Thinking over the *gender* of "the definition of [hu]man," then, has yielded productive insights and can continue to do so. Both Condit and Bate have questioned Burke's work and used it to support their own arguments for the importance of thinking through the implications of gender and language. This we seem to have arrived at a broad agreement over the first line in Burke's definition.

However, like the gendered language in the first part of Burke's original definition, the second part of that line, "symbol-using animal," also reflects a particular way of viewing and thinking about the world. The language of symbol-using "directs attention toward some things and away from others" (Bate, "Generic Man" 83), to borrow Bate's wording—particularly in this case the range of communicative acts in which humans engage. In what follows I consider how we might "haggle" with Burke's definition of humans as symbol-using animals. I draw on scholarship in disability studies that has questioned the historic and contemporary tendency to ignore differences in language use across humans, as well as Bate's reasoning about the importance of language to identity, to interrogate how language comes to be privileged as a key determinant of humanity.

RETHINKING SYMBOL-USING: AUTISM AND LANGUAGE IMPAIRMENT

According to Bate the term "man" places women at a disadvantage when used to refer to all humans. One could similarly argue that the term "symbol-using" places individuals with communicative disabilities at a disadvantage, directing attention away from alternative ways of communicating without traditionally recognized symbols. Among those with communicative disabilities, we might include individuals with aphasia or apraxia of speech (which can occur due to a brain injury or stroke), auditory processing disorder, selective mutism, and in some cases autism. To broaden this group further, we might consider how individuals with mental disabilities, such as intellectual or cognitive disabilities, psychiatric conditions, and the like may sometimes have difficulties being understood by individuals tuned only to certain kinds of symbol-using. One might also note that humans begin life without the ability to communicate through language, may experience periods of communicative disability throughout their lives, and may end their lives with communicative disabilities.

As Cynthia Lewiecki-Wilson has argued, the case of individuals with communicative disabilities challenges us to consider "rhetoric's received tradition of emphasis on the individual rhetor who produces speech/writing, which in turn confirms the existence of a fixed, core self, imagined to be located in the mind" (157). It is important for us as rhetoricians to consider what we mean when we define humans as symbol-users, and to consider whom we might unwittingly marginalize or exclude in our privileging of symbolic language. Just as we have questioned and now rejected gendered language, we should question how the language we use conveys ableist assumptions about communicative practices.

Burke's definition of humans as the "typically symbol-using animal" rests on the assumption that humans emerge into personhood through language. In "(Non-symbolic) Motion/(Symbolic) Action" (1978), Burke suggests, "In terms of symbolic action, it [the Self] becomes a 'person' by learning the language of its tribe" (814). Burke made this suggestion as early as 1956, in "Symbol and Association," an essay he published in the *Hudson Review*. In that essay, Burke notes "once man has emerged from the state of infancy, his approach to *things* is through a fog of *words*" (213). Infancy, Burke writes, is "a condition somewhat analogous to the speechlessness of other animals" (224).

This statement implies that those who have not yet learned (or those who lose) the "language of the tribe" are neither fully human nor fully rhetorical. As Catherine Prendergast notes, these kinds of assumptions mean that "to be disabled mentally is to be disabled rhetorically" (202). Thus people with communicative difficulties might under Burke's definition be grouped alongside infants in a kind of animal-like state of symbolic ineptitude. In this way Burke's definition of human enacts what preeminent disability studies scholar Lennard Davis calls "one of the foundational ableist myths of our culture: that the norm for humans is to speak and hear, to engage in communication through speaking and hearing" (15). Davis points out that these norms privilege particular forms of speech and hearing, such as oral speech rather than sign language.

Burke's definition comes awfully close to making language a requirement for humanity, and such an assumption can dehumanize people with disabilities. Our dominant assumptions about appropriate language and symbol-using—assumptions embedded in Burke's thought—clearly can have troubling implications, since they imply that people with language impairments may be somehow less than human. One might be tempted, then, to jettison "symbol-using animals" alongside the generic Man.

Like Bate, though, who found value in Burke's theories even as she rejected his use of the generic Man, I too find value in Burkean concepts for understanding alternative forms of communication. I argue here that three concepts from Burke's own repertoire help us to expand how we understand the phrase "humans are the symbol-using animal" or "bodies that learn language": orientation, symbolic action, and piety. To show how these concepts might help us to understand alternative communicative practices from a rhetorical perspective, I use autism as one example of a condition commonly considered a communicative disorder.

Burke's notion of orientation might provide rhetoric scholars with a framework within which to understand language patterns that do not reflect the cognitive habits and brain functioning commonly ascribed to "normal" people, or what some have termed "neurotypicals." In Burkean terms, we might view neurotypical human communication as an orientation, a system of interpretation and a set of assumptions "as to how things were, how they are, and how they may be" (*PC* 14). For instance a Western neurotpyical orientation values eye contact (at least in most Western cultures), which has come to be associated with a range of qualities: directness, honesty, confidence, intimacy. Lack of eye contact is commonly mentioned as one of the key features of autism (although autism is itself a diverse condition, usually understood as a spectrum). Seen as part of an orientation, though, eye contact is important not for its intrinsic value but because of the way it is linked to other communication practices, habits, and values in a neurotypical system of interpretation. From the perspective of a neurotypical orientation, differences common in autistic individuals can be seen only as deficits, as failures of symbolic action; from the perspective of a neurodiverse orientation, eye contact might be seen as uncomfortable, intrusive, and domineering.

Burke's own thinking might also encourage us to include embodied communication as symbolic action. For instance one behavior commonly associated with autistic people is self-stimulating behavior, or "stimming." Stimming practices might seem to fall into the realm of "nonsymbolic motion"—rocking, hand flapping, watching dust specks in the air, humming, and so on.[4] Burke might lead us to consider how these motions function as symbolic action. In "Symbol and Association" Burke takes up the case of the "neurotic" as a kind of test for his theory. Here he suggests that neurotics might carry out acts that seem asymbolic (that is, "nonverbal or extra verbal *motions*") that are "nonetheless motivated by strongly symbolic compulsions, of which the act could be seen as *symptomatic*, once you know how to read the signs" (214).[5] While neurosis is no longer a recognized diagnostic category in psychological practice, we can guess that Burke might read stims as "symbolic compulsions" as well. Often autistic writers suggest that stimming offers a solution to sensory bombardment. One blogger, Aleph, writes: "Stimming is a way to relieve tension, it is a way to provide the body with a controlled sensation which serves as a channel through which to focus the chaos and let everything else out a little." From a Burkean perspective, we might understand stimming as an alternative form of communication, grounded in the sensory experiences of individuals with autism and imbricated in a unique orientation to the world.

Burke himself was willing to recognize that each individual is unique in his or her "underlying physiology of sheer motion," the "realm of sensations" (814) characterized by "the centrality of the nervous system" ("[Nonsymbolic]" 813). Stims such as rocking, used to soothe the nervous system, can thus be seen as symbolic actions; rather than sheer motions, they are *symptomatic* of situational factors, such as stress or sensory bombardment. Thus while stimming might be categorized as nonsymbolic motion by some—and hence not a form of human language—from a Burkean perspective these acts can be understood as symbolic action.

Drawing on Burke's notion of *piety,* we might note that what counts as language depends on the sense of appropriateness that guides our assessments of symbolic action. This sense of the appropriate typically privileges only certain kinds of symbolic actions, typically oral or written alphanumeric discourse. Yet in other instances Burke extends the concept of piety to include acts that seem impious. Burke noted for instance that drug users are deemed "fiends" if they use heroin at a party but that medical patients could use morphine in a hospital without taking on the trappings of a criminal or "drug fiend" (*PC* 77–78). We might similarly note that some stims practiced by neurotypicals *are* a form of communication or body language. When we see someone tapping their toes, twirling their hair, or biting their nails, we understand those acts as symbolic actions indicating nervousness or anxiety. However to flap one's hands is considered abnormal and nonsymbolic. Seen as a form of piety, though, autistic stims might be understood as acts of pious system-building for people with autism, part of the sense of "what goes with what" that drives all human communication. Some autistic people note that their stims "go with" certain activities, emotions (stress or boredom), or situations. Others have resigned themselves to substituting finger tapping or playing with a stress ball for their preferred stims in order to pass as neurotypical.

The sense of piety is precisely that which is ironically denied in some mainstream descriptions of autism. Such discriminations posit that people with autism lack "central coherence," what autism researchers Francesca Happé and Uta Frith define as "a processing bias for featural and local information, and relative failure to extract gist or 'see the big picture' in everyday life" (6). People with autism may insist on sameness between situations, so that if a small detail is out of place, the situation loses meaning (5). In this way, we might actually see autistic behavior as a stronger than average drive for piety, a consuming desire to "round things out" or "to fit experiences together into a unified whole" (Burke, *PC* 74).

To return to the first clause of Burke's definition, then, the example of autism begs us to stretch, and potentially reject, the criterion of symbol-using as a determinant of humanity. While it is indeed possible to use Burkean notions of orientation, symbolic action, and piety to reinterpret autistic communication, doing so risks imposing a neurotypical framework on neurodiverse actions. Thinking of embodied actions as forms of *nonsymbolic language* suggests a category between Burke's binary of symbolic action/nonsymbolic motion.

As an example of how a neurodiverse perspective might lead us to rethink assumptions about language, consider one autistic blogger and filmmaker, Amanda Baggs, who created a video titled "In My Language." Baggs begins by showing herself interacting with the material world—looking at a slinky-like toy, waving a piece of paper, running her hand over a keyboard. In the second part of the video, Baggs uses a computerized speech technology to add a voice over that defines these various interactions as language. In the voiceover, Baggs disavows symbolicity as a motivation for her language: "Many people have assumed that when I talk about this being my language that means that each part of the video must have a particular symbolic message within it designed for the human mind to interpret. But my language is not about designing words or even visual symbols for people to interpret. It is about being in a constant conversation with every aspect of my environment."

To illustrate this point, in the video Baggs places her hand under a stream of running water, but she warns her viewers, "In this part of the video the water doesn't symbolize anything. I am just interacting with the water as the water interacts with me." Baggs goes on to question why this "language" is not usually recognized as such, why it is that "it is only when I type something in your language that you refer to me as having communication" and subsequently personhood.

Rather than describing her movements as "nonsymbolic motion," Baggs insists that they form a language, if not a symbolic one in the traditional sense. Instead we might position this wide range of embodied action within the framework of orientation, suggesting instead that humans are orientation-builders, expressing *preferences* "as to how things were, how they are, and how they may be" (*PC* 14). Thinking about communication from Baggs's perspective, then, encourages us to consider what we mean by the language itself, and whether we can expand that term to include a wider range of communicative strategies and technologies.

Taking seriously this expanded definition of "language" might shift our attention to alternative communication technologies (such as the computerized voice Baggs uses) or types of languages, and how they might be included among the tools used by "bodies that learn language."

CONCLUSION

Burke stated that humans are "the kind of animal that can haggle about the definition of himself" (*LSA* 23)—and in fact Burke encouraged such haggling. When he first introduced his definition in a *Hudson Review* article in 1963, he extended this invitation: "I am offering my Definition of Man in the hope of either persuading the reader that it fills the bill, or of prompting him to decide what should be added, or subtracted, or in some way modified" ("Definition of Man" 491). Burke envisioned this definition as a work in progress, a group project of sorts that would lead rhetoric scholars to a better understanding of human communication.

Prompted by Bate's inquiry over thirty years ago, I have here continued Burke's and Bate's questioning of the "definition of human." To do so, I used Bate's encounter with Burke as an heuristic, or source of invention. After I read through the archival materials, I asked myself, What other terms in Burke's definition might place individuals "at a disadvantage" (to borrow Bate's phrasing)? How do other terms in the definition of human "intertwin[e] with modes of thinking" ("Generic Man" 83) that might be archaic or ethically questionable? Such an approach seems valuable to me because it means that the archive will never be exhausted, even when Burke's extensive documents have been thoroughly mined for new insights or missed connections (however long that endeavor takes!). While such work is clearly valuable (and I have engaged that approach myself), I argue here that seeing archival materials as heuristic can shift scholars' focus from *what was* to *what might be* or *what might have been.*

Even this one episode with Bate can yield further analysis. While gender and disability perspectives provide opportunities for questioning that definition, we might also identify other haggles with Burke's terminology. For instance the growing field of animality studies might prompt us to question the distinction Burke makes between humans and animals—a distinction that seems increasingly difficult to uphold, both from a scientific and an ethical perspective.

Reconsidering Burke's "definition of human" might even lead us toward a new area of study, which we might call "rhetorics of humanity." Rather than accepting the universal man as a neutral term, Bate insisted that such gendered language mattered because it excluded women. I have argued similarly here for an expanded view of human communication that does not assume symbol-using should be a criterion for humanity. Instead we might position a wide range of embodied action within the framework of orientation, suggesting instead that humans (and potentially animals as well) are orientation-builders, expressing *preferences* "as to how things were, how they are, and how they may be" (*PC* 14). Both feminist and disability studies perspectives, then, encourage us to reflect on our own definitions (of man, of language, of human), and consider whether we can expand that term to include a wider range of communicative strategies, actors, and technologies.

More fundamental is that these perspectives might lead us to question our privileging of symbolic action as a key determinant of humanity. Drawing on insights from gender, disability, and animality studies (to name a few), we might ask how "exclusively human" traits are actually produced and embodied through what Una Chaudhuri calls "line-drawing exercises" (522), the rhetorical acts of definition that distinguish among humans and between humans and other beings. In Burke's terms, we might examine the "scope" and "circumference" of the term human, and how that territory has changed in different historical circumstances.[6] Studies in "rhetorics of humanity" should continue to examine how the lines between human and not-human are drawn and institutionalized through language.

We might consider how definitions of "human" that rest on certain forms of linguistic or rhetorical competence carry with them ethical implications, since they exclude people who do not communicate according to preferred standards and methods. Rhetoricians might accordingly rethink the lack of verbal expression as something other than a deficit, especially when we define speech according to neurotypical, human preferences. The goal of such an endeavor would be to take seriously the communicative capabilities of all beings (symbol-using or not, human or otherwise), as "bodies that learn language."

NOTES

1. Burke's notes appear on a photocopy of Bate's "Generic Man" article that does not include the page numbers for the article as published. The notes appear on the first page of the photocopy, which corresponds to page 83 of the published article.

2. The father-authority symbol relationship is drawn out in Burke's burlesque "Electioneering in Pyschoanalysia," which dramatizes the tendency for nations to use symbolic parricide, ousting one "father-symbol of accepted authority" in favor of a new one with each election "benignly getting nowhere," doing nothing to change the actual situations in which they are embedded (*PLF* 136).

3. Burke's notes appear on a photocopy of Bate's "Generic Man" article that does not include the page numbers for the article as published. The notes appear on the eighth page of the photocopy, which corresponds to page 90 of the published article.

4. For a longer list of "stims," see International Christian Association of Neurodevelopmentalists, "The Stim List," at http://www.icando.org/images/thestimlist.pdf.

5. See also *PLF,* where Burke argues that bodily ailments "may be a 'symbolic' action the part of the body which, in this materialization, *dances* a corresponding state of mind, reordering the glandular and neural behavior of the organism in obedience to mind-body correspondences" (11).

6. For instance women have historically been positioned as defective men, and as somehow closer to animals; people with disabilities have been dehumanized, depicted as "creatures" or "beasts" rather than people. Rosemarie Garland-Thompson points out that women are both historically and currently associated with people with disabilities (citing for example Aristotle's declaration that women were "mutilated males") (6-8). Rosi Braidotti makes a similar point in her essay "Animals, Anomalies, and Inorganic Others."

WORKS CITED

Aleph. "Positive Stims." *Malakhim* June 17, 2007.

Baggs, Amanda.(2007, January 14). In *My Language* (video file). Retrieved from http://www.youtube.com/watch?v=JnylM1hl2jc.

Bate, Barbara. *Communication and the Sexes.* New York: Harper Collins, 1987.

———. "Generic Man, Invisible Woman: Language, Thought, and Social Change." *University of Michigan Papers in Women's Studies* 2.1 (1975): 83–95.

———. Letter to Kenneth Burke. Nov. 19, 1975. Kenneth Burke Papers. Paterno Library, Pennsylvania State University.

———. Personal communication. Aug. 8, 2009. E-mail.

———."A Rhetorical Approach to the Nonsexist Language Controversy: An Exploratory Study Using Interviews with Selected University Faculty." Diss. University of Oregon, 1976.

Braidotti, Rosi. "Animals, Anomalies, and Inorganic Others." *PMLA* 124.2 (2009): 526–32.

Burke, Kenneth. "Colloquy I: The Party Line." *Quarterly Journal of Speech* 62 (1976): 62–68.

———. "Dancing with Tears in My Eyes." *Critical Inquiry* 1 (1974): 23–31.

———. "Definition of Man." *Hudson Review* 16.4 (1963/1964): 491–514.

———. "Dramatism and Logology." *Communication Quarterly* 33.2 (1985): 89–93.

———. "Dramatism as Ontology or Epistemology: A Symposium." *Communication Quarterly* 33.1 (1985): 17–33.

———. *A Grammar of Motives.* Berkeley: University of California Press, 1969.

———. *Language as Symbolic Action.* Berkeley: University of California Press, 1966.

———. Letter to William Rueckert. Oct. 6, 1972. *Letters from Kenneth Burke to William H. Rueckert, 1959–1987*. Anderson, S.C.: Parlor, 2002. 188.

———. "Methodological Repression and/or Strategies of Containment." *Critical Inquiry* 5.2 (1978): 401–16.

———. "Ms. Universe." *Late Poems—1968–1983: Attitudinizings Verse-wise, While Fending for One's Selph, and in a Style Somewhat Artificially Colloquial.* Ed. Julie Whitaker and David Blakesley. Columbia: University of South Carolina Press, 2005. 69–70.

———. "(Nonsymbolic) Motion/(Symbolic) Action." *Critical Inquiry* 4 (1978): 809–38.

———. Notes on Barbara Bate's "Generic Man." Undated. Kenneth Burke Papers. Paterno Library, Pennsylvania State University.

———. *Permanence and Change.* 3rd ed. Berkeley: University of California Press, 1954.

———. *Philosophy of Literary Form: Studies in Symbolic Action.* 3rd ed. Berkeley: University of California Press, 1973.

———. "Post-Roethkean Translations." *Johns Hopkins Review* 6 (1952–53): 6–7.

———. *A Rhetoric of Motives.* Berkeley: University of California Press, 1969.

———. *The Rhetoric of Religion: Studies in Logology.* Berkeley: University of California Press, 1961.

———. "Symbol and Association." *Hudson Review* 4.2 (1956): 212–25.

———. "Theology and Logology." *Kenyon Review* 1 (1979): 151–85.

———. "The Vegetal Radicalism of Theodore Roethke." *Sewanee Review* 58.1 (1950): 68–108.

Chaudhuri, Una. "'Of All Nonsensical Things': Performance and Animal Life." *PMLA* 124.2 (2009): 520–25.

Coe, Richard M. "Defining Rhetoric—and Us: A Meditation on Burke's Definition." *Composition Theory for the Postmodern Classroom.* Ed. Gary A. Olson and Sidney I. Dobrin. Albany: State University of New York Press, 1994. 332–44.

Condit, Celesete Michelle. "Post-Burke: Transcending the Sub-Stance of Dramatism." *Quarterly Journal of Speech* 78 (1992): 349–55.

Davis, Lennard J. *Enforcing Normalcy: Disability, Deafness and the Body.* New York: Verso, 1995.

Garland-Thomson, Rosemarie. "Integrating Disability, Transforming Feminist Theory." *NWSA Journal* 14.3 (2002): 1–32.

Happé, Francesca, and Uta Frith. "The Weak Coherence Account: Detail-Focused Cognitive Style in Autism Spectrum Disorders." *Journal of Autism and Developmental Disorders* 36.1 (2006): 5–25.

Lewiecki-Wilson, Cynthia. "Rethinking Rhetoric through Mental Disabilities." *Rhetoric Review* 22.2 (2003): 156–67.

Prendergast, Catherine. "On the Rhetorics of Mental Disability." In *Towards a Rhetoric of Everyday Life: New Directions in Research on Writing, Text, and Discourse.* Eds. P. Martin Nystrand and John Duffy. Madison: University of Wisconsin Press, 2003. 189–206.

Rountree, J. Clarke, III, Richard Kostelanetz, and Kenneth Burke. "Richard Kostelanetz Interviews Kenneth Burke." *Iowa Review* 17.3 (1987): 1–14.

KEITH GIBSON

BURKE AND THE POSITIVE POTENTIALS OF TECHNOLOGY

Recovering the "Complete Literary Event"

Kenneth Burke often wrote in his published work about the effects of science and technology on society. The majority of those writings have left readers with the impression that Burke was at least skeptical and perhaps even downright negative about the consequences of our modern scientific rationalization. One set of documents from the Kenneth Burke Papers at the Penn State archives challenges the simplicity of that notion, and this essay will consider how they provoke us to refine our understanding of Burke's view of science and technology. I begin with his published work, and I demonstrate that Burke had a well-established (and well-deserved) reputation as a skeptic of the virtues of technology. I then introduce a little-known interview Burke gave to a Swedish radio station that complicates our idea of Burke as technological pessimist; in this interview he described some positive uses of technology, especially in relation to literature and the preservation of what he regarded as the "complete literary event." I conclude by applying the ideas from this interview to contemporary multimedia technologies. Burke's writings on technology and literature were important in the 1950s, and they continue to be relevant as literary and rhetorical scholars learn to deal with rapidly changing technology today.

BURKE'S TECHNOLOGICAL SKEPTICISM

Finding explicit skepticism regarding science and technology in Burke's writings is a very simple task. Burke's criticisms of science and technology have tended to follow three themes: (1) critiquing those who see science as an unerring boon to society; (2) warning us about the negative consequences of science and its application; and (3) pointing out the weak epistemological position of science. While I lack the space here to provide an exhaustive list of Burke's criticisms of science, I will provide a representative sample to illustrate each of these motifs that appear in his work, and I conclude the section with a summary of the scholarly community's views of Burke's attitudes toward science and technology.

Critiques of Science as "an intrinsically good power"

One of Burke's best-known treatments of technology occurs in his description of the modern occupational psychoses in *Permanence and Change*, among them the agrarian psychosis, the investor's psychosis, and the criminal psychosis. As Burke traced the history of rationalization through magic, religion, and science, he noted that each of these had been brought to bear to control a certain aspect of society: magic to control nature, religion to control humans, and science to control machinery. The technological psychosis ("mainly responsible for their [the other modern psychoses'] perplexities") arose when the "doctrine of use, as the prime mover of judgments, formally established the *secular* as the point of reference by which to consider questions of valuation" (*PC* 45). Burke claimed this led to a series of confusions for philosophers working in this rationalization. Marx for instance "tended to confuse the *is* and the *ought to be*," and he had difficulty making "the subtle distinction between *what is to a man's interests* and *what he is interested in*" (*PC* 45).

Burke did not see a particularly easy way out of this "problematical approach to questions of value," given that it is intensified by "the occupational diversity that is part of this same technological framework" (*PC* 47). Burke further explained in *Attitudes toward History* that this new scientific rationalization will lead to an even more debilitating social side effect than the technological psychosis: naïve capitalism (*ATH* 142–58). And though many saw science and technology as the liberators freeing society from the falsehoods of magic and religion, Burke did not see this as liberating at all; instead he foresaw a prolonged struggle that would result in an uneven distribution of wealth and eventual class warfare (*ATH* 158; see also Gibson). It was not just that science *could* lead to undesirable side effects; Burke persuasively argued that it *would*.

In *The Philosophy of Literary Form* Burke took to task some specific thinkers who saw science and technology as nearly unerring forces for good. In his critique of John Dewey's *Liberalism and Social Action* for instance, he noted that Dewey took this leap: "if the author's merging of science as technique with science as charitable attitude towards people were made the express subject of analysis and rationalization, Dr. Dewey's volume would be more enlightening" (*PLF* 391). Burke continued this theme in *A Rhetoric of Motives*, where he became even more forceful in his contention that too many scholars had come to see science as a virtue, or in some cases even the definition of virtue. In describing the "autonomy" of science, he noted that "liberal apologetics" were not even willing to concede that the science leading to cruel animal experiments is vicious: "The liberal is usually disinclined to consider such possibilities because applied science is for him not a mere set of instruments and methods, whatever he may assert; it is a *good* and *absolute*, and is thus circuitously endowed with the philosophic function of *God* as the grounding of values" (*RM* 30).

Burke observed that there was plenty of explicit cheerleading of science, but he seemed even more concerned about the more implicit "claims for science as a substance which, like God, would be an intrinsically *good* power" (*RM* 30). Burke insisted that this was a mistake, pointing out that technology "could become identified with motives good, bad, or indifferent, depending upon the uses to which it was put, and upon the ethical attitudes that, as part of the context surrounding it, contributed its meaning in the realm of motives and action" (*RM* 30). Science is merely a tool with no intrinsic character of its own; whatever good or bad flows from it is a product of the agents that wield it and the motives they possess.

Warnings of "technological pollution"

Even when Burke seemed to appreciate science, he was skeptical of science's technological products. In *The Philosophy of Literary Form* he confessed an admiration for the "aesthetic" traits of "the speculations of pure science": "enterprise, independence, spiritedness, imaginativeness, critical keenness" (419). But he was much less enthusiastic about the actual products of science, which he labeled "adventurous speculations harnessed for business purposes" (*PLF* 420). His chief fear was that we would become a society bound to the trappings of progress. It is ironic that he saw applied science as diametrically opposed to pure science, creating "the opposite type of mind, with more and more demands upon our acquiescence . . . our loss of fluid, physical, 'earthy' living, our development of cogwheel thoughts to match the cogwheel methods of production. . . . the most brilliant aspects of human thought . . . being steadily converted, by men of a different order, into human impoverishments" (*PLF* 420).

This concern over the technological paraphernalia with which we surround ourselves remained a theme throughout Burke's work. His famous "Definition of Man" (which Jordynn Jack considers at length in this volume) included the clause that "man" is "separated from his natural condition by tools of his own making" (*LSA* 16), and these tools are, he claimed, reshaping our very natures. As he writes, "The implements of hunting and husbandry, with corresponding implements of war, make for a set of habits that become a kind of 'second nature,' as a special set of expectations, shaped by custom, comes to seem 'natural'" (*LSA* 13). By the late 1960s Burke was clearly worried about the massive consumption he had witnessed over the previous twenty years. In a review of Marshall McLuhan's *Understanding Media*, for example, he notes that "though men's technical innovations are but a fraction of the 'human condition' in general, the great clutter of such things that characterize modern life adds up to a formative background" (*LSA* 410). Later, in the 1970s, Burke spoke often of writing a satire about this "technological pollution" and the effects it was having on contemporary society (*On Human Nature* 72). The tools that had originally served to improve our lives had instead distracted us, injured us, and eventually taken us over.

Admonitions against the Weak Epistemology of "Technologism"

Burke's later work led him to think more philosophically about science and its effects on society. In *The Rhetoric of Religion* (1970), Burke contrasted "dramatism" with "scientism," the former being a focus on action and motive, the latter being a focus on knowledge. An epistemology based on dramatism, Burke claimed, stimulates questions such as "'From what, through what, to what, does this particular form proceed?'" (*RR* 39). These questions focus our attention on action and motive, leading us to sophisticated examinations of our circumstances. Scientism, on the other hand, leads to overly simplistic epistemological questions, such as "'What do I see when I look at this object?' or 'How do I see it?'" (*RR* 39). Though these inquiries may be worth pursuing, they concentrate on relatively simple issues of perception. Investigations into the fundamental properties of the universe, such as those conducted by physicists and chemists, could thus never lead to the kind of illumination into the human condition that can be gained through studies of philosophy, rhetoric, and dramatism.

Scientific epistemologies can lead to plenty of new knowledge of course, and Burke warned that the seemingly impressive accomplishments of scientism have caused many to take science too seriously: "the undeniable material reality and might of the technologist's engines" inspired what Burke called "technologism," and this quickly became more than just a point of view. He claimed "technologism" was functioning in society as a religion: "it is a 'religion' to the extent that technology is viewed as an intrinsic good, so that its underlying, unspoken assumption is: 'the more technology, the higher the culture'" (*RR* 170–71). With this we see a return to one of Burke's original critiques of science and technology—that no one was really criticizing it.

These three interwoven themes of scientific criticism in Burke's work have been noted by many scholars who have studied and written about Burke, even to the extent that skepticism is often regarded as Burke's only attitude toward science and technology. William Rueckert observed, "The counterpart to rhetoric in our material, empirical dealings with nature is technology, which, Burke says, is made possible by symbolicity. It is by means of technology that we coerce, manipulate, persuade, transform, and try to 'improve' nature" (174). Dale Keller pointed out Burke's warning that technology "creates many unintentional by-products which . . . easily lead to the creator becoming slave to the created" (par. 6), and Star Muir described dramatism generally as a reaction against "a pervasive and pernicious scientism, an improper attitude that extends scientific methods to all aspects of life, that truncates human purpose, uses language as a means of mystification, and dominates Nature to the point of ecological imbalance." She saw this "preoccupation with technology" throughout Burke's work, asserting that it is one of the most formative themes in his scholarship (35–37). Burke's epistemological and philosophical leanings were clearly opposed to what he saw as a simplistic scientific perspective, and many of his contemporaries seized on this opposition as a way to help their readers better understand Burke's scholarly positions.

Given the political environment of the 1930s and 1940s, it is no surprise that a fair amount of Burke's resistance to science and technology is tied to politics as well. Robert Wess called technology "the antagonist in Burke's politics" (76), and Trevor Melia furthers this agonism by linking portions of our modern environmentalism to some of Burke's writings of more than seventy years ago: "Burke views technology as a logical and even, given our "rottenness with perfection," an inevitable outcome of our symbol-using genius. He has been warning since at least as early as 1937 about the danger of ecological disaster, and nowadays, as our symbols coalesce into more and more powerful technology, he contemplates the possibility that we are not only *apart from* but *against* nature" (71). For Burke, as science and technology took us away from nature, appropriate political systems could be a tool for bringing us back.

Of course Burke's views on technology were not entirely monolithic, and some critics have complicated the notion of Burke as anti-science. Stanley Edgar Hyman described Burke as having "an agrarian, backward-looking ideal that he shares with Thoreau, the Jeffersonians and Populists . . . which has led Henry Bamford Parkes to write, with a certain accuracy: 'he would like to have lived in Confucian China'" (219). But Hyman admitted there is something of a range to Burke's attitudes toward technology. At one extreme there "is even a dislike of science itself"; at the other "he is prepared to find some good in technology . . . finding such real, if negative values as its lessening the ravages of crop failure, pestilence, and other natural disasters" (219). Hyman ultimately concluded that Burke is "somewhere in the middle . . . combining the simple, immobile, and agrarian life with the technology necessary to get him, by car, train, and subway, to the New York Public Library" (219). Richard Thames claimed that though Burke "appears opposed to science and technology[,] the more careful reader knows he resists only their enshrinement" (19). Ian Hill also argued against the notion of Burke as Luddite, offering a more nuanced Burkean concept of technology: "rhetoric motivates technology and . . . technology motivates behavior" (par. 6). These motivations are not necessarily negative; our job as cultural critics is to distinguish the good from the bad, and Hill insists that Burke did more of this than he is credited with having done.

Even if Burke is not viewed as a Luddite, the bulk of his published work and the majority of the critical responses to that work do indeed leave us with the idea that he is clearly skeptical of science and technology. He was especially pessimistic about our ability to properly deal with the technological toys science would provide us, and our current culture of acquisition does not offer much evidence that we know how to deal very effectively with the "technological pollution" he decried.

BURKE'S RADIO INTERVIEW ON TECHNOLOGY AND LITERATURE

Though Burke had a pretty clear and largely consistent record in his published work detailing his skepticism of science and technology, the richness of Penn State's Kenneth Burke Papers provides a much fuller, more complete view of Burke's thought. One example is the written response Burke made to a request from Swedish public radio for an interview. In 1956 Radiotjanst, the Swedish version of National Public Radio in the United States, distributed an "international questionnaire" to determine the opinions of intellectuals worldwide on the effects television was having on our appreciation and reception of literature. Burke received the questionnaire on September 28, 1956, which consisted of the following two questions:

1. According to your view, what part does literature play in a society increasingly dominated by radio and television?
2. Is it possible for an appreciably large television audience to share in the cultural experience which lies at the back of every high-class literary production? (Linmann)

Burke was given five minutes to provide a recorded answer that would be translated and broadcast by the Swedish Broadcasting Corporation on October 17. In the nearly three weeks he had to prepare for the broadcast, he wrote four drafts of his response, all of which are preserved in Penn State's Kenneth Burke Papers. The drafts and the finished response (reproduced, in their entirety, in appendices A–D) provide us with a glimpse into his writing process and a more complex view of Burke's perspectives on science and technology than the simple skepticism and antagonism we are used to reading in his work. In the remainder of this essay I describe and analyze three aspects of Burke's answer: (1) his use of ancient rhetoric to address a very modern question; (2) the evolution of his thought, as evidenced in his successive drafts, on the importance of "the language of technology and factual information"; and (3) the contribution Burke believed technology could make to the appreciation of literature. His responses indicate a much more optimistic view of technology than is present in much of Burke's published work. He points specifically to two positive effects radio and television can have on literature: they employ recording devices "much superior in fidelity of representation" to writing; and they have the capability to restore "tonality and gesture" to literature, thus helping us to "keep from forgetting what a *complete* literary event really is" (see appendix D, this essay). This "complete literary event" is the natural state of literature for Burke, and he sees in technology the potential to "round out the circle" and return us to that natural state. Indeed Burke's response points to a more general claim about technology, and I conclude by explaining and employing a test Burke offered to determine if a particular technological application is to be "feared": does it "take us away" from nature, or does it "bring us back"?

"Plato and the living word"

The first draft of his response to the Swedish Broadcasting Corporation contains a full paragraph (123 words) of notes on Plato's *Phaedrus*: "Plato and the living word (Phaedrus)—we depart from it at our peril—yet thank God Plato turned to the written word, even in admonishing against it—(great value of it—even with the kind of literature that lends itself most perfectly to purely vocal perfection, the critic must also have the details in their fixity, as with the written word, so that he can, at his leisure, study them in their internal relations and developments. To hear the performance as such is analogous to a physiologist's study of the body—to view the work in its written details like the anatomist's dissecting of a body's tissues. We need both methods, to understand fully the miraculous workings of the artistic structure (poetic organism)." This peek into Burke's brainstorming reveals much more of his writing process than we are typically privy to; the informal comments and sentence fragments almost make it seem as if we are sitting and listening to him talk through the issue. The most developed portion of this paragraph is the extended medical analogy explaining Socrates' view of language ("to hear the performance as such is analogous to a physiologist's study of the body—to view the work in its written details is like an anatomist's dissecting of a body's tissues"). The influence of Plato's dialogues here is noteworthy: Burke's first thoughts on technology and literature bring him back to the Phaedrus. Indeed it would seem that Plato's writings form the foundation of Burke's initial thoughts on the question, and that should probably not be surprising. Plato's emphasis throughout his work on the "natural" is a clear predecessor to Burke's preference for technology that helps bring back the natural experience of poetry. It is clear that Plato's work was on Burke's mind more than any other scholar as he built this first draft: Plato is the only person mentioned in it, and the paragraph Burke wrote on the Phaedrus is one of only two fully formed paragraphs, the rest being little more than notes in sentence-fragment form.[1]

In the second draft Burke's discussion of the *Phaedrus* was less than one-third the size, comprising only two sentences and thirty-seven words: "In Plato's *Phaedrus*, Socrates speaks ill of the written word; he cares only for the living, spoken word, he says. For it is pliant; adapting itself to each new situation, whereas the written word is forever fixed." The medical analogy has been replaced with a simple recognition that Socrates believed the spoken word is "living," "pliant," and capable of "adapting itself to each new situation." The omission of the physiologist versus anatomist view of language greatly simplifies Burke's description of Socrates' position, though the meaning is maintained through Burke's focus on "the living, spoken word." By removing the anatomist half of the metaphor, Burke focuses his attention on the more important aspect of the technology—the capacity for live performance. Burke's use of Plato is briefer and simpler, but it is also speaks more clearly to his main point.

The other noteworthy change in the Plato portion of this draft is its position in the response. In the first draft the Plato paragraph was penultimate, but little meaning can be drawn from that: the draft was not an organized answer, but a mere collection of thoughts. This second draft is the first in which Burke began shaping a cohesive response, and in this draft the discussion of Plato is now in the first full paragraph. He notes that his answer will have two positions, the first of which is the difference between the written and the spoken word. The notes on Plato (followed now by two new sentences on Aristotle's *Poetics*) clearly form the foundation to this first position and an introduction to the entire response. Burke's use of and emphasis on ancient rhetoric to answer a modern question is evidence for his belief that the ancient writings are still relevant today. He demonstrates this relevance as he ties the ancients' preference for live oratory to his own appreciation of radio and television. Just as a recited poem is more "living" than a written one, so too is a televised play more "pliant" than a copy of the script.

The third draft and the finished response feature the same text about Plato, and Burke has trimmed it even further, featuring only two simple sentences and a total of twenty-six words: "In Plato's *Phaedrus,* Socrates speaks ill of the written word. He cares only for the living, spoken word, he says (with its powers of doctrinal impregnation)." These sentences comprise the clauses from only the first sentence of the previous draft; Burke has then conceptually cut his discussion of Plato in half, and the medical analogy is now down to a single word: "living." In an interview in which Burke had only five minutes to provide a rather complex answer, it is not surprising that he pared this section twice, dropping nearly 80 percent of the original text, and the final version is a clear, concise description of Plato's portrayal of Socrates' skepticism of writing. The existence of all four drafts of his response, though, helps us see just how much intellectual weight can lie behind a single adjective: when Burke called the spoken word "living," he was representing a complex and illustrative medical analogy.

Burke also made one significant addition to in this draft: he notes that the spoken word has "powers of doctrinal impregnation," which by implication the written word lacks. With this note Burke demonstrates the dangerous potential of what he has so far praised: the "living" spoken word. At the time of this interview, the world had just witnessed the perils of a powerful orator, and Burke acknowledges here that the spoken word, propagated by radio and television, has inherent risks. The phrase "doctrinal impregnation," though, has more than simply rhetorical roots. It was used at this time in the speaking and writing of Plinio Correa de Oliveira, a Catholic activist who spent much of his career decrying the influence of communism on religion. His most famous essay, "The Church and the Communist State: The Impossible Coexistence," features the following: "The officially philosophical and sectarian Communist State carries out a *doctrinal impregnation* of the masses with intransigence, amplitude, and method" (par. 67; emphasis added). Burke does not specifically mention de Oliveira, but given his interest in both communism and religion, it seems possible, perhaps likely, that Burke was subtly tweaking a critique of communism with this late addition.

The positioning of the Plato section also changed in these drafts. Serving as an introduction to the second draft, Burke's notes on Plato moved to the bottom of the second page in the third draft. This draft features Burke's more focused argument about the positive uses of radio and television to help us recreate the "complete literary event," and his positioning of Plato and Socrates as support for this argument indicates Burke's increased focus on the concept of technology that "rounds the circle." And though its place is not quite as prominent, his specific use of Plato, Socrates, and Aristotle further evidences Burke's belief in their relevance to even the most modern of questions.

"Purely signpost kind of words"

Though Burke was clearly interested in the possibility of technology helping reconnect audiences with the natural state of literary performance, he was not necessarily concerned with all forms of language being reconstituted through the technology of radio and television. Indeed one passage in the drafts of his response demonstrates Burke's clear differentiation between literary language that is meant to be heard and more technical language—"purely signpost kind of words"—that should only be read. Indeed as the progression of the drafts demonstrates, Burke eventually builds his argument for the recovery of the "complete literary event" around his concern that language is becoming too technical, losing its poetic value.

In the first draft of his response, Burke introduced the idea of technical language with the following:

> We omit from this discussion the purely signpost kind of words—words without tonal value—statistics, facts, the vast amt. of purely informative material needed for running a complex technological world—like the names and numbers in a telephone directory—the sort of words which people are taught to skim through rather than to read (and properly so—ideally, they should be read, if that were possible, not just in blocks as big as sentences, but in whole pages sized up at a single glance—ironically, many in being taught to read such stuff in the wholly non-dramatic way proper to it, lose their ability to appreciate the other kind of word, the kind that is to be appreciated, like a flavor, not gulped down like raw whiskey. Performance in the new mediums may correct this error somewhat.

Although, as noted earlier, Burke had not at this point crafted a cohesive, organized answer, this paragraph about "words without tonal value" is clearly meant to be an afterthought. He drew the distinction between literary and technical language, but it was the last thing Burke typed, and his indication that he intended to "omit from this discussion" this "purely informative material" is strong evidence that he did not, at this point, believe this technical language was very important to the matter of technology and literature.

By the second draft, however, Burke had already changed his mind somewhat about the importance of the issue. In this version, the fourth paragraph reads: "Much modern writing is not made for speech—after reading something of that sort for a while, I have a feeling in my head as though I had been shaking dice in a dice-box. Words of that sort are not made to be enjoyed as a flavor; they must be gulped down, like raw whiskey—and there are actually techniques taught now for reading in chunks (like running the eye down the columns of a telephone directory)—some people who master the art can become so good at it, that written words addressed to the ear (as with much good poetry) become almost unintelligible to them." Perhaps most notable here is that Burke does not begin this paragraph with the dismissive "We omit from this discussion"; he has instead decided that this is a relevant part of his answer to the question, providing it as a transition from Socrates' disdain for writing to the usefulness of "the new mediums" in reminding us what language sounds like. Though Burke is no longer omitting the "signpost kind of words" from his answer, he introduces two similes that make clear how he feels about such instrumental language: the reading of such words makes his head feel "as though I had been shaking dice in a dice-box," and these words are not meant to be savored but "gulped down, like raw whiskey." These figures of speech are distinctly Burkean in tone and subject, and their inclusion in this draft demonstrates Burke's evolution of feeling toward technical language from neglect to simple distaste.

The third and final drafts contain the same paragraph on this topic (with a two-word penciled addition in the third draft becoming typed text in the final):

> The further we go from the language of poetry and oratory towards the language of technology and factual information, the further we go from words that are *designed for the ear*. And there are even techniques taught now, for reading purely informational sentences in chunks, like running the eye down the columns of a telephone directory. With people who hear internally as they read, after they have punished themselves for a while by painfully listening to each successive syllable, of a style that was not meant to be heard at all, they may have an empty, rattling feeling in the head, as though they had been shaking dice in a dice-box. But the other sort, who have learned to take in whole sentences at a glance, like gulping down raw whiskey, become so good at the art of purely visual reading that written words addressed to the ear (as with much good poetry) become almost unintelligible to them.

The language is very similar to that in the second draft, with only a bit of rearranging; fortunately for his original listeners and for us, both similes survived. The most notable change in this paragraph is not the wording, but the position—it is now the lead paragraph in Burke's response. This is a remarkable evolution in Burke's belief in the importance of "the language of technology." It started as an afterthought, a topic he intended to gloss over quickly; it became a relevant piece of evidence, but still little more than support for his broader point about the natural state of literature; and it ended as the introduction to his response, with the shift "from the language of poetry and oratory towards the language of technology and factual information" acting as the chief reason radio and television need to rescue the spoken word.

"THE MACHINES THAT BRING US BACK"

While the drafts of Burke's response can help us understand the evolution of his thinking on technology and literature, the most meaningful content, that which Burke intended for public consumption, is worth a closer look as well. In the final draft of his response to the question about the intersections of radio, television, and literature, Burke did not simply retreat to the technological skepticism that had become such a feature of his published work. Instead he offered an insightful commentary on some of the positive aspects of technology, especially those that "round out the circle by restoring the initial supremacy of the spoken word." He makes this point by describing two benefits of radio and television on our consumption of literature, and far from worrying about the deleterious effects of these new technologies on literature, Burke suggests we embrace them: "The machines that take us away are to be feared until they are corrected by the machines that bring us back."

Burke's first argument in defense of radio and television is the superiority of recording devices over writing for preserving the author or poet's words. Though writing and printing were clearly important tools in preserving literature and poetry, Burke points out that they left out those poets who were not literate. Recording technology removes this limitation, and it does so in a way that more accurately represents the poet's wishes; it brings us back to our more natural state.

Burke's second argument is the restoration of the complete literary event. He here retreats back to Plato and Socrates, taking their case against Aristotle, who, as Burke points out, "rates the reading of a Greek tragedy higher than the witnessing of an actual performance." Burke dismisses this argument of Aristotle's, however, noting that it was easy for Aristotle to make that claim, having routinely seen and heard the "seventeen thousand tragically purged Athenian citizens"; he could provide that background as he read. Modern audiences, in contrast, rarely have the opportunity to experience plays or poetry off the page, and radio and television can rectify that shortcoming (though Burke admits "that much of even the best modern poetry is poor in auditory appeal"). Television will be especially useful, Burke claims, in allowing audiences to "enjoy those expressive moments that defy words. . . . those moments that flicker beyond the borders of the Word." Though words are obviously a major part of literature, they were not originally intended to be the totality of the experience, and Burke is pleased that radio and television will help us return to the "complete literary event."

These two points helped Burke make the claim that, at least in the case of literature, radio and television are machines that "round out the circle." He illustrates this figure of speech by pointing to two other examples: "Air conditioning in a theatre, for instance, but cancels off the atmospheric abnormalities caused by the gathering of people unnaturally. The water system in a city but restores, to each family, ready access to a spring, thereby correcting an earlier departure from nature." These examples clearly demonstrate Burke's complexity of thought regarding technology: scientific advancements that can correct a departure from our natural state are useful. For literature, printing and publishing (even if making the work more widely accessible) removed it from its original venue—the stage. A television broadcast, then, returns the audience to its rightful place as listeners and watchers of a performance. They are not the machines to be feared because they have taken us away from nature; rather, they are to be embraced for bringing us back.

How is this optimism, even enthusiasm, for technology to be squared with so much scientific and technological skepticism in Burke's published works? First we should note that Burke was here analyzing a specific piece of technology and a particular use of it. In many of his books and articles, he was writing much more broadly about science and technology and their place in society as a whole. Given the seeming inability of so many critics to find anything but good in science, Burke found himself in the role of naysayer, pointing out the risks and dangers of this new rationalization. This task required Burke to repeatedly point to the negative side of technology, thereby casting himself in a role as technological pessimist. This interview, however, asked Burke to address a much more specific rhetorical situation than he usually dealt with, and there is (in Burke's view) simply less risk of television harming literature than of technological advancement harming humanity generally.

More important though, this document provides evidence that Burke's position on science and technology is more complex than many critics have acknowledged. A quick scan of Burke's books and major articles has led many to characterize Burke too easily as a scientific skeptic, or as Hill describes, as a Luddite. Burke's response to the Swedish Broadcasting Corporation and the sequence of drafts through which he composes it indicate that even if he has reason to fear some technologies, he is certainly able to see the positive potential in others. Indeed this interview has provided a Burkean principle that can be useful as we assess the potential impacts of contemporary technology: that of rounding out the circle.

CONCLUSION: "ROUNDING OUT THE CIRCLE"

Numerous scholars have applied Burkean principles in the analysis of a variety of technologies.[2] Their analyses usefully explore how particular technologies affect our lives and suggest how we might best interact with them. Burke's interview with the Swedish Broadcasting Corporation serves this function as well, providing us with a general principle to help us assess whether a specific machine is to be "feared": does it "take us away" from nature or does it "bring us back"? Do our current technologies help us recover the "complete literary [or, more broadly, artistic] event"?

An extended example may help illustrate this principle. Let us apply this test to mp3 files and players to see how it works in practice. On one hand, mp3 technology makes more music available to more people, removing the separation between musician and audience that was caused by expensive formats and more expensive concerts. This is clearly a benefit, helping music lovers the world over recover a musical experience that had been impossible due to geography, economics, or both. On the other hand, the personalized nature of mp3 players removes the listener from the community of other audience members; the shared experience of public performance is gone. This community is certainly an important part of the complete musical event, and mp3 technology removes the listener further from it. A technology as relatively simple as mp3 files and players has at least two different results when subjected to Burke's "rounding out the circle" test; more complex technologies, such as iPads or smart phones, would clearly have many, many more.

This is not to say however that the test is too ambiguous to be useful. Burke's pentad is a broad analytical tool that can yield many different results if employed most generally on a work of literature or real-life rhetorical situation. Used in a more focused manner however—as Burke suggested with the focus on ratios—it is much more productive. The "rounding out the circle" test is similar. If we simply apply the question to an entire machine, we are likely to come up with a number of varied, perhaps contradictory, results. We need to instead use the test to examine particular aspects of specific technologies. Precisely because so many of our technological tools have multiple traits and uses, we need to focus our theoretical lens to get the most efficiency out of it. For instance if we want to better understand the way price and ease of distribution of mp3 technology affects music accessibility, we will find it rounding out the circle and completing the musical event. The accessibility of mp3 files has brought music to people in a way no technology before it has. This is especially true among young people: a recent Edison Research study has found that the percentage of Americans age twelve to twenty-four who "have ever downloaded mp3s or other digital music files from the internet" has more than doubled from 31 percent in 2000 to 65 percent in 2010 (23). The relative simplicity of using inexpensive recording technology and mp3 compression has furthermore allowed many more musicians than ever before to record, preserve, and distribute their music to the public. Thanks to this new technology, audiences have access to a range of complete musical events unheard of a mere quarter century ago.

On the other hand, if we want to analyze the effect of mp3 technology on our sense of musical community, we may find that it is further removing us from our natural state. Though we now have access to much more music than consumers before us, we have much less reason to go experience music in the way it was originally presented: in concert. The same Edison Research study cited above found, over the same ten-year period as the doubling in mp3 downloads, a drop in concert attendance among twelve- to twenty-four-year-olds: in 2000 they attended an average of 2.1 concerts per year, and in 2010 they attended 0.9 concerts per year (19). This 57 percent drop is likely not entirely due to mp3 technology—Americans had less disposable income in 2010 than 2000 for instance—but the concurrent rise in mp3 downloads is almost certainly a factor.

Penn State's Kenneth Burke Papers is a valuable archive of material that will help us better understand one of the leading figures in twentieth-century rhetorical scholarship. As we continue to explore this resource, we are likely to find many more texts that will help us comprehend Burke, our society, and ourselves. The four drafts of Burke's response to two questions about literature and technology give us insight into the complexities and evolution of Burke's thought on the topic, and they provide a useful test that can help us better understand our constantly changing technologies. Burke's test is not a tool that will allow us to simplistically put machines into piles of good and bad. It will, however, help us better understand specific attributes of our technology as we are led to productive questions to ask. This understanding can then inform how we use our tools. If we are concerned with recovering the complete artistic event, as Burke clearly was, we can use this test to help us make more sophisticated decisions about our uses of technology, and we will be able to more consistently round out the circle with our own technology.

APPENDIX A

Each of the drafts contained in the appendices and quoted in the text are quoted with the permission of Rare Books and Manuscripts, Special Collections Library, Pennsylvania State University Libraries. Permission is also provided by the Kenneth Burke Literary Trust. I am very grateful for the permission provided.

First Draft

Talking to one's neighbor, over a nation-wide hookup (as vs. going down and knocking at his door)

(perhaps a dialogue of two people, Thumbs-up and Thumbs-down) with third, synthesis, All-Thumbs

What is the essence of the new mediums?—our notion, spontaneity (plus revision by montage—omission, pointing up, recording, etc)—no problem of the Lost Chord

Rounding the circle—to arrive back at illiteracy, but by the most completely literate route—there, I think, is the condition for good art—the new mediums are of this nature

Those in authority haven't, I think, completely understood the resources, and what to do about them—they either stage a program (and many, of course, should be of this sort)—or they record discussion just as they occur (forum of the air programs)—they stumble on the right form, when quoting selections from investigations, etc. (an audience can readily accept the transitions supplied by a narrator, commentator, etc.—and can promptly swing into the spirit of the citations)

Impromptu discussions—could imagine a studio with all sorts—all being recorded—with the intention of using only those that turn out well—or that could, by cutting, etc. be made efficient

Plato and the living word (Phaedrus)—we depart from it at our peril—yet thank God Plato turned to the written word, even in admonishing against it—(great value of it—even with the kind of literature that lends itself most perfectly to purely vocal perfection, the critic must also have the details in their fixity, as with the written word, so that he can, at his leisure, study them in their internal relations and developments. To hear the performance as such is analogous to a physiologist's study of the body—to view the work in its written details like the anatomist's dissecting of a body's tissues. We need both methods, to understand fully the miraculous workings of the artistic structure (poetic organism)

We omit from this discussion the purely signpost kind of words—words without tonal value—statistics, facts, the vast amt. of purely informative material needed for running a complex technological world—like the names and numbers in a telephone directory—the sort of words which people are taught to skim through rather than to read (and properly so—ideally they should be read, if that were possible, not just in blocks as big as sentences, but in whole pages sized up at a single glance)—ironically, many, in being taught to read such stuff in the wholly non-dramatic way proper to it, lose their ability to appreciate the other kind of word, the kind that is to be appreciated, like a flavor, not gulped down like raw whiskey. Performance in the new mediums may correct this error somewhat.

APPENDIX B

Second Draft

(*Italics* indicate handwritten additions)

When answering the first question, I think *here* are the two positions to work with, *and work from:*

In Plato's Phaedrus, Socrates speaks ill of the written word; he cares only for the living, spoken word, he says. For it is pliant; adapting itself to each new situation, whereas the written word is forever fixed.

But Aristotle, in his Poetics, rates the reading of a Greek tragedy higher than the witnessing of an actual performance. (And one knows of music lovers who *have* learned how to read a musical score so as to hear the music internally; even the best renditions *may seem to them a come-down*) (of Keats: heard melodies are sweet, but those unheard are sweeter)

I personally, when reading, have to hear every word. So I can't read faster than one ordinarily speaks. And since much modern writing is not made for speech—after reading something of that sort for a while, I have a feeling in my head as though I had been shaking dice in a dice-box. Words of that sort are not made to be enjoyed as a flavor; they must be gulped down, like raw whiskey—and there are actually techniques taught now for reading in chunks (like running the eye down the columns of a telephone directory)—some people who master the art can become so good at it, that written words addressed to the ear (as with much good poetry) become almost unintelligible to them.

-page 2-

The new mediums (such as radio and television—and recording devices generally) can help make up for this deficiency. And though mechanisms are always to be distrusted where matters of culture are concerned, I do think it is good when they have taken us all the way round the circle:

Imagine a wholly illiterate poet; give him a sound-recorder, a mechanism made possible by nothing less than a whole dictionary of technical terms that are almost zero as far as their auditory appeal is concerned

And he can leave you with such a record of his intentions as the early bard could not. For as regards literary action of this sort, writing is an extremely inferior medium.

APPENDIX C

Third Draft

(*Italics* indicates handwritten additions)

The further we go from the language of poetry and oratory towards the language of technology and factual information, the further we go from words that are *designed for* the ear. And there are even techniques taught now, for reading purely informational sentences in chunks, like running the eye down the columns of a telephone directory. With people who hear internally as they read, after they have punished themselves for a while by painfully listening to each successive syllable, of a style that was not meant to be heard at all, they may have an empty, rattling feeling in the head, as though they had been shaking dice in a dice-box. But the other sort, who have learned to take in whole sentences at a glance, like gulping down raw whiskey, become so good at the art of purely visual reading that written words addressed to the ear (as with much good poetry) become almost unintelligible to them.

I see good cultural possibilities in the new mediums because they bring the word so spontaneously back to its beginnings. Whatever my distrust of mechanisms *(and it is great),* I like them when they round out the circle. Air conditioning in a theatre, for instance, but cancels off the atmospheric abnormalities caused by the gathering of people thus unnaturally. The water system in a city but restores to each family ready access to a spring, thereby correcting an earlier departure from nature. *The machines that take us away are to be feared—until they are corrected by the machines that bring you back.* And, as regards the new mediums (radio, television, and recording devices in general): do they not round *out* the circle by restoring the initial supremacy of the spoken word?

-page 2-

Note the tremendous difference between "rounding the circle" and mere "return to origins." Primitives and Neo-Primitivism are thousands of years apart. Neo-Primitivism has rounded the circle; primitives have never yet begun, hence through lack of inoculation they are over-susceptible to the *disease of false* promises. Now, as regards the new technological mediums of communication, think of this: Give a poet a modern sound-recorder, and even though he could not read or write, he could leave you a record of his intentions much superior in fidelity of representation to that left by the old clerics who wrote down the songs of an early bard. As regards language of that sort, the written word is an exceptionally poor recording instrument. But though these new mediums can permit even a wholly illiterate man to make a faithful record of his poetic intentions, note that the devices themselves can be produces only through the sheerly literate vocabularies of technology. Lose these, and the technical precision needed for the production of such machines would soon dwindle away.

In Plato's Phaedrus, Socrates speaks ill of the written word. He cares only for the living, spoken word, he says (with its powers of doctrinal impregnation). But Aristotle, in the Poetics, rates the reading of a Greek tragedy higher than the witnessing of an actual performance. (How I have yearned, just once, to hear the mighty shout that must have arisen, from the throats, of seventeen thousand tragically purged Athenian citizens, when

[end of page; remainder of draft missing]

APPENDIX D

Final Draft

Reply to the questionnaire

As regards the first question:

The further we go from the language of poetry and oratory towards the language of technology and factual information, the further we go from words that are designed for the ear. And there are even techniques taught now, for reading purely informational sentences in chunks, like running the eye down the columns of a telephone directory. With people who hear internally as the read, after they have punished themselves for a while by painfully listening to each successive syllable, of a style that was not meant to be heard at all, they may have an empty, rattling feeling in the head, as though they had been shaking dice in a dice-box. But the other sort, who have learned to take in whole sentences at a glance, like gulping down raw whiskey, become so good at the art of purely visual reading that written words addressed to the ear (as with much good poetry) become almost unintelligible to them.

I see good cultural possibilities in the new mediums because they bring the word so spontaneously back to its beginnings. Whatever my distrust of mechanisms (and it is great) I like them when they round out the circle. Air conditioning in a theatre, for instance, but cancels off the atmospheric abnormalities caused by the gathering of people unnaturally. The water system in a city but restores, to each family, ready access to a spring, thereby correcting an earlier departure from nature. The machines that take us away are to be feared until they are corrected by the machines that bring us back. And, as regards the new mediums (radio, television,

-page 2-

and recording devices in general): do they not round out the circle by restoring the initial supremacy of the spoken word?

Give a poet a modern sound-recorder, and even though he could not read or write, he could leave you a record of his intentions much superior in fidelity of representation to that left by the old clerics who wrote down the songs of an early bard. As regards language of that sort, the written word is an exceptionally poor recording instrument. But though these new mediums can permit even a wholly illiterate man to make a faithful record of his poetic intentions, note that the devices themselves can be produced only through the sheerly literate vocabularies of technology. Lose those, and the technical precision needed for the production of such machines would soon dwindle away.

In Plato's Phaedrus, Socrates speaks ill of the written word. He cares only for the living, spoken word, he says (with its powers of doctrinal impregnation). But Aristotle, in the Poetics, rates the reading of a Greek tragedy higher than the witnessing of an actual performance. (How I have yearned, just once, to hear the mighty shout that must have arisen, from the throats of seventeen thousand tragically purged Athenian citizens, when Aeschylus had contrived at the end of his great Orestes trilogy, to call upon them in a body to exult.)

Aristotle did not need the record beyond the writing; for his everyday experience enabled him spontaneously to supply the rest. We, lacking his everyday experiences, know how inferior that record is. Yet, speaking as a critic, I would note another respect in which we want both the auditory reception (the living "physiology" of speech) and the written record (the dead "anatomy"

-page 3-

of speech). For in a great writer's utterance, there are formal developments, and relationships among terms, that could not be properly studied on the run. Only by the help of the fixed, written word, can we analytically dissect a work's tissues, to understand the workings of it, as a structure, a poetic organism.

That brings us to the second question:

The more you like words, it seems to me, the more you can enjoy those expressive moments that defy words. If a tonality or a gesture occurs—and, to our knowledge, there is no word for it—that experience can be a delight too. The expression is in a different order of terminology from words—and the more you love the arts of the Word, the more you can enjoy those moments that flicker beyond the borders of the Word. The new mediums can give us many such. (After a few years, we may have caught up with this lore. But meanwhile, the many centuries of the exclusively written record have allowed for much neglect and imprecision here).

Literature can do well, in adding such dimensions to its study. I wish I had time to cite some moments of tonality and gesture (on radio and television) that have delighted me, as one who loves language in all its forms—and finds such elusive kinds of gesture-speech a perpetual challenge to our powers of conceptualizing in words.

-page 4-

Certain kinds of great literature must be lost to large audiences of any sort; so they'll be lost to large audiences of radio and television. But I dare think that other kinds can profit by the medium.

To hear contemporary poets on sound recorders is to realize that much of even the best modern poetry is poor in auditory appeal ("vocality"). It is largely for eye-reading alone, like the telephone directory, alas. And I have heard poetry readings on the radio that try to make up for this deficiency piously by devices such as mood-music for background, like a smell. But the poems were for reading alone, in one's study, not even aloud, not even hearing internally—and the greater the effort to make them palatable under other conditions, the greater the infelicity of the result.

Such poetry certainly will not flourish in this medium. But there are kinds of poetry—and of good literature in general—that spontaneously suggest an accompaniment of tonality and gesture. And I see no reason, no technical reason at least, why such kinds of literature could not positively profit by the new mediums.

The issue, you will note, splits into two major aspects. One concerns the problem of large audience as such. Many good kinds of expression are for small audiences, and we should not even attempt to extend their range of direct appeal (though through other works, differently constructed, they may be "stepped down"). Second, there is the nature of the mediums, technically, as recording devices. On this score: since tonality and gesture

-page 5-

go naturally with certain kinds of expression, the new kinds of recording should have a good effect, in helping us to keep from forgetting what a <u>complete</u> literary event really is.

NOTES

1. It is not surprising that Burke began his ruminations on technology with the Phaedrus: it had been a significant part of his work on both the *Grammar* and the *Rhetoric*. *A Grammar of Motives* features a particularly in-depth discussion of the Phaedrus; Burke discusses it at length in his analysis of merger, division, and "Socratic transcendence" (420).

2. In 1975 William Gage Chapel used Burke as "a good foundation for a discussion of the persuasive quality of TV programs" (82) and specifically the pentad as "a useful beginning tool for analyzing the dramatic action and ultimately the ideas and meanings behind television messages" (91). In 1996 Dale Keller applied Burke's warnings about the creator becoming enslaved to the creation of modern computer technology; as he writes, "Technology, as a human creation, seems to have taken on an existence and power of its own. Although not inherently bad, if left unchecked, Burke suggests it will increasingly self-perpetuate to become rotten with perfection" (par. 12). More recently Fernheimer and Nelson have employed the Burkean parlor to describe the rhetorical situation surrounding blogs (par. 13), and Robert MacDougall uses Burke's dramatistic emphasis and his action/motion distinction as part of an epistemological analysis of news blogs.

WORKS CITED

Burke, Kenneth. *Attitudes toward History*. 3rd ed. Berkeley: University of California Press, 1984.

———. *A Grammar of Motives*. Berkeley: University of California Press, 1969.

———. On Human Nature: A Gathering while Everything Flows, 1967–1984. Ed. William H. Rueckert and Angelo Bonadonna. Berkeley: University of California Press, 2003.

———. *Language as Symbolic Action.* Berkeley: University of California Press, 1966.

———. *Permanence and Change.* 3rd ed. Berkeley: University of California Press, 1984.

———. *The Philosophy of Literary Form.* 3rd ed. Berkeley: University of California Press, 1973.

———. *A Rhetoric of Motives.* Berkeley: University of California Press, 1969.

———. *The Rhetoric of Religion: Studies in Logology.* Berkeley: University of California Press, 1970.

Chapel, Gage William. "Television Criticism: A Rhetorical Perspective." *Western Journal of Communication* 39.2 (1975): 81–91.

de Oliveira, Plinio Correa. "The Church and the Communist State: The Impossible Coexistence." *American Society for the Defense of Tradition, Family, and Property.* Aug. 1, 1963.

Edison Research. "Radio's Future II: The 2010 American Youth Study." *Digital Music News* Sept. 29, 2010. 1–50.

Fernheimer, Janice Wendi, and Thomas J. Nelson. "Bridging the Composition Divide: Blog Pedagogy and the Potential for Agonistic Classrooms." *Currents in Electronic Literacy* 9 (2005): n. pag.

Gibson, Keith. "Burke, Frazer, and Ritual: Attitudes toward *Attitudes.*" *KB Journal* 3.1 (2006): n. pag.

Hill, Ian. "'The Human Barnyard' and Kenneth Burke's Philosophy of Technology." *KB Journal* 5.2 (2009): n. pag.

Hyman, Stanley Edgar. "Kenneth Burke and the Criticism of Symbolic Action." *Critical Responses to Kenneth Burke, 1924–1966.* Ed. William H. Rueckert. Minneapolis: University of Minnesota Press, 1969. 208–21.

Keller, Dale. "A Rhetorician Ponders Technology, or Why Kenneth Burke Never Owned a 'Personal' Computer." *Electronic Journal of Communication* 6.1 (1996): n. pag.

Linmann, Nils. Letter to Kenneth Burke. Sept. 28, 1956. Kenneth Burke Papers. Penn State University Archives, University Park.

MacDougall, Robert. "Identity, Electronic Ethos, and Blogs: A Technologic Analysis of Symbolic Exchange on the New News Medium." *American Behavioral Scientist* 49 (2005): 575–99.

Melia, Trevor. "Scientism and Dramatism: Some Quasi-Mathematical Motifs in the Work of Kenneth Burke." *The Legacy of Kenneth Burke.* Ed. Herbert W. Simons and Trevor Melia. Madison: University of Wisconsin Press, 1989. 55–73.

Muir, Star A. "Toward an Ecology of Language." *Kenneth Burke and the 21st Century.* Ed. Bernard L. Brock. Albany: State University of New York Press, 1998. 35–70.

Rueckert, William H. *Encounters with Kenneth Burke.* Urbana: University of Illinois Press, 1994.

Thames, Richard H. "Nature's Physician: The Metabiology of Kenneth Burke." *Kenneth Burke and the 21st Century.* Ed. Bernard L. Brock. Albany: State University of New York Press, 1998. 19–34.

Wess, Robert. *Kenneth Burke: Rhetoric, Subjectivity, Postmodernism.* Cambridge: Cambridge University Press, 1996.

JEFF PRUCHNIC

BURKE IN/ON PUBLIC AND PRIVATE

Rhetoric, Propaganda, and the "End(s)" of Humanism

> No wonder so many nineteenth-century writers were prodigious in output. A shift in the angle of approach must disclose an infinity of ways in which our former classifications can be reclassified. After a lifetime of productivity we find Bentham wishing that he could become a dozen selves, since his perspective showed him that he had work for all. Indeed, he has in time become thousands of selves, as Darwin also has.
>
> Permanence and Change, 1935

In his early work Kenneth Burke was fond of noting the multitude of "selves" that individuals represent, the subjective or perceptual positions produced both by the variety of orientations of a given subject as well as the diversity of interpretations others might have of them.[1] Studies of Burke's work often begin or end by noting the quixotic legacy in twentieth-century intellectual history produced by two such "selves." On the one hand, Burke is regarded as one of the century's preeminent humanist thinkers; on the other, he is seen as rhetoric's most influential proto-post-modern theorist.[2] There is of course much in Burke's large corpus of work to justify both of these conceptions. In addition to his sympathies with landmark writers in the Western humanist tradition (from Aristotle to Rousseau to John Dewey), Burke would in later works explicitly suggest that many of his concepts and terms (the comic corrective, dramatism) were meant to be synonyms for humanism. Although not necessarily presenting the two options as exclusive, Burke would also in late life express his lack of interest in aligning his work with postmodern criticism. When asked in a 1990 interview if he "was a postmodernist," Burke responded simply "I hope not" (qtd. in Brock 310). At the same time however, while many of his writings prize traditional humanist sentiments (the universality or commonality of human thought and perception, the power of rational reasoning, an emphasis on consensus), they are simultaneously marked by an abiding suspicion of the os-tensibly unbiased nature of various frames of interpretation and more specifically a resistance to liberal humanist notions of agency. Thus inasmuch as Burke has been often canonized in rhetorical scholarship as "our kind of humanist" (Blair 154), he has equally been claimed as our forerunner to the poststructuralist "big theory" era, a movement that largely first defined itself around the rejection of humanist touchstones.

Recently this opposition has been mediated in Burke scholarship by tracing Burke's "progression" from humanism to proto-postmodernism, concomitantly emphasizing his later works at the expense of the earlier texts *Counter-Statement* and *Permanence and Change*. In addition to being more generally cohesive, the later works' focus on the symbolic and discursive make them easier to contextualize within postmodern theory and poststructuralist philosophy, particularly the "linguistic turn" of the humanities and the social sciences occurring around the time of their publication. Thus Robert Wess for instance reads the sequence of Burke's works as one of increasing sophistication, culminating in the most "mature" concept of his last works, dramatism; others pick up Burke's work from the late 1930s or 1940s with *Attitudes toward History* and *A Grammar of Motives*, making only passing reference to the earlier texts (Biesecker; Bygrave). To give just one more dramatic example, Burke's longtime friend and critic William Rueckert goes so far as to declare the early works as "stylistic and terminological underbrush," "an irritation, a distraction, the rank growth of a fecund mind" (*Kenneth Burke* 5).

My interest in this essay however is to return to those earlier works—not to recuperate a humanist Burke, but instead to consider the prominent tensions in these works that have led to disparate conceptions of Burke in relation to humanism. More specifically I read Burke's interest in prototypical humanist notions of the "universal" or "common" (and the possibilities and limitations of both) as part of his broader investment in two related areas: an intellectual inquiry into the boundary between rhetoric (as both a hermeneutic toolbox and a method of persuasive civic dialogue) and propaganda (as self-interested persuasive manipulation); and his more personal consideration of the extent to which his public writings should be used to forward his own political beliefs and desires.[3]

I use the terms "public" and "private" in this essay to refer to two pairs of conceptual categories that have implicit intersections (and, I will argue, more specific relationships) within Burke's work. The first is the notion of "public" and of "private" most often hailed in critical writings on the "public sphere" (from Machiavelli to Arendt to Habermas) to connote the boundaries of communication and behavior recognized as legitimate within dominant rhetorical environments versus those that circulate within smaller communities and/or not accepted in the public sphere. Although Burke does not always refer to the "public" in this way, his interest in this category, and particularly in what Habermas codes the "legitimation crisis" haunting twentieth-century social life under global capitalism, has drawn many scholars to integrate Burke's work into contemporary publics theory (for example, Biesecker 74–103; Farrell; Stob). The second pairing of the public and private considered in this essay encompasses the relations between the collective and individual in more overtly political theories of social power and persuasion (or to put it more simply the ways that the communal interests of a society influence or determine the "private" thinking of its members). Here one might find the modern start of critical reflection on this concept in Enlightenment humanism through Kant's essay on the "question" of enlightenment and his famous distinction between the appropriate "public" and "private" uses of reason ("Answer" 55–57). More immediately relevant to Burke's audiences, however, and running counter to the Kantian tradition, would be the treatment of this pairing found in Hegel's early work on the "Ruse of reason," and later conceptions of ideology in Marx and after, discourses very much in the air at the time Burke was working on his early texts.

As readers might expect, given the theme of this collection, I also intend the terms "public" and "private" to refer to categories of Burke's available writings. In the following I trace Burke's work on these questions by reading Burke both "on" the relations between public and private spheres of discourse, judgment, and persuasion, and his works on these concepts "in" public (his published writings) and "in" private (correspondence and archival materials not intended for broad publication). In terms of his public documents, I attend to *Counter-Statement, Permanence and Change,* "My Approach to Communism," and other essays of the same period. The "private" materials under examination include various manuscript versions of the published material, much of which has only recently been acquired as part of the Kenneth Burke Papers at Penn State. I also consider private correspondence composed in the 1930s that addresses controversies over the "popular front" of American communist discourse as well as the broader impact of changes in mass media and cultural trends on public political discourse.[4]

Taken together these texts illustrate Burke's consistent engagement with the need to consider not only how a discourse might be received divergently by various audiences but also how a rhetorician must think through the relations between his privately held values, the values he emphasizes in his discourse, and the ethical or political actions he is attempting to foment through such discourse. I argue specifically that reading Burke's work "on" and "in" public and private shows the development of a particular strategy in his writing, one in which his work written for public audiences takes on an increasingly prescriptive, even propagandistic register, while simultaneously presenting in the same work a conception of the intersection of rhetoric and ethics that would make such an approach justifiable. These two itineraries in Burke's writings show him taking up the question—one endemic to humanism—of how one balances the "means" and "ends" of ethical and political praxis. Finally I conclude by arguing for the value of Burke's intersections with, and divergences from, versions of humanist and proto-postmodernist thought in his writings of the 1930s in thinking through the transitional moment of critical theory today, one wherein the so-called "death" of postmodern theory or the "big theory" era of the humanities as a whole is an increasingly common refrain.

BURKE'S APPROACH(ES) TO COMMUNISM

It is not at all surprising that Burke's early engagements with both the idea of "propaganda" and the question of the appropriate relationship between his political investments and his public writing would emerge in the early 1930s through his involvement with American communist thought. In this decade Burke published several works that explicitly address capitalism and communism as economic and social systems—"Boring from Within" (*New Republic,* 1931), "The Nature of Art under Capitalism" (*Nation,* 1934), "My Approach to Communism" (*New Masses,* 1934). His private correspondences meditate on the import of these publications, revealing him to be increasingly concerned about how his public support of communism might affect the reception of his writing (a concern he would carry into the 1940s and 1950s).

"My Approach to Communism" offers a perfect case in point. In comparing earlier drafts of the essay to the published version, Stacey Sheriff finds that Burke's support of the movement in his earlier manuscript version is actually *less affirmative* than in the published version. The published version, appearing in a 1934 issue of the *New Masses* and generally considered to be Burke's most unqualified support for communism, emerged from a talk Burke gave earlier in the year at the John Reed Club. Even though the primary audiences for the essay and the talk were decidedly Marxist, one would expect Burke to be more explicit in his endorsement of communism in the oral (and ephemeral) presentation. Burke had previously voiced concerns about his public identification with communist movements and about how publishing any endorsement would put him "on the record." And yet, as Sheriff details, the typescript based on the original lecture presents a "less decisive, more defensive Burke" (286). Sheriff makes a strong case for reading the difference between the two as not the result of any proleptic presumption of audience response by Burke, but rather as a result of the very real response he received at the JRC. This response prompted Burke to reconsider his approach in drafting the published version so that it was less ambiguous in promoting, and standing more firmly in support of, his own views on communism.

The drafts and related correspondence referring to the essay suggest that this is almost certainly the case.[5] However I would also like to suggest that Burke's self-correction via revision here is of a piece with a larger and recurrent theme in Burke's writings: his consideration of the relation between his private beliefs, in particular political or ethical principles, and his desire for concrete political and ethical transformations in society. Burke's revisions to this lecture reflect specifically his career-long struggle with the question of whether he should present his work as a disinterested "mapping" of social and communicative forms or as an explicit argument for his readers to take particular actions (as well as how he should position his own experiences and desires within these possible approaches).

Such a focus foregrounds what otherwise might be taken as a fairly innocuous change in the revisions of Burke's speech and essay: its title. As recorded in the typescript of the essay draft Burke composed, the original oral performance carried the title "Approaches to Communism" rather than the published title of "My Approach to Communism." In the introductory letter Burke prepared for submission of the typescript to print, he provides rationales for both plural and singular (personal) versions of the title (Cover letter). On the one hand, he defends the multiplicity of extrinsic approaches to communism outlined in the essay and their possible divergence from traditional "Marxian" conceptions. He writes, "All of these approaches are under the justifiable suspicion of being non-Marxian—and on this score the only defense I can offer is the following: I believe that there must be many approaches to Communism." On the other hand, Burke emphasizes the personal nature of both how individuals come to support communism and how that support is maintained, how "one's reasons for going may differ from reason's for staying Communists."

All of these reasons, he argues, are more specific and singular than we might traditionally expect. As for his own reasoning, the introductory letter for the typescript references both hostile responses to the JRC speech and the relationship between doctrinaire and personal approaches to the movement: "As for the charge that I was presuming to 'tell' Communists about their movement when they knew much more about it than I did, in this there is unfairness. I was simply trying to 'tell' them something about which I could very easily be expected to know much more than they did; namely: the kind of consideration which led me to deem Communism desirable." In this sense then, at least in retrospect Burke's lecture was less a full-throated rationale for communist principles than it was a public narrative of how he became personally committed to communist principles narrated for a public audience.

Although again it is clear that the specific circumstances of his reception at the JRC speech motivated the revisions of what would become "My Approach to Communism," these shifts can also function as a synecdoche for Burke's consistent reformulating of how he should balance his personal experiences and desires with his public roles as a critic of communication systems and a partisan for particular political causes. This tension would also lead Burke to continually reconsider the relation between his investments and the style of his work in two ways, both of which might be mapped on divergent interpretations of *ethos*. Burke consistently questions what register in which to present his work, whether it will take (or proclaim to take) the form of *diagnosis* (the mapping of communicative systems), *prescription* (explicitly suggesting what readers should do), or *advocacy* (forwarding the interests of a particular group or movement).

The first term has a particular resonance for Burke in the 1930s in representing his work. In publicly responding to Granville Hicks's critique that *Counter-Statement* lacked an ethics and ignored contemporary social conditions, Burke asserted that "a moral imperative is not proper to a rhetoric." He compares the rhetorical scholar studying discourse to a mechanic studying motors without concern for whether they be used "for warfare or trade" (Burke and Hicks). In a 1937 letter to Richard McKeon he continues to imagine the merging of "technical" and "sociological" approaches into a single criticism that would lay stress "upon *how effects are got,* rather than upon what *effects should be got.* Ballistics, not politics. Not exhortation but diagnosis" (KB to *RM* March 12, 1937, qtd. in Heath 11).

As Burke called for diagnosis, however, he was also going "on record" at the time in other works to advocate particular political systems (communism) and goals (changes in currency systems and in drug legislation). Indeed his concern over the conceptual slippage risked by works that appear to be prescriptive for certain ideals through their negative critique of others would haunt his 1930s works as a whole. An essay from this period later collected in *Philosophy of Literary Form,* "The Virtues and Limitations of Debunking," provides perhaps Burke's most intense engagement with this dilemma. In analyzing debunking's reliance on "deflating" popular notions by revealing the hidden motivations of their proponents and/or the hidden consequences of their functioning, Burke finds it both a corrupt methodology for critical work (because it must always ignore or in some way protect the author's own investments or motivations) and a constitutive operation of progressive political movements (*PLF* 168). "In brief," Burke writes, "the history of debunking is interwoven with the history of liberalism" (169); as individuals lose their investment in dogmatisms and traditions, they concomitantly are likely to become increasingly critical of formal systems of knowledge and belief structures as a whole.

Although Burke's late public writings on motivation and religious belief systems would continue to attend to this dilemma, his public and private 1930s works show Burke trying out at least one possible resolution: a rhetorical strategy of encrypting the more prescriptive elements of his work while overtly presenting a critical view of rhetoric that would make such a strategy ethically and politically defensible. One can follow the unfolding of these strategies in the various extant versions of what would become *Permanence and Change,* particularly through the differences between the manuscript material and the first published edition, as well as the changes Burke made between the original edition and the revised 1954 version.

The deletions Burke made in preparing the 1954 edition of the text, about six pages in total, fit into three broad categories. "Rationalizations" for the viability or necessity of communism comprise the largest number of passages and (by word count) the longest passages. Indeed the original title of the final section of part 1 of the text was "Communism: A Humanistic, or Poetic Rationalization," with the first term excised from the later edition. A second category includes references to inherent contradictions within capitalism or the inevitable decline of what Burke codes "the collapsing capitalist economy." Finally, in the third, there are still other references deleted from the text that focus not so much on communism as a general movement or philosophical standpoint but on a particular goal of the same: the benefits of eliminating private property.

When noting the deletion of these passages in the foreword to the third edition of *Permanence and Change,* Burke states that while he remains firm in believing that "communication is grounded in material cooperation," he has decided to remove text "speculating on the form that such material cooperation should take" (1984, xlix). The reason for the removal, he goes on to write, is twofold. First, "under present conditions, the pages could not possibly be read in the tentative spirit in which they were originally written." Second, and presumably due to the "tentative spirit" of their original composition, Burke states that, as paradoxical it may seem, the "omissions could be called a kind of 'restoration' since they bring the text back closer to its original nature." In other words, although the removal of material original to the book would hardly be considered a "textual" restoration, it does achieve a "conceptual" restoration because Burke's more prescriptive suggestions were (or are, or should be) not vital to his primary objective in writing *Permanence and Change.*

Depending on how one reads Burke's "tentative nature," his explanation provides support for either (or both) of the usual interpretations for the omissions of these passages. Certainly Burke's reference to "the present time" upon reissue of the work—the present time being the red-baiting American 1950s—suggests he may have been concerned about possible associations with communist movements. Thus Schiappa and Keehner observe that the present currency of considering Burke's omissions is in asking ourselves "if we, too, are faced with the choice of making our writings more 'theoretically significant,' and acceptable to future generations at the potential cost of lessening their explicit political relevance to our own" (196–97). At the same time, his suggestion that the omissions restore the work to its original intention is clearly in line with other comments Burke made about his ambivalence toward communist orthodoxies and strategies, one voiced in an oft-quoted 1932 letter to Malcolm Cowley. He notes there, "I can only welcome Communism by converting it into my own vocabulary. I am, in the deepest sense, a translator" (Burke and Cowley 202–3). Thus the "tentative nature" referenced by Burke is also often read as reflecting not so much a concern with the public reception of his work but rather a confusion about his investments; he was "a man committed to the need for social change, but torn between support for Communism's promise and concern over its potentially orthodox and exclusivist development in America" (Sheriff 285).

However we might read Burke's omissions here in yet a third way: as part of an ongoing attempt to reformulate his own work to have (however cryptically) propagandistic power. Such a reading, perhaps only hinted at by the omissions made between the first and later editions of *Permanence and Change,* is much more powerfully suggested by a much earlier series of erasures performed by Burke: deletions made from manuscript versions of *Permanence* before its first publication. Around one hundred pages of recently acquired archival materials titled after various sections of *Permanence and Change* contain dozens of pages Burke eliminated from the published text. In addition to content on psychoanalytic theory and relationship between religious and secular belief structures (both of which remain in streamlined form in the final text), these typescripts and handwritten pages include frequent deleted and revised passages on the (mis)uses of propaganda and digressions on the relationship between communicators' rhetorical styles and their ideational agendas. Especially relevant, given my purposes, are reflections by Burke on the best way to forward communism in America. These passages, particularly when read in relation to other private and public writings of the time, suggest a Burke who embraces a propagandistic role for his own work at the same time he is eliminating many of the overt references to communism in the same.

For instance in the published version of the third edition of *Permanence*, Burke remarks on the difference between "fatalist" versions of Marxism that draw their power on the predicted inevitability of capitalist decline and those that, in the style of Lenin, stress the need for "intellectualistic effort"; the passage ends with the rather generic suggestion that "socialization" strategies for forwarding Marxist goals can only be evaluated in reference to their particular circumstances (183). In the manuscript version, however, Burke concludes by explicitly advocating the superiority of the propagandistic approach. Capitalism's collapse and concomitant "proletarian anguish" may happen spontaneously, but, Burke writes, "a definite policy of propaganda is required before this anguish and resentment can be turned into the channel of rational action." Similarly the longest single passage on communism deleted between the first edition and third edition of *Permanence* exists in a different version in the manuscript. Although it begins and ends in the same way, the manuscript version includes an additional digression on the difficulty of convincing individuals to get behind socialist "reform" without "converting" them through "inducement": "you cannot induce man to accept deterioration, unless you can radically 'convert him to new meanings.'"

To give just one more example, in a wholly deleted passage, Burke applies a distinction regarding Marxism that is prominent elsewhere in *Permanence*—a distinction between rhetorical strategies of "domination" and more viable ones of "inducement." He reflects specifically on the failure of "Marxians" to persuade their audiences because they have repeated Marx's mistake of "commingling" two existing belief structures: technocracy (through an appeal to utilitarianism) and paradoxically laissez-faire capitalism (through their reliance on appeals to "revolutionary or emancipatory slogans"). Their failure, Burke suggests, is in their inability to "play off" different parts of the same, extant belief structure, one that would allow a strategy of "inducement" as "opposed to dominance."[6] These and other passages show Burke eliminating not only references to communism, but also references to the appropriate rhetorical means for forwarding communist objectives. In surviving manuscript versions of the preface to the original edition of *Permanence and Change*, back when Burke was working on his "Treatise on Communication" (an earlier title Burke had considered), both of these issues would be foregrounded. The first line of one version reads: "All social activities—commerce and invention as well as formal art—now seem capable of discussion in terms of rhetoric, the 'strategy of appeal.'" Another version does not progress far until Burke openly states, "In the field of practical exhortion, our position is Communistic. The strictly Marxian approach to Communism is not observed, yet we believe that our statements are in no important particular antagonistic to the Marxian attack upon the commercial structure." The final version of *Permanence and Change* would omit not only these overt allegiances but also almost all references to both communism and rhetoric. (Reading the book now it seems strange that the latter term appears only in passing.) At the same time, however, the two themes would be all the more pervasive, in many ways because of these omissions. Trimming his explicit references to communism, propaganda, and rhetoric allowed Burke to perform a more subtle rhetorical strategy for promoting communist ideals.

Although these passages alone may not in and of themselves be enough to confirm that Burke was increasingly seeing himself as an organ of propaganda for the communist cause (while simultaneously deleting explicit references to propaganda as a whole and "softening" his work on communism), such an approach would be in fidelity with Burke's private correspondence about his work. For instance in a letter to an individual identified only as "Perce," dated February 14, 1935, Burke explicitly suggests *both* that his rhetorical strategies in fomenting communism, as opposed to those of his more doctrinaire contemporaries, make him particularly well-suited for such a function, *and* that his own "revisionary" strategy (one that would become in the future quite literal in editing the reissue of *Permanence*) is justified:

> Though a "rotten Communist," I find myself with a mode of argument which can carry the business of propaganda in quarters which "Good Communists" cannot reach. I can accept my ambiguous position, and the partial distrust of my "allies," with understanding and good humor. . . . I do feel that Communism requires a caritas mythology as well as a mere vindictive one, and I believe this purely because of my experiences with the problems of suasion. Art is, by nature, wheedling rather than force—and one is not merely cutting off his balls in recognizing this fact. . . . *Das Kapital* is a vocabulary, pure and simple. There is no more nor less surrender in poetry than in politics (in each case, one takes the recalcitrance of his material into account—the versifier, changing from one word to another in the interests of rhyme is making the same "compromise" as the politician who changes from one measure to another in the interests of his cause—it is only an accident of speech that one is called "revision" and the other "opportunism)."

Indeed it seems that as early as *Counter-Statement* Burke was using his work as a recondite platform to forward particular political and ethical agendas. Despite his public proclamations that the work was purely "diagnostic," in a letter marked "unsent" to Cowley dated June 2, 1932, Burke would confide that the "Program" essay of the text is "is based specifically, explicitly, on the doctrine that the confiscation of wealth is an economic necessity" (qtd. in Heath 11). In a letter Burke did send to Cowley dated two days later, he would expand on this sentiment: "Having agreed fully with the communists as to objectives, and having specifically stating in my sinful Program that I considered nationalization of private wealth the fulcrum of the new economy, I diverged solely in my notion of the tactics for arriving at these objectives" (Burke and Cowley 203).

Such an approach would be in line with Burke's most straightforward public description of the appropriate tactics for forwarding communist goals, the 1931 essay "Boring from Within." Whereas "Approaches to Communism"/"My Approach to Communism" is a work explicitly about communism and only implicitly about the best persuasive methods for forwarding its objectives, "Boring from Within" is only implicitly about communism and explicitly about the most effective means for persuading others to forward its goals. The essay, written in response to Edmund Wilson's "An Appeal to Progressives" published a few months earlier in the *New Republic,* approves of Wilson's general suggestions—that progressives dissociate themselves from the formal Communist Party and use more populist means of persuasion to recommend communist principles. However it suggests that the latter means must be less radical and more attuned to the extant, shared ideals of Americans, "the mentality already at hand" (327). Being outside the "party" is not enough, Burke suggests; successful persuasion in support of the cause must "bore from within" by adapting the appearances and practices of the group they are trying to affect: "We must all become Republicans and Democrats . . . shaking hands with the worst of them, frequenting their speakeasies and gambling dens, attending churches, patronizing their brothels. We must join Rotary Clubs; we must play checkers at the Y.M.C.A. We must demand unceasingly the expulsion of the reds. We must be conformity itself" ("Boring" 328).

In opposition to Wilson's call for an increased radicalism, as expressed through demands for the socialization of industry, Burke calls for increased conventionalism—"We must be conformity itself"—expressed through a subterfuge. Rather than call for the socialization of industry directly, Burke suggests the slow forwarding of an increased taxation scheme that would achieve that result—a sly seduction, rather than polemical exhortation, that will be voiced not in political pamphlets, but "over drinks and a cigar," when Burke's ideal conventional-radical asks his "boon companions" the question "Why don't the big fellows have to part with more of their incomes in times like these?" (328).

Although Burke's incredibly specific description of the ideal situation for such a strategy ("over drinks and a cigar") might suggest nothing so much as a very heterodox depiction of the now famous "Burkean Parlor," it also seems to be our best extant description of the tactics Burke would increasingly take in his work on communism as well as the overall question of how to forward particular ethical and political objectives within critical works. This strategy shows Burke continuing to obscure overt prescription in his work while using his writings to suggest the ideal "forms" for persuading others toward progressive practices and simultaneously performing these "forms" himself. Such an approach to reading Burke's work of and on "propaganda" may have the unfortunate requirement of speculating on Burke's "intentions" or taking his writings on communism, or as a whole, at something other than face value.[7] However such a consideration might be not only unavoidable, but also particularly appropriate, when approaching a thinker for whom both "motive" and "perspective" would become key terms.

The "Burke" composed in this section offers one way to approach to Burke's ambivalent relationship with critical postmodernism. Burke's novel strategies for writing (on) propaganda and tempering the "debunking" impulse allow for a critique of broad political or ethical systems. Though the latter move would in many ways put the "critical" in "postmodern critical theory," Burke, while acknowledging the potential (and even ease) of practicing critique in such a manner, chooses instead to "bore from within" or leverage the possible commonalities (real or feigned) between his own partisan interests and those of his audience. In the following I argue that a broader application of this same strategy (albeit thematized more than performed) in *Permanence and Change* might also be useful to contextualize Burke's equally ambiguous relationship with humanism.

PIOUS AND CONGRUOUS BURKE: AFFECT, AESTHETICS, AND ETHICS

An advertisement in the *New Republic* for the first edition of *Permanence and Change* read: "Burke, in the present volume, attempts to trace interrelationships among phenomena, many of which are superficially very different, such as motives, interpretations, expectations, style, piety, hyperbole, virtue, metaphor, guilt, nudism, and war. He subjects to rigorous consideration our notion as to what action is, showing how it is affected by our vocabulary, so that a slight difference in words may lead to a radical difference in the choice of means" ("Permanence and Change"). And in his unpublished outline for this edition, Burke wrote: "If we *must* be good, let us be good *secondarily*, as a kind of by-product arising out of heartlessness, out of the goodness of our medicines, dynamos, and traffic regulations."

Burke was not shy in showing his humanist credentials. However, his particular articulation of humanist principles of commonality and universality would take a fairly heterodox form. Rather than suggest some enduring quality of human "spirit" or "being" that transcends historical circumstances, Burke instead insisted on a biological coordination: "the fact that man's neurological structure has remained pretty much of a constant through all the shifts of his environment would justify us in looking for permanencies beneath the differences, as the individual seeks by thought and act to confirm his solidarity with the group" (*Permanence*, 1935, 159). Burke's interest in manipulating affective capacities (mutual abilities to feel and respond to stimuli) shared by humans due to a common neurology would in many ways be the baseline notion that ties together the various themes within *Permanence and Change:* the conflation of aesthetics, ethics, and politics; the use of physiological theories of emergence and sensation to describe contemporary rhetorical interactions; the focus on "form" as a master trope for analyzing both the public sphere of communicative practices and private realm of subjective belief systems. Indeed the link between the "natural" of human physiology and the "artificial" of contemporary social life would be Burke's point of entry for the broad sweep of *Permanence and Change*. As Burke describes it in the typescript for one of the discarded prefaces, "we might call the book an essay in human ecology, where the 'environment' trails off into the infinite." Though he would drop this particular way of describing the text, connecting the human (as both a bodily organism and a subject of reason) with the ostensibly "infinite" forces of culture that shape human motivation and perception would remain the central concern of *Permanence and Change*.

While this theme is pervasive throughout the text, it might receive its most intense working out in "perspective by incongruity," Burke's methodological program for linking seemingly disparate terms or sentiments together to create novel associations between phenomena. References to this method in scholarship on Burke tend to emphasize the "destabilizing" results of cultivating incongruity and its service in emphasizing the transitory and contingent relationships between terms and meanings. In this sense perspective by incongruity can be (and has been) read as a conceptual avatar or forerunner for a host of similar methodologies that emerge in the early days of the "big theory" era in the critical humanities—deconstruction, genealogy, language games, social construction, and so on. Such a reading and its concomitant comparisons are certainly warranted. Burke himself often foregrounds the destabilizing vectors of the method, its potential for "experimentally wrenching apart all those molecular combinations of noun, substantive, and verb," of undermining "every last linkage that remains with us merely as the result of piety or innate propriety" (*Permanence,* 1935,119). Burke's references to the use of strategies of incongruity by Nietzsche in his critique of dominant systems of morality also similarly suggests the uses of "perspective" to critique dominant social and communicative systems.

However at many other times Burke is very ambiguous as to whether he is advocating the use of the concept as a generic tool for pointing out the inconsistencies of human associations, whether he is simply mapping what is already currently happening in various fields (he refers frequently to the uses of "perspective" by assorted artists, philosophers, politicians, and mass media personnel), or whether "perspective" is meant to be appropriated as a tool that leads not to a "debunking" of communicative systems but to a careful introduction of novelty into the existing tendencies of a particular audience. In this last iteration, perspective is a "prescription for change" through the strategic manipulation of existing associations that can be translated over to other phenomena as part of a broader persuasive strategy.[8]

Although the first reading has received the lion's share of attention, much of the published text of *Permanence and Change*, and perhaps even more in the passages contained in the typed and handwritten manuscripts labeled "Perspective by Incongruity" in the Kenneth Burke Papers at Pennsylvania State University, suggests that the third reading, one that prioritizes the manipulation of "congruity" rather than the blanket introduction of "incongruity," was at least one of Burke's considerations. For the sake of brevity, these passages might be divided into two thematic categories.

First, various excised passages focus not on the problems caused by rigidity or pervasiveness of one or more orientations, but rather on the strain on social life fomented by the lack of such orientations. In one passage Burke suggests that the breakdown of reliable congruities has made us particularly vulnerable to manipulation by mass media: "Perhaps today it is only in the poorest sense that congruity remains with us. The most delicate 'rightnesses' are lost—wherefore we are all the greedier to be 'right' when a given fashion, or fad, or war turns up. So vague are our expectancies, so fluid in our orientation, that a new direction for our 'interests' can be established over night. The 'power of the press' to remake us quickly exists only because our basic interests are in confusion. Its power to attract readers lies in its agility at jumping with the cat in obedience to the fluctuations of our psychoses." Slightly earlier in the typescript Burke suggests a more specific iteration of this process. Burke writes that as "the old scheme or orientation" provided by early religious doctrines broke down, "myriad reorganizations, of varying complementary and antagonistic ingredients arose to 'profit by'" this fact: "Like carpetbaggers in the disorganized South, people with plausible 'lines' swarmed across the civilization of Europe in hordes. The breakdown of the broad cultural orientation made of individual orientations a *business*." These passages show Burke focusing not on the need for disrupting a "dominant" orientation (or orientations). Instead he focuses on how the waning of such has made individuals increasingly susceptible to adopting new orientations, provided they promise the same structure and solace of previous versions. Thus while the majority of orientations Burke discusses are portrayed negatively, he also insists on the value of mining the forms of these orientations to produce more ameliorative associations and motivations in individuals.

Second, several passages focus on how the success or failure of perspective by incongruity depends on its practitioner's ability to key in on terms that will affect their audience while also being "fluid" enough to allow for them to project their own meanings onto them. In a passage excised from the section on "Exorcism by misnomer"—the "renaming" of phenomena to make it appear less intimidating or powerful—Burke emphasizes this strategy, particularly its successful use by Freud: "Bertrand Russell has said that a vague term, like a chunk of putty, is more likely to hit the bull's-eye, by splattering over everything, than is something sharp and precise, which must either hit or miss. Now Freud's terms, if only his customers were not too exacting, had the great value that, precisely because of their amorphousness, they could 'rationalize' anything." In another passage Burke reflects on how pieties and "orientation devices" are distinguished by their intuitive nature and are often "not only undiscussable, but undiscussed" until challenged by other systems. At the same time, however, he also reflects on how associations form through recurrent experiences and the breakdown in communication that can occur when one cannot account for, and modify their approach to appeal to, these associations.

In the final analysis then, Burke's "perspective by incongruity" may be taken as a more expository and expansive version of the approach he earlier coded as "boring from within." Although the 1954 edition of *Permanence* retains cryptic endorsements of at least some version of communism, Burke's systematic focus on the need to draw upon, rather than destabilize or "debunk," the existing sentiments of interlocutors is at the same time a more general strategy of suasion, one that perhaps best collects the sometimes ambiguous programs for critical analysis, political intervention, and ethical praxis he develops in the 1930s work.

This strategy most notably can help us mediate two other dominant themes of his 1930s texts: the conflation of aesthetics and ethics, of form and value. The reliance on the manipulation or slow subversion of others' existing sentiments (rather than the critique or direct challenging of them) is, on the one hand, highly empathetic in its form, while on the other, it is (at least potentially) highly manipulative in its intentions. In an interview near the end of his life, Burke would provide perhaps his best defense of how such a praxis could still be attuned to ethics, both as a system and in the specific actions of the individual practicing such a strategy: "The word ['ethics'] means custom. But there are two kinds of customs. One means that you've got to do it, the other means that you ought to do it. That's a big difference. And the more strain you put on the 'ought' kind of ethics, the tougher things are" ("Counter-Gridlock" 370–71). It was always "custom" rather than critique that would be Burke's most multivalent rhetorical tool, and his various attempts to "bore from within" were not premised as much on the "ought to" of a practiced judgment or morality as on the "got to" of the partisan seeking a greater good.

This finally is also perhaps the best way to contextualize the ambiguous relationship between Burke's work and humanist and postmodern conceptual systems with which this essay began. Although Burke would share postmodernism's jaundiced view of human agency and its emphasis on communicative practices as drivers of social power, he would also persist in his belief that human motivations held the potential to be progressively moved toward a greater or more cooperative good. Given the sometimes manipulative activities necessary to foment such change, however, Burke had at least partially to reconceive what became the bedrock humanist ethical principle: the Kantian imperative to "act so that you use humanity, whether in your own person or in any other person, always at the same time as an end, never merely as a means" (Kant, *Groundwork* 38). Insofar as Burke considered humans' ability to be manipulated as constitutive of their "humanity" itself, his own description of strategies for such manipulation might be taken as both violating and preserving the human as an "end" rather than a means. Or, in other words, we might say that as a figure who straddled the historical moment in which humanism's dominance of Western education and culture was being eclipsed, Burke's own work was not so much a contribution to the "end" of the effort as such as much as it was a redefinition of the "ends" of that effort.

AFTER BURKE: RHETORIC AND SOCIAL POWER TODAY

The *New Republic* advertisement for first edition of *Permanence and Change* states that Burke "pursues with great, though highly readable obstinancy, his central purpose, which is to work out a usable attitude toward the present" (Advertisement for *Permanence and Change* in *New Republic*).

I have argued that juxtaposing Burke's public and private work of the 1930s helps explain the ambiguous position of his thinking between humanist notions of the "universal" or "common" and proto-postmodern suspicion of the same. Reading these public and private texts in conjunction illustrates that while Burke spilled considerable ink questioning the legitimacy of various beliefs or cultural commonplaces that had become to seem "natural" or universal, he increasingly drew on the universality of human vulnerability to persuasion and habituation as both the center of his conception of rhetoric and the ethical core of his strategies for intervening in the political. In what follows I want to shift ground by thinking through the value of Burke's 1930s work and more generally his liminal position between humanist universals and the proto-postmodern critique of universals, for thinking through the transitional moment of present-day theory.

I refer here to the trajectories of contemporary critical theory forming in the wake of its so-called "death," the declarations of the demise of postmodern theory and/or the "big theory" era of the academic humanities.[9] What these implicit or explicit memorials share, despite their many other differences, is the argument that the traditional critical strategies of postmodern theory—emphasizing the "social construction" of knowledge, challenging essentialism and foregrounding marginality and difference—have become not so much tools to "resist" social power but rather the fundamental ways through which whatever we might call "power" operates today. Recent indictments of the contemporary validity of such strategies argue that the institutions that were the targets of postmodern critique (global capitalism, governmentality) themselves have become increasingly flexible and responsive, or may even find their function via the very forces of destabilization, difference, and antifoundationalism that were once leveraged against them. Given such broad changes in the structures of social power, Hardt and Negri for instance suggest that those who continue basing their strategies on the touchstones of postmodern theory may well "find themselves pushing against an open door" (138).

Although the best response to such a shift in the terrain of contemporary cultural production is still very much at issue—indeed this is perhaps *the* question of contemporary critical theory—I focus on two possible responses that have been popularly leveraged as remedies to the problems of postmodern theory: ontology and affect. Both movements take us back to the questions of the "common" or "universal" that were so unavoidable during the transition between humanist and postmodernist thought—and that so occupied Burke's work—giving it special relevance today.

Although a (re)turn to ontology over the past few years has been forwarded from many corners of the critical humanities, the recent work of Badiou and Žižek has most relentlessly and explicitly positioned ontological reasoning as a solution to what they take to be the failures of postmodern theory.[10] In the work of both, ontology is configured not as a given condition of the human but as one created by an extreme commitment to a particular cause or belief. For Badiou, such commitment comes though the individual's extreme fidelity to the "event," the occurrence (or conditions of occurrence) for moments of revelation and potential revolution. This fidelity is what makes the "subject" worthy of the name; subjectivity is maintained by the persistence of that dedication, the individuals' ability to adhere to "his own principle of continuity, the perseverance of being what he is" (47). Žižek's reinvention of political ontology takes a similar contour in describing in place the actions of the individual as prior to its manifestation as an ontological being. He writes in *The Ticklish Subject*, "the subject is the contingent emergence/act that sustains the very universal order of Being," and in his more recent works the foundation of the "ethical act" that produces authentic subjectivity has increasingly taken on the register of an extreme commitment to a cause or belief (160). The baseline innovation of both of their attempts to thematize a new political ontology is their ability to bypass what has constitutively haunted liberal approaches to the same: the difficulty of deciding precisely what commitment should be favored. As Peter Hallward writes in reference to Badiou's work, the strength of such an approach lies in its deployment of an "axiom," "a principle we posit in such a way as to take it for granted" (773). By focusing not on the content of an ontological commitment but rather on its pure form, they are thus able to reaffirm a category of the universal against the focus on fragmentation, ambiguity, and contingency they code as a debilitating tendency in postmodern leftist political theory.

However, as much as such an "axiomatic" logic might free its practitioners from endless hand-wringing over the contingency of individual interpretations or ideological investments (as well as the ethics of enforcing one's views as universally applicable), it also seems to celebrate the act of commitment itself while ignoring the conditions that might prompt the decision to "commit." Thus as Daniel Bensaid argues, Badiou's celebration of commitment *tout court* looks much like a mere exhortation toward a blank volunteerism, his rationale an unfortunate "combination of theoretical elitism and practical moralism" (101). On the other hand, and perhaps more dangerously, investment in the act of commitment itself might also require support for commitment to movements that have had highly problematic historical consequence, a move Žižek flirts with in seeking the "redemptive" lessons in Jacobinism, Leninism, Stalinism, and Maoism in his recent *In Defense of Lost Causes.*

Burke's value in thinking through such questions of political ontology today might lie in his configuration of "being" around not the universality of some constitutive human identity nor the singular commitment to a cause or belief, but rather in human capacities for suasion and gratification. As he writes in the section of "Toward a Philosophy of Being" that concludes part 2 of *Permanence,* if only basic neurological similarities are transituational, then any totalizing conception of ontology can be based only on the ability of humans to be affected by suasive forces. This is one way of reading Burke's intuitively odd retrospection that in *Permanence* he "used rhetoric and ontological as synonymous terms": the only force that can be deployed as "axiomatic" in his schema is the possibility of rhetoric itself (Burke qtd. in Brock 309).

Though taking a very different form than contemporary work on ontology, the renewed interest in affect or precognitive emotional response has also been forwarded as a "corrective" to postmodern theories of constructivism. To give just two examples, Brian Massumi positions affective theory as a way to avoid both the "Scylla of naïve realism" and the "Charybdis of subjectivism" by thinking more concretely about the relations between human bodies and human cultures (4). Eve Kosofsky Sedgwick similarly presents her influential work on affect as a counter to the "antibiologism" of postmodern critical theory (101) and our tendency to identify social forces as either "repressive" or "liberatory" (10). Although their work, and the turn to affect as a whole within contemporary critical theory, has indeed been salutary in challenging the latter's potential overreliance on analyses of discursive or social construction, it is worth asking whether the investment in affect as an abstract category may suffer from the same weaknesses as the similar investment in abstract "commitment" I just mentioned. As Clare Hemmings wrote in reference to Massumi and Sedgwick, affect has perhaps been too easily aligned with base "hope of freedom from social constraint" (550), seen in the privileging of affect as primarily a disruptive force, or one that somehow "escapes" or undermines the negative effects of social conditioning.

Burke was unusually prescient within 1930s humanistic research in accounting for affect as a vital part of rhetorical and cultural systems. His work on the same still holds the potential to be a "recalcitrant" or "corrective" influence—to use his terms for such conceptual tempering—on contemporary approaches to affect. First and foremost, Burke's positioning of affect emphasized, if anything, the harmful associations or rigid manifestations of affective response, and their potentially negative role in supporting trained incapacities and self-defeating orientations and pieties. Second, and concomitant, such a positioning led Burke to focus not so much on the uses of affect as a wedge against social conditioning, but on their role as conditioning forces and the subsequent importance of manipulating affective response and affective associations within persuasive strategies. Such a conception, and the stated need for such strategies, paints a rather darker picture of the role of affect within subjectivity. However such a picture is in line with the sometimes mercenary strategies I have outlined that Burke at least for a time considered necessary. As Burke states in *Counter-Statement*, a sentiment he would repeat in subsequent works, erring on the side of the negative is almost always a safer bet: "once you postulate human virtue as the foundation of a system, you are a dullard indeed if you can't make up a thousand schemes for a good society. A society is sound only if it can prosper on its vices, since virtues are by very definition rare and exceptional" (114). From the vantage point of the present, Burke's conception of affect and ontology, along with his interest in propagandism and the redirection of some of the less enlightened impulses of individuals, looks increasingly like some of our best tools for building on "vices" in such a manner.

CODA: APTITUDES TOWARD HISTORY

Any attempt to recover an earlier version of a canonical work, to compare manuscript and published versions of the text, or to contexualize an influential author's work within his private writing, runs at least two necessary risks. On the one hand, such an investigation might undermine a reading of the text that has become venerable or particularly salient to readers. On the other hand, and in the opposite direction, it might remove an ambiguity or aporia in the reading of the text that has become useful to critics. Both of these risks are perhaps intensified in leveraging such material to argue for the potentially disparate motivations and conceptions evinced in public and private venues as I have done here. At the same time however I hope this approach has not run too far afield of the advice Burke himself provides in a passage excised from *Permanence*. This passage, which would have appeared in the "Toward a Philosophy of Being" section of the first published edition, is worth quoting in full as it not only considers the appropriate way to approach venerable works but also relates to Burke's views on "being" and the humanist tradition:

> A philosophy of "being" has one great advantage over the philosophies of "becoming." It opens up to us once more the ancient arcana of wisdom, instead of isolating us upon a little island of modernity. It enables us to see the devices of the past as "correct," rather than as "erroneous" (they can be seen as either). It gives us a greater range of authorities to model ourselves after. We must, of course, learn how to "translate" the words of earlier thinkers or teachers. Much that they said was framed for the particularities of their day, within the terminology of their day—and our genius for archaeology (paradoxically flowering at a time when the cult of the future

was in the ascendancy) will not be complete until we are able to "restore" earlier modes of thought in the truest sense, not as museum pieces, to be viewed under glass, but with genuine sympathy. We must consider the past not in the way of trophy hunters, but as listeners.

In this spirit it is tempting to end here with a reiteration of the sentiments that concluded an essay by James Anrt Aune, written on the occasion of the publication of the most recent edition of *Permanence and Change*. Arnt Aune ends, just as this essay begins, with a description of the "plural" Burkes that have met generations of scholars (237). Noting that to each generation Burke periodically looks more as though "he may have been up to something else" than is suggested in previous interpretations, Aune ends by suggesting one transhistorical lesson of the text— a lesson about "how, in dangerous times, to go about reinventing liberalism." Given both that a partial focus of this essay has been on the difficulties of such a "reinvention" and that the Burke offered in these pages is meant to be relevant to the present, it might be fitting to merely echo these earlier statements. This too could lend another (double) meaning to Burke's observation about the various "selves" of an influential author. Burke found himself being at least two (if not more) "selves" to balance his personal political objectives and his public critical work, and this initial duplication has paved the way for the multitude of "Burkes" called to service by progressive scholars in various times and circumstances.

At the same time, however, given the synonymy of "revision" and "opportunism" I have noted, the sometimes mercenary tasks of rhetoric, and the effectiveness of drawing on existing inclinations to redirect them in another way, it is equally tempting to conclude with a more steely-eyed or cynical conception of the Burke presented in this essay. Here the presentation could be seen as the author's opportunistic act—one of leveraging Burke's material to make him do the work I find relevant or necessary in the present moment.

It is fortunate for me, then, that Burke's own schema may have made both options possible. After all, this reading of Burke's 1930s work suggests that one might have to be a propagandistic to be an ethical individual: you must "sin" (by omission, by misdirection) in order to "save" others or serve a greater good. Or, to reproduce one final deleted passage from the typescript of *Permanence and Change:* "One could thus remain both pious and forgiven: one could respond to the symbolic implications of the act, since one had a technique for 'cleansing' him of his 'sin' he had committed."

NOTES

1. In addition to this epigraph, see for instance Burke on "sub-personalities" in *Grammar* (169) and multiples selves in "(Nonsymbolic) Motion/(Symbolic) Action."

2. For observations of these two legacies of Burke's work see, in addition to Blair, Biesecker (9–11), Hawhee (responding to Blair, 130–31), Nelson (164), Pruchnic, and Rueckert ("Some").

3. Propaganda as term and concept was a consistent interest of Burke's throughout his work. At times he uses the term in its common, pejorative sense to discredit discourses or arguments that are driven less by factual fidelity and more by partisan interest (e.g., *Grammar* 395), or as a way to distinguish the "pure" literature of poetry from what Burke calls, in one of the introductions to "Auscultation, Creation, and Revision," the "applied literature" of propaganda (55; also addressed in *Grammar* 289). At other times he subsumes all or almost all instances of communication within the realm of propaganda, arguing that the charge of propagandism can be leveled against any discourse that does not come out of an attitude of pure disinterest (a realm that, as Burke so often reminds us, is incredibly scarce in contemporary life) (*Permanence* 81, 1984, 272). At still other times he conceptualizes his own work (most often in unpublished planning notes for projects or in private correspondence) as propaganda—as attempts to sway an audience toward particular causes or toward the production of particular actions or effects through less-than-transparent means of persuasion.

4. Both the typescript of Burke's "My Approach to Communism" (originally delivered as a talk to the John Reed Club) and much of the manuscript material for *Permanence and Change* have recently been acquired by the Kenneth Burke Papers of the Pennsylvania State University, forming part of the "Burke-3" collection that joins two earlier holdings of Burke's material. Some of this material has already been discussed in print. See Sheriff for a comparison of the spoken and published versions of "Approach" and essays by Burks and by Schiappa and Keehner published in the 1991 issue of *Communication Studies* dedicated to Burke. When referring herein to excised portions from manuscript versions of *Permanence* that are reproduced more fully in these articles, the page numbers of those reproductions are parenthetically cited. References to correspondence between Burke and Malcolm Cowley that are included in Jay's *Selected Correspondence* are likewise cited within that work. I have additionally done the same when appropriate with correspondence reproduced in Robert L. Heath's *Realism and Relativism,* one of the first and one of the most expansive uses of Burke's archived correspondence to contextualize his early written works.

5. This is particularly clear in a letter from Burke to Cowley quoted by Sheriff, which mentions that the accepted essay was "voted clear by several" whereas the oral performance was voted "obscure by all" (Burke and Cowley 294).

6. The latter two terms would reappear, without Marxism as a reference, in multiple places in the third edition of the book (*PC* 1984, 34, 65, 270, 272).

7. Of course the same is true of the two most popular ways of reading Burke's "self-censoring": as Burke's "honest," ongoing attempt, as he himself states, to "translate" communist principles in into his own "vocabulary" or as an attempt to stiff-arm the dangers of being pegged as a communist or sympathizer.

8. For the sake of brevity I omit consideration here of another vector of Burke's "perspective"—its use an inventional or self-experimental device for changing the associations of its speakers. It is undoubtedly true, as Ann George and Jack Selzer gloss the term, that Burke presents "perspective" as a heuristic for "productively disrupting the assumptions both of the writer/critic who suggests the translation and of the audience who responds to it" (128).

9. For a consideration of how such memorials fit into the past and future of critical theory, as well as a more extensive checklist of its proclamations, see Nealon's "Post-Deconstructive?"

10. See Strathausen's "A Critique of Neo-Left Ontology" for a more comprehensive look at how contemporary theorists such as Jean-Luc Nancy, Jacques Ranciere, and Ernesto Laclau have returned to questions of "being" as a partial response to the challenges posed to postmodern theories of subjectivity.

WORKS CITED

Advertisement for *Permanence and Change*. *New Republic* 82 (Mar. 27, 1935): 193.

Arnt Aune, James. "Burke's Palimpsest: Rereading *Permanence and Change*." *Communication Studies* 42.3 (1991): 234–37.

Badiou, Alain. *Ethics: An Essay on the Understanding of Evil*. Trans. Peter Hallward. London: Verso, 2001.

Bensaid, Daniel. "Alain Badiou and the Miracle of the Event." *Think Again: Alain Badiou and the Future of Philosophy*. Ed. Peter Hallward. London: Continuum, 2004. 95–105.

Biesecker, Barbara A. *Addressing Postmodernity: Kenneth Burke, Rhetoric, and a Theory of Social Change*. Tuscaloos: University of Alabama Press, 1997.

Blair, Carole. "Symbolic Action and Discourse: The Convergence/Divergent Views of Kenneth Burke and Michel Foucault." *Kenneth Burke and Contemporary European Thought*. Ed. Bernard L. Breck. Tuscaloosa: University of Alabama Press, 1995. 119–65.

Brock, Bernard L. "The Evolution of Kenneth Burke's Philosophy of Rhetoric: Dialectic between Epistemology and Ontology." *Extensions of the Burkeian System*. Ed. James W. Cheseboro. Tuscaloosa: University of Alabama Press, 1993. 309–28.

Burks. Don M. "Kenneth Burke: The Agro-Bohemain 'Marxoid.'" *Communication Studies* 42.3 (Fall 1991): 219–33.

Burke, Kenneth. *Attitudes towards History*. Berkeley: University of California Press, 1984.

———. "Auscultation, Creation, and Revision: The Rout of the Esthetes, or, Literature, Marxism, and Beyond." Cheseboro 43–172.

———. "Boring from Within." *New Republic* 65 (Feb. 4, 1931): 326–29.

———. "Counter-Gridlock: An Interview with Kenneth Burke." *On Human Nature: A Gathering while Everything Flows, 1967–1984*. Ed. William H. Rueckert and Angelo Bonadonna. Berkeley: University of California Press, 2003. 336–89.

———. *Counter-Statement*. Berkeley: University of California Press, 1968.

———. Cover letter for "My Approach to Communism." Kenneth Burke Papers, Pennsylvania State University. Folder P27. Box P23–P31.

———. *A Grammar of Motives*. Berkeley: University of California Press, 1968.

———. Letter to Richard McKeon. Mar. 12, 1937. Kenneth Burke Papers, Pennsylvania State University.

———. Letter to Perce. Feb. 14, 1935. Kenneth Burke Papers, Paterno Library, Pennsylvania State University

———. "Misc. notes, typescripts, etc. ca 125–135." Kenneth Burke Papers, Pennsylvania State University. Folder P09. Box 01–03.

———. "My Approach to Communism." *New Masses* 10 (Mar. 20, 1934): 16, 18–20.

———. "The Nature of Art under Capitalism." *Nation* 137 (Dec. 13, 1934): 13–14.

———. "(Nonsymbolic) Motion/(Symbolic) Action." Rueckert and Bonadonna 139–71.

———. *Permanence and Change*. New York: New Republic, 1935.

———. *Permanence and Change: An Anatomy of Purpose*. Los Altos, CA: Hermes, 1954.

———. *Permanence and Change: An Anatomy of Purpose*. 3rd ed. Berkeley: University of California Press, 1984.

———. *The Philosophy of Literary Form: Studies in Symbolic Action*. 3rd ed. Berkeley: University of California Press, 1973.

Burke, Kenneth, and Malcolm Cowley. *The Selected Correspondence of Kenneth Burke and Malcolm Cowley*. Ed. Paul Jay. New York: Penguin, 1988.

Burke, Kenneth, and Granville Hicks. "Counterblasts on *Counter-Statement*." *New Republic* 9 (1931): 101.

Bygrave, Stephen. *Kenneth Burke: Rhetoric and Ideology*. London: Routledge, 1993.

Farrell, Thomas B. "Comic History Meets Tragic Memory: Burke and Habermas on the Drama of Human Relations." *Kenneth Burke and Contemporary European Thought: Rhetoric in Translation*. Ed. Bernard L. Brock. Studies in Rhetoric and Communication. Tuscaloosa: University of Alabama Press, 1994. 34-75.

George, Ann, and Jack Selzer. *Kenneth Burke in the 1930s: Studies in Rhetoric/Communication*. Columbia: University of South Carolina Press, 2007.

Habermas, Jürgen. *Legitimation Crisis*. Trans. Thomas McCarthy. Boston: Beacon, 1975.

Hallward, Peter. "The Politics of Prescription." *South Atlantic Quarterly* 104.4 (Fall 2005): 769–89.

Hardt, Michael, and Antonio Negri. *Empire*. Cambridge, Mass.: Harvard University Press, 2001.

Hawhee, Debra. "Burke and Nietzsche." *Quarterly Journal of Speech* 85.2 (1999): 129–45.

Heath, Robert L. *Realism and Relativism: A Perspective on Kenneth Burke*. Macon, Ga.: Mercer University Press, 1986.

Hemmings, Clare. "Cultural Theory and the Ontological Turn." *Cultural Studies* 9.5 (Sept. 2005): 548–67.

Kant, Immanuel. "An Answer to the Question: 'What Is Enlightenment?'" *Kant's Political Writings*. 2nd ed. Ed. Hans Reiss. Trans. H. B. Nisbet. Cambridge, UK: Cambridge University Press, 1990. 4–60.

———. *Groundwork of the Metaphysics of Morals*. Trans and ed. Mary Gregor. Cambridge, UK: Cambridge University Press, 1998.

Massumi, Brian. *Parables for the Virtual: Movement, Affect, Sensation*. Durham, N.C.: Duke University Press, 2002.

Nealon, Jeffrey T. "Post-Deconstructive? Negri, Derrida, and the Present State of Theory." *symploke* 14.1–2 (2006): 68–80.

Nelson, Cary. "Writing as an Accomplice of Language: Kenneth Burke and Poststructuralism." Simons and Melia 156–73.

"Permanence and Change." Advertisement. *New Republic* 82 (Mar. 27, 1935): 193.

Pruchnic, Jeff. "Rhetoric, Cybernetics, and the Work of the Body in Burke's Body of Work." *Rhetoric Review* 25.3 (2006): 275–96.

Rueckert, William. *Kenneth Burke and the Drama of Human Relations.* 2nd ed. Berkeley: University of California Press, 1982.

———. "Some of the Many Kenneth Burkes." *Representing Kenneth Burke.* Ed. Hayden White and Margaret Bose. Baltimore: Johns Hopkins University Press, 1982. 1–30.

Sedgwick, Eve Kosofsky. *Touching Feeling: Affect, Pedagogy, Performance.* Durham, N.C.: Duke University Press, 2003.

Sheriff, Stacey. "Resituating Kenneth Burke's 'My Approach to Communism.'" *Rhetorica* 23.3 (Summer 2005): 281–95.

Stob, Paul. "Kenneth Burke, John Dewey, and the Pursuit of the Public." *Philosophy and Rhetoric* 38.3 (2005): 226–47.

Strathausen, Carsten. "A Critique of Neo-Left Ontology." *Postmodern Culture* 16.3 (May 2006).

Wess, Robert. *Kenneth Burke: Rhetoric, Subjectivity, Postmodernism.* New York: Cambridge University Press, 1988.

Williams, William Carlos, and Kenneth Burke. *The Human Particulars: The Collected Letters of William Carlos Williams and Kenneth Burke.* Ed. James H. East. Columbia: University of South Carolina Press, 2003.

Žižek, Slavoj. *In Defense of Lost Causes.* London: Verso, 2008.

———. *The Ticklish Subject: The Absent Centre of Political Ontology.* London: Verso, 1999.

MICHELLE SMITH

THE DRAMATISM DEBATE, ARCHIVED

The Pentad as "Terministic" Ontology

Burke begins *A Grammar of Motives* with the following passage: "What is involved, when we say what people are doing and why they are doing it? An answer to that question is the subject of this book. The book is concerned with the basic forms of thought which, in accordance with the nature of the world as all men necessarily experience it, are exemplified in the attributing of motives. . . . We shall use five terms as generating principle of our investigation. They are: Act, Scene, Agent, Agency, Purpose" (xv). This deceptively readable passage, introducing the five terms of the pentad, has prompted two main interpretations.[1] The pentad, the central terminology and analytical tool for Burke's dramatism, offers either a means to uncover and understand human motives—ontology—or a means to understand the attributing of motives through language—epistemology. To put it differently, the pentad helps with either the analysis of acts or the analysis of how we talk about acts. Both views have been contested by readers and scholars since the publication of the *Grammar* in 1945.

Burke's initial presentation of the pentad in the *Grammar* lends itself to an epistemological reading. Epistemology is best defined, for our purposes, as the "theory of knowledge" or "knowledge of knowledge" (Crable 327). The epistemological reading of the above passage might be stressed as follows: "What is involved, when we *say* what people are doing and why they are doing it?"; "The book is concerned with the basic forms of thought which . . . are exemplified in the *attributing* of motives." The passage can easily be read as presenting the pentad as a set of terms that function in *statements* about motives. Indeed much of the *Grammar* presents the pentad as a means of analyzing the attribution of motives through language, which Burke reads as a component of virtually all communication—"every judgment, exhortation, or admonition, every view of natural or supernatural reality, every intention or expectation involves assumptions about motive, or cause" (xxii). The pentad, in this light, offers a way of unpacking statements about human motives through the terminology of drama. Dramatism, in the epistemological view, is a metaphor, a perspective for understanding human motivation.

In contrast a typical ontological reading of the same passage from the *Grammar* would direct its gaze towards human motives themselves. Within relevant scholarship, ontology is typically approached as the "science of being" or the "study of being"—the essence of a thing "in itself" (Crable 327). Thus an ontological view would read the passage for its resonances regarding "being," "in itself," and motives as they really exist. The stresses might fall accordingly: "What is involved, when we say *what* people are doing and *why* they are doing it? . . . The book is concerned with the basic forms of thought which, *in accordance with the nature of the world* as all men necessarily experience it, are exemplified in the attributing of motives." The ontological view, then, seems to involve a more literal approach—human motivations *are* a drama that necessarily involves the pentadic elements—whereas the epistemological view investigates human motivation through the *lens*, or perspective, of drama. Given Burke's general emphasis on metaphor throughout his work, many scholars found the epistemological view more defensible and cohesive with Burke's overall project—the ontological view seemed ripe with "theoretical hubris" and an unusual insistence upon accuracy and literality (Crable 330). Ontology seemed anti-Burkean.

Given this attitude, it is no wonder that Burke scholars were surprised when, at a conference in 1982 and through an interchange with Bernard Brock and Herbert Simons, Burke insisted that the overall project of dramatism (with the pentad as a key component) was ontological. At the 1982 meeting of the Eastern Communication Association in Hartford, Connecticut, Bernard Brock presented "The Role of Paradox and Metaphor in Kenneth Burke's Dramatism," to an audience that included Burke himself. Brock's discussion centered on dramatism as a whole, but his remarks about the pentad reveal his epistemological leanings. Brock asserted: "Having described reality as symbolizing in response to the 'human situation,' . . . Burke presents the pentad as a means of unlocking human motives, thereby understanding symbolic reality" (Brock et al. 20). Though Brock explains that symbolizing is a seeming ontological "reality" for Burke, his distinction between symbolic reality and the "human situation" to which symbolizing responds maintains a view of dramatism as a metaphor, as one perspective on reality.

Burke's response to Brock's ECA paper homes in on the question of the relationship between reality and symbolic action. Burke asks whether symbolic action is literal and concludes, "it is a literal statement to say that people really do act in using symbolic action[,] which is a different kind of action than other species on this earth carry out which do not use symbolic action" (Brock et al. 23). Given Burke's comments, symbolic action is literal; thus it makes more sense to view the pentad, a study of the forms of symbolic action, as an ontological tool. As the conference debate progressed, the discussion continued around the concerns of whether symbolic action is literal, whether dramatism is a metaphor, and the like—all questions seemingly related to the underlying ontology/epistemology distinction. Indeed one key feature of this debate, as Bryan Crable has persuasively argued, is the interlocutors' insistent coupling of epistemology with metaphor and ontology with literality, pairings that have contributed to the confusion over what exactly Burke meant by ontology (324).[2]

Because of the importance of this debate, *Communication Quarterly* published not only the transcript of the conference proceedings, but also a post-conference correspondence between Burke, Brock, and Simons. In the published exchange, Brock and Simons continued to argue for dramatism as epistemology (a theory of how acts are known or talked about), while Burke forwarded the claim that his system is, rather, an ontology (a theory of the nature of acts).

Burke's *Communication Quarterly* contribution articulated the ontological view by directing his audience to his 1968 article "Dramatism," where he had tried to clarify his stance regarding the nature of dramatism and the pentad. This article describes "act" as central to the entire system, "a 'god-term' from which a whole universe of terms is derived" (445). It also explicates symbolic action as literal, not metaphorical. Brock too supplemented his conference paper argument with some meditations on the "Dramatism" article. Focusing on Burke's later writings, Brock identifies a dramatism based upon "act," an overly literal approach to language and a reality-oriented philosophy, as opposed to a "method for understanding the social uses of language" (Brock, "Epistemology and Ontology" 94). Brock and Simons thus conclude that Burke had changed his perspective: having presented an epistemological system in the *Grammar* (1945), Burke was now (in the 1968 "Dramatism" article and the 1982 debate) presenting dramatism as a metaphysical ontology.[3] It seemed that Burke was now arguing that the pentad could uncover human motives themselves and could account for all other philosophies. This perspective struck Brock and Simons as distasteful because it seemed to destroy the pluralistic tone of dramatism, presenting it as "the intellectual equivalent of a King of Kings" (Brock et al. 30).

This essay responds to this debate by leveraging archival documents to argue for a view of dramatism as ontology, without resigning dramatism to the wholesale realist ontology that Brock attributed to Burke's later articulations of the theory. Reading dramatism as "terministic ontology," I suggest, retains much of what Brock, Simons, and many others found valuable in their initial reading of the pentad as a form of terministic analysis. My aim here is not to argue that the pentad be understood, once and for all, as ontological or epistemological; nor is it to dismiss particular applications of the concept.[4] Yet this interpretation also proceeds under the assumption that scholars can learn something from Burke's association of dramatism (and thus the pentad) with ontology. My interpretation of the pentad as ontological in its original formulation is grounded in several archival sources from the years when Burke was writing the *Grammar*, including the longer original version of the "Dramatism" article that he deployed in the 1982 debate. I first show that "act" was the generative term behind dramatism; and second, that Burke proposed the pentad as a "linguistic" or "terministic" ontology, a system that demonstrates truths about linguistically constructed reality. I conclude by briefly considering how such a terministic ontology might help scholars consider the place (and the paradox) of archival scholarship in rhetorical studies.

FROM ACTION TO THE PENTAD

In a letter to Matthew Josephson (September 11, 1940), Burke wrote, "I found that, in trying to get a *beginning* for my stuff On Human Relations, nothing else would serve but a kind of paradigm for all possible discussion of human relations." The question of the centrality of "act" to the pentad is a key concern for scholars who resist the classification of the pentad as ontology. Brock in particular expressed concern during and after the 1982 debate over Burke's privileging of act in this discussion, a privileging he argues was absent from the original version of dramatism in the *Grammar*. However Burke's letters as he was writing and revising the *Grammar* suggest that act was in fact the genesis of the entire project. In the *Grammar*, Burke explains that the terms of the pentad are stressed differently in different philosophies: "each school features a different one of the five terms, . . . with the other terms being comparatively slighted or being placed in the perspective of the featured term" (127). In this presentation each philosophy will be more grounded in some pentadic components than others, but every approach is equally a symbolic attempt to express the ineffable, the "reality" we feel is out there (which of course may bear little similarity to our symbolic attempts to capture it in pentadic emphases and ratios). In this earlier view, no one perspective or philosophy is more accurate than another; the pentad cannot answer "the question as to which characterization is 'right' or 'more nearly right'" (*Grammar* xvii).

But in "Dramatism" and the 1982 debate, Burke argues for act as the central term. As he writes in "Dramatism": "'Act' is . . . a terministic center . . . a 'god-term'" (445). Brock argues that this new emphasis on act signifies that Burke is now privileging an act-centric philosophy (realism) over other philosophical views. The centrality of act is spelled out even more clearly in the original introduction to Burke's "Dramatism" conference presentation: "D[ramatism] is a method of terministic analysis (and a corresponding critique of terminology) designed to show that the most direct route to the study of human relations and human motives is via a methodic inquiry into the cycle or cluster of terms and their functions implicit in the key term, 'act'" ("Dramatism talk" 1). Brock explains his problem with this new emphasis: "In the first instance, Dramatism is a method that allows for a variety of perspectives to exist, and in the second, Dramatism is 'reality' because Burke argues that a single philosophy is dominant" (Brock, "Epistemology and Ontology" 100–101).

But this focus on act was not a new addition to Burke's thought in the second half of the twentieth century. Rather, "act" was already the "key term" behind

Burke's conceptualizing of the pentad in the 1940s, because human action itself was the primary focus of the project that became the *Grammar.* The archives remind us that Burke did not intend to sit down and write *A Grammar of Motives* the way he had composed his work in the late 1930s and early 1940s. The *Grammar* began as a book on human action and interaction titled "On Human Relations." As Burke explains in a letter to Norman Guterman, the original starting point for the book was an investigation of "constitutions as a representative public act," and Burke intended to use this "constitutional theme" as an "opening and organizing device throughout" the work (KB to NG November 25, 1939). Burke's interest in action derived from his goal of challenging the methods of social science. This purpose is evident in a 1940 letter to Lewis Dexter, in which Burke refers to his project in the *Grammar* as his "great conspiracy . . . to prove that the perspective of sociologists cannot be thorough and accurate without being that of 'dramatic criticism method-ized.' That, otherwise, sociology can have only the kind of organization one gets in a mail order catalogue" (KB to LD September 2, 1940). Thus Burke hoped that dramatism could be a sort of corrective to the current attitude of social scientists, whom Burke saw as confusing their field with the physical sciences.

In Burke's distinction, the goal of the physical sciences is to describe the scene of human action, the physical world, which follows the rules of motion. The social sciences however are meant to analyze the drama of human action itself, which is not reducible to the laws of motion. As he explains in *The Philosophy of Literary Form:* "The physical sciences are a calculus of events; the social sciences are a calculus of acts. . . . The error of the social sciences has usually resided in the attempt to appropriate the scenic calculus for a charting of the act" (114). Dramatism as a whole is meant to correct the tendency to ignore that humans are forever torn between motion and action, neither wholly free nor wholly constrained; as Burke writes, "The ideal calculus of dramatic criticism . . . would be required to employ the coordinates of *both* determinism *and* free will" (*PLF* 116). Burke's project, then, sought to provide the social sciences with a calculus for human acts that acknowl-edges human motives and free will, elements irrelevant for the physical sciences.

This overarching purpose for the *Grammar,* while clearly demonstrating Burke's privileging of act, does not entail that humans really do act in some realistic and knowable manner. The action/motion distinction between things that move and people who act may be inherent to how humans see their world, but this distinction is not necessarily a "truth" about the world itself. As Clarke Rountree explains: "the philosophical issue of whether humans really do act (rather than merely move as a bag full of chemicals or genetic programming or neuronal circuits might 'move') is not Burke's concern, but only the recognition that we do, indeed, 'pragmatically' treat other human beings *as if* they were acting rather than merely moving" ("Coming to Terms" 1). And this pragmatic distinction that humans make between action and motion surfaces when Burke tries to clarify dramatism and the pentad: "Within the practically limitless range of scenes (or motivating situations) in terms of which

human action can be defined and studied, there is one over-all dramatistic distinction. . . . This is the distinction between 'action' and 'sheer motion'" ("Dramatism"
447). Dramatism begins, then, with the tension between action and motion that
plays out in human life.

However as he attempted to write an introduction to "On Human Relations,"
Burke discovered that there was more ground to cover before he could begin to
discuss human action itself. The pentad, embraced afterwards as the heart of dramatism, actually began as an afterthought, something that Burke felt he had to write
because it was "logically prior" to what he wanted to say about human action and
interaction. In a letter to Matthew Josephson, Burke describes this process: "Am at
present (outside and around the interruptions and interregna) trying to show what
you can do by taking five very simple words (act, scene, agent, agency, purpose) and
looking at them long and hard . . . . However, to my great disgruntlement, this business was not my intention at all. But I found that, in trying to get a *beginning* for my
stuff On Human Relations, nothing else would serve but a kind of paradigm for all
possible discussion of human relations. And so, from that, I found my introduction
becoming rather what ought to be a separate book in itself' (KB to MJ September 11,
1940; emphasis in original). The pentad, then, is a paradigm for how we talk about
human action, which Burke felt needed to be established before he could broach
human relations themselves.

This information regarding the composing process of the *Grammar* clarifies
Burke's subsequent claim that act is the key term of the pentad. In his initial project,
Burke intended to write a book about human relations and action proper: action
was the focus of his analysis. But in order to write this text, Burke felt he needed an
introduction discussing how we talk about action, and this consideration grew into
the pentad. At this point, judging from the passage just cited, the project seems to
have taken on a life of its own, maturing into something that "ought to be a separate book in itself." Because the pentad grew out of a primary desire to inquire into
human action itself, action can be seen as the genesis for the entire system.[5]

In digesting this information about Burke's initial project, "On Human Relations," readers may have noted that the project Burke set out to accomplish—one
on human action—sounds more ontological than this second project—one about
how we talk about action. I now turn to why and how Burke insists that this second
project, addressing statements about motives, was itself ontological.

A "TERMINISTIC" ONTOLOGY

To better understand Burke's ontological claims, I look again to his letters, especially
those that explained what he thought he had accomplished in the *Grammar*. Gain-
ing a stronger understanding of what Burke meant by "ontology" also provides a
response to scholars' concerns about the totalizing, "container"-esque nature of
ontologies. The problem here has more to do with the nature of ontology itself
than with a specific aspect of Burke's description of the pentad that changed over

time. That is, by calling his system an ontology, Burke has raised the specters that haunt the term.

In the issue of *Communication Quarterly* immediately following the publication of the 1982 debate, Brock published an article summarizing his post-debate understanding of dramatism. In this piece Brock highlighted his concern about the totalizing nature of ontologies and stated his view that the nature of Burke's dramatism had shifted over time: "Kenneth Burke initially established Dramatism as a method for understanding the social uses of language. . . . However, recently Burke has shifted Dramatism towards a philosophy" (Brock "Epistemology and Ontology" 1985, 94). And for many scholars, defining dramatism and the pentad as ontological seemed to strip Burke of the ambiguity and pluralism championed in much of his earlier work. In the debate, Simons protested that accepting Burke's view would mean acknowledging dramatism as a master system, such that "Dramatism is a container, logic is a thing contained in it, and it is so powerful and so all-encompassing that other container-makers [ontologies] cannot avoid it, much as they might try" (Brock et al. 30). Brock similarly argued that dramatism was initially a pluralistic method, but Burke later described it as a statement about "reality," identifying the essence of "human motivation" and thus precluding other perspectives (Brock, "Epistemology and Ontology" 100–101). These scholars were likely not reassured by Burke's 1968 "Dramatism" article and its claim that the system offers "the most direct route to the study of human relations and human motives" (445), as this description seems to claim access to the Real.

Since the 1982 exchange Burke scholars have continued to debate the question of dramatism's potential ontological status. As one would expect, the elements of the debate have changed over the last twenty years, and two of the major camps today describe two different kinds of ontology that might encompass the pentad. In *Addressing Postmodernity: Kenneth Burke, Rhetoric, and a Theory of Social Change*, Barbara Biesecker makes one case for viewing the pentad as ontology. Biesecker describes the pentad as a metaphysical ontology, a way to get at the true, underlying nature of human action (25).[6] Burke however is eager in his letters to assure readers that he is not forwarding this kind of metaphysical ontology.

Instead Burke asserts that dramatism is "terministic." Robert Wess provides some insight as to what kind of ontology this description might represent. In contrast to Biesecker, Wess argues that the pentad illustrates an objective truth about human *discourse* and thus constitutes what he calls a *rhetorical* ontology (*Kenneth Burke* 185). Where Biesecker reads Burke as attempting an "investigation of the ontological foundation of motives" *themselves* (*Addressing* 25), Wess suggests that dramatism offers the pentad as a tool for investigating the ontological linguistic foundations of *statements about* motives. By forwarding a view of the pentad as terministic ontology, I situate the pentad within Wess's brand of ontology and borrow Burke's description of it as "terministic." Moreover I read the pentad as belonging to this atypical genre of ontology from its first instantiation in the *Grammar.*[7]

Ontology is generally understood to be nearly identical to metaphysics, defined by the *Cambridge Dictionary of Philosophy* as "the philosophical investigation of the nature, constitution, and structure of reality" (qtd. in Wess, "Pentadic Terms" 156). As an ontology, then, the pentad should reveal some aspect of reality. In my reading, Burke's view of the pentad as an ontology is not a declaration of the pentad's ability to reveal true motivations, or even a statement that such a revelation is possible. Primary to understanding the nature of a terministic ontology is clarifying the aspect of "reality" Burke feels the pentad accounts for: the reality of statements about human action. In a markedly clear and charismatic letter to Richard McKeon, Burke describes the pentad as a means of accounting for the way that philosophies are developed and expressed. "Fact is that I have finished my Grammar (of the five Miraculous Terms, act, scene, agent, agency, purpose), and would greatly prize a chance to discuss it with you under grovelike conditions. It all gets down to a 'dramatist' approach to the category of substance—and an attempt to show that, if one begins by considering the relations among these five terms (as revealed in the contemplation of drama), one will best understand why philosophies (being theories of motivation, action, etc.) assume the forms they do" (KB to RM May 19, 1942). This passage clarifies that the pentad is not meant to uncover motives, but to uncover some truth behind descriptions of motives, whether in formal philosophies, as discussed here, or in more colloquial commonplace accounts of why people act as they do. If the pentad is meant to describe any aspect of reality, it is meant to describe symbolic reality. Such an ontology is not metaphysical, but linguistic—or, in Burke's description, "terministic."

To consider the meaning of a terministic ontology, we must return to Burke's understanding of language and action. While Burke does not discount the fact that we often understand and use language for its referential capacities, dramatism is based around Burke's understanding of language as action. Burke's "paradox of substance" is key here. In the *Grammar* Burke famously explains this paradox that inheres in definition and language: as we attempt to define a thing "in itself," we inevitably define it in terms of what it is not—that is, we define the thing by that which is outside and apart from it (21–23). In other words, "a thing is not so much *represented in* as *constituted by* language" (Crable 328; emphasis in original). Language, for Burke, is "constitutive action," helping to constitute the world as we perceive it. A terministic ontology, then, inquires into the constitutive, world-making capacities of language as symbolic action—not language as representation.

Burke's own understanding of ontology is certainly relevant here. Consider his definition from *The Philosophy of Literary Form*: "Implicit in a perspective there are two kinds of questions: (1) what to look for, and why; (2) how, when, and where to look for it. The first could be called ontological questions; the second, methodological" (68). The *methodology* of dramatism tells us to look at statements about motives, but the pentad itself tells us what to look for, meeting Burke's criteria for *ontology*. In statements of motives, we look for the grammatical components of act, scene, agent, agency, and purpose. The reason we should look for the five pentadic elements is that any discussion of action necessarily utilizes these five concepts. In other words, it is the nature of language itself that when humans discuss action, they impute motives. As Rountree states in his defense of dramatism as literal: "No recognizably human society ever existed that was not able to draw the distinctions we draw in answering the questions Who, What, When, Where, How, and Why. In other words, these questions and the answers they call for are *universal*" ("Revisiting"; emphasis in original). Burke thus establishes the pentad as the grammar for any discussion of motives.

The pentad is an ontology, then, not in the sense that it provides access to some reality *underneath* language, but in that it provides access to the reality that *is* language (or the reality that becomes *through* language). By analyzing statements about motives at the terministic level, Burke can get at the grammatical rules that these statements apply—the components and their ratios. Because he is trying to articulate the rules and forms of language itself, Burke's analysis stays at this terministic level, not positing a relationship between symbolic reality and some sublinguistic reality. Burke articulates this focus in a letter to Lewis Dexter, writing that the pentad is a tool for investigating "the *purely internal* relationships prevailing among these five terms (their 'syntax')" (KB to LD September 2, 1940; emphasis added). A metaphysical ontology would presumably look beyond language in its analysis in order to make assertions about being, about human action in the world; the pentad however, as terministic ontology, stays in the terministic realm, the realm of symbolic—but no less "real"—action.

As a terministic ontology, the pentad introduces the terms and concepts that will appear in *any* statement of motivation. This claim to universality is a clear mark of an ontological system, not an epistemological perspective. Burke's sense of the pentad as the unavoidable means of expressing motives is clear in a letter to Goodwin Watson, where Burke identifies his project as "an analysis of the various dialectics employed consciously or unconsciously in the imputation of motives" (KB to GW December 21, 1940). The true motive itself may be forever blurry and indistinct, but in expressing and describing motivation, we are nonetheless subject to the pentad's grammar. This relationship between the actual "substance" of human motives and the pentadic terminology can now be recognized in the *Grammar* itself: "And so with our five terms: certain formal interrelationships prevail among these terms, by reason of their role as attributes of a common ground or substance . . . From the central moltenness, where all the elements are fused into one togetherness, there are thrown forth, in separate crusts, such distinctions as those between freedom and necessity, activity and passiveness, cooperation and competition, cause and effect, mechanism and teleology" (xix). Acts, like prelinguistic substance more generally, argues Burke, are unified, based in a "central moltenness" of experience, but language breaks down the unified whole into the components required for linguistic expression (and quite possibly human perception itself). And of course the mind breaks down this moltenness via language in a process that is largely unconscious—in other words, there is no claiming access to a true expression of motives that is not prey to this linguistic translation.

Even as the pentad and dramatism were fresh in his mind and on the page, Burke was aware that his ontological claims would seem problematic to some of his contemporaries (and to future scholars as well). As he continued his letter of triumph to McKeon upon finishing the *Grammar,* Burke expressed the possibility that people (including McKeon himself) might read his ontology of language as a traditional metaphysical ontology: "I hear you murmur 'platonizing.' But I think I can show you that it is, rather, 'terministic.' I.e., I take the five terms; consider their relations to one another; then show what ambiguities, resources, necessities reside in these relations; then show how different philosophical and rhetorical strategies take form from these ambiguities, resources, necessities" (KB to RM May 19, 1942). In this passage, which counters the accusation of a platonic ontology with the assertion of a terministic one, Burke describes the pentad as illustrating a truth about the nature of language, hinting at some of the strengths of his system for rhetorical analysis.

Still, categorizing Burke's ontology as a "terministic" or linguistic ontology does not entirely excuse his system from the problematic tendencies of ontological systems. For one, an ontology is a statement about "reality," and it thus cannot allow other perspectives on reality; an ontology is, as Simons claims, first and foremost a container. Burke clearly depicts the pentad in this vein in a heady letter to Matthew Josephson: "If I were a mathematician, I could tell you, now, how many hundreds of thousands of philosophies are possible, by tinkering with these five words and making various permutations and combinations of the tinkering. And if I were a historian of philosophy, I could show you just how many of said variants have already been exploited (I think every philosophy in history can be adequately located by these terms and their subdivisions)" (KB to MJ September 11, 1940). While this passage illustrates Burke's notion that the pentad *contains* and accounts for "every philosophy in history," he is also aware that such claims are, according to his own philosophical tenets, dangerous. Several months later Burke wrote to Josephson again, but this time with a more humble tone: "In an age of fumbling such as ours, I suppose nobody should dare claim not to be lost himself. I claim only that speculations along these lines are in the 'right direction.' They are at least *in the direction* of a proper vocabulary of motives" (KB to MJ December 17, 1941). Even in the second letter, the faith that a "proper vocabulary" is attainable shows that Burke believes that there is an ontological basis to statements of motive.

While Burke might be excused from charges that he viewed dramatism as an accurate reflection of reality, he does still argue that dramatism is a more persuasive and all-encompassing calculus for human actions and motives than other preeminent philosophies. In part 2 of the *Grammar,* "The Philosophic Schools," Burke analyzes philosophies such as pragmatism, mysticism, and idealism to illuminate their emphasis on one component of the pentad over the others. But these analyses are not meant to undermine these metaphysical ontologies; rather they are meant to show that all such philosophical systems employ their own unique motivational calculus, each composed of elements of the pentad. We need these perspectives, but Burke believes that dramatism is part of the constitution of those perspectives. As he claimed in the 1982 debate, "Such perspectives always exist. But, Dramatism functions on another level. It accounts for the fact that these views exist, that these views are literal" (Brock et al. 25). Crable uses Burke's discussion of science and medicine to help explain this idea. These fields approach people, at times, as though they were machines, or animals, in order to effectively treat patients for example. And these metaphors are useful, but they never override our general sense of one another as acting beings and users of language. "Dramatism, as literal, allows us to see the whole of the human condition and, from there, trace the various possible fictions that are generated to account for parts of it" (Crable 335).[8] Burke sees dramatism as occupying a special place because, while dramatism can account for our ability to conceive of people as machines or animals, we cannot start with a philosophy that approaches people as machines or animals and thus arrive at language use.

In introducing dramatism as ontology, Burke highlights not only the importance of language but also his faith that we can discover ontological truths about how language works. The various philosophies to which we adhere all come with their own terministic emphases that guide our sense of the possibilities of human action. As their grammars of motives shape our understanding of how we act and react in the world, they shape our future choices as well. Through use of the pentad, we might better trace how such motivational philosophies inform all assertions about action. Such work will demonstrate how motivational equations function— and function rhetorically—through discourse, be it philosophical, political, or personal. Thus one of the main benefits of this interpretation of the pentad is a new perspective on rhetorical analysis. Without disavowing the value of pentadic readings that proceed from an epistemological interpretation, I think we have yet to capitalize on the affordances of ontology.

Burke's pentad suggests that any description of human action will invoke the terms/concepts of the pentad. When analyzing a text, then, one would not look at the rhetor as the agent, the text as the act, and so on but rather look *within the text itself* to identify the acts, agents, scenes, purposes, and agencies in play. From this dissection of the *motivational equations within the text,* one could generalize about the dramatistic calculus ascribed to by the rhetor, or at least invoked for this occasion, this audience, and so on. While there is no need to forego more traditional analyses of rhetors, their purposes, their contexts, and so on, I find Burke's suggestion of the pentad as a dramatistic calculus to be a provocative first step for analysis, before turning to questions of why a certain philosophy of action (motivational equation) might have been embraced or invoked in a certain instance. Read as terministic ontology, the pentad offers a way of seeing how rhetors' worldviews weave themselves through their rhetoric.

ONTOLOGY AND/OF THE ARCHIVE

I want to conclude by considering how these musings on ontology might speak to our archival practices within rhetorical studies. In a 1999 *College English* forum on the topic, Linda Ferreira-Buckley reminds rhetoricians that their employment of archival materials is not "news": "Archives have long been understood as providing the stuff from which histories are constructed" (578). And over the past several decades, (re)examinations of methods for producing histories and historiographies of rhetoric have focused much attention on explaining how archival work can help scholars construct responsible histories. But rhetoricians who use the archives to illuminate the concepts of rhetoric *theorists* (as many in this collection do) have not been as vocal or public in their descriptions and defenses of their archival methods. This essay has aimed thus not only to offer some new perspectives on the debate over the pentad, but also to invite a more explicit discussion of how archival materials can assist in unpacking rhetorical theory. I employ two methods for enriching rhetorical theory through the archive.

In the first section, discussing Burke's emphasis on act, I use the archive to reconstruct the composing process of the *Grammar*. The evolution of the *Grammar* (how it went from thought to paper to revised and completed text) clarifies that the initial focus of the project was on *act*—not as a component of the pentad, but on act *in itself*, with the pentad conceived as a sort of preamble that ended up demanding its own space. In this way the archive unsettles the sense of the *Grammar* as a fixed entity.[9] By reminding us of the materialities and vagaries of writing and revising, archives can reawaken our sense of interpretive freedom, opening texts for further interpretations and creating new possible texts, texts that might have been.

In my second section, arguing for the pentad as terministic ontology, I look to Burke's letters for their varied presentations of the goals of the *Grammar*. Rather than use the archive to undermine the printed text, I try to leverage these individual letters as a source for additive, not corrective, meaning. In his letters Burke presents his project differently to different audiences. Not every re-presentation of his project added to my understanding of the pentad, which underscores how our own goals and perspectives filter what the archives say to us. For example the letter to Richard McKeon, where Burke distinguishes between "Platonizing" and "terministic," jumped out at me because the counterargument Burke predicted was the very one that the scholars raised at the 1982 conference. But another reader would have found something else. Still, I maintain a pragmatic faith that the more variations on the theme of dramatism we read, the better our chance of understanding what Burke was up to. By exposing us to versions of published ideas tailored to specific, often personal, audiences, archival sources can complement our understanding of theorists' printed texts.

One danger of the methods employed in this essay, and a common tendency in archival scholarship of any sort, is to grant the archive the status of "Truth," or at least that of the "better truth." Archival materials are thus privileged over published texts as the "more real"—as a less constructed, less mediated, version of events or ideas. Barbara Biesecker shares this concern over the privileged status of archival materials and quotes Helen Freshwater's reminder that archival texts are as unstable as all the other texts we (more reflectively) use to construct our histories and theories: "Here the archive's inherently textual nature must interrupt our blissful encounter with its contents" (qtd. in Biesecker, "Of Historicity" 126). Balancing the thrill of archival discovery against textual skepticism is a tricky maneuver.

Indeed the temptation abounds to see archives as ontologically real. Our "blissful encounters" with archival sources reassure us (falsely) that this time, we'll definitely get it right, get it straight. I wonder if this was the initial hope, too, of the scholars who found Burke in the audience as they discussed his works in 1982. *There's the man himself: he'll tell us whether we're on the right track.* Of course this exchange did not go as planned. Brock and Simons found themselves confronted with a very real Burke, who insisted they'd gotten it *wrong*. Burke found himself dismayed at how this audience for his published works quickly morphed, in an "ironic development," into "opponents" (Brock et al. 31). To be honest, when I first read this exchange, I was surprised at the audacity of the scholars who insisted on their reading in the face of the ur-text of Burke himself. This reading—steeped in my own assumptions that when Burke says you've gotten Burke wrong, you concede the point—might bespeak our attitude towards archival sources in general.

Yet while I can now admire the audacity of these scholars, I still find the exchange troubling. In response to Burke's opposition, Brock ultimately gave up on the Burke he'd met in the *Grammar* and whose dramatism inspired his own work. The conclusion that Burke had just changed his mind over the years did allow Brock to continue to read the *Grammar* in the way that made it most useful and valuable for him. But it prevented him from exploring the possibility of using both perspectives simultaneously; that is, it prevented him from hanging on to the paradox and ambiguity while also taking seriously Burke's claim that the system was ontological. In using the archive to revive both Burkes, I hope I've shown that what we find in the archive need never overdetermine our readings. Instead the more we have to "cope with," the more resourceful we can and must be.

The academic hankering for the archive as the Real becomes almost paradoxical in the case of rhetorical studies. As rhetoricians we have a distrustful relationship with concepts like reality, truth, and literality—and yet we long for our scholarship to get down to what Burke or other theorists "really" meant. We long for language itself to have some power over (or at least contact with) the real, the true, the literal. This paradox emerges front and center in the historical and contemporary debates over how to read the pentad, and dramatism. Those who first resisted Burke's categorization of dramatism as ontology feared losing the Burke who undermined literal approaches to language and thus helped show that language builds the world—it does not just reflect it. But the more recent defenders of Burke's claims to ontology belie their own discomfort with the place of rhetoric (as a phenomenon and a field) vis-à-vis reality.

In order to defend dramatism as ontology without giving up prized aspects of Burke's theory, scholars have to redefine, even water down, ontology. (My own argument, positioning Burke's ontology as "rhetorical" or "terministic," makes just such a move.) In doing so, we drain the venom of ontology at the risk of also draining its power. Thus one defender of ontology criticizes another of having "sacrificed too much" in his redefinitions of ontology and literality (Rountree, "Revisiting"). The old guard feared granting dramatism the status of ontology because it seemed so literal and inflexible; the new guard fears diluting ontology so much that the power of symbolic action itself is undermined, along with dramatism and the pentad. But the fear of a domesticated ontology need only intimidate those who refuse Burke's ultimate challenge: to see language as nonrepresentational yet still constitutive of human reality. And perhaps this reminder applies as well to archival work. The archive, too, may not bear a direct correlation to Truth; yet it is the stuff our disciplinary truths are made of.

NOTES

1. The author acknowledges the cooperation of the Kenneth Burke Literary Trust for permission to quote from Kenneth Burke's unpublished notes, drafts, and letters. Permission is also granted from Rare Books and Manuscripts, the Pennsylvania State University Libraries, for quotations from unpublished notes and letters in the Kenneth Burke Papers, Rare Books and Manuscripts, Special Collections Library, Pennsylvania State University Libraries.

As is well known, Burke later considered adding a sixth term: attitude. Since Burke never formally did in revision of the *Grammar* and, more importantly, since my project focuses on the initial development of the concept, I concentrate on the original five terms of the pentad.

2. In Crable's account, "Burke thus asserted that dramatism is literal—and implied that dramatism is ontological. The others in the debate assumed that Burke equated those two terms" (324). Crable's argument helpfully explores the potential of reading ontology and literality as two separate characteristics of dramatism.

3. Chesebro's *Communication Quarterly* article and Brock's more recent work continue this trend of reading Burke's system as shifting over time from epistemology to ontology. Burke himself noted a shift from his earlier system of dramatism to his later project of logology (Brock 103). But according to Wess, Burke describes this shift as one from ontology to epistemology—in other words, the exact opposite of what the scholars at the 1982 conference asserted ("Pentadic Terms" 172n1).

4. Over the more than half a century since the pentad was first introduced, both ontological and epistemological interpretations have provided valuable applications of

the concept. Indeed Wess suggests that there may be no need to choose between the two terms. Wess argues that the two concepts entail one another: one cannot make a claim about the nature of reality (ontology) without some justification for how one gains access to knowledge of reality (epistemology); further, a statement of how humans know reality (epistemology) is itself a claim about the nature of that reality (ontology) in the sense that an epistemology is a claim that reality is, in fact, knowable ("Pentadic Terms" 157).

5. It might be helpful to distinguish between "action" as the starting point for Burke's investigation and "act" as one of the five terms of the pentad. Speech about human action tends to break down along the fault lines of the pentad, but that doesn't mean that the fault line of "act" is more important or central than that of "scene." Rather act functions both as the overall genesis for the other terms and then as one of the terms itself. In considering a human act, we understand that act in terms of the pentadic components of act, scene, agency, agent, or purpose, whereas analyzing a scene does not necessarily entail employing the terminology of act, agency, agent, or purpose. Thus, considering the genesis of the *Grammar* illustrates that the centrality of act that Burke discusses in his later work, especially "Dramatism," stems from the fact that the pentad originated as a paradigm for understanding the way we discuss acts.

6. In fact Biesecker maintains that the pentad serves both an epistemological and an ontological purpose (*Addressing* 25). I focus on her ontological reading here because my interest lies in distinguishing between metaphysical and terministic ontologies.

7. However atypical, in his "Pentadic Terms and Master Tropes," Robert Wess defends Burke's ontology as the only kind of ontology possible for a post–linguistic–turn philosopher, comparing Burke and McKeon to show that Burke belongs to that category.

8. Crable's analysis includes a fascinating discussion of the difference between metaphorical and literal speech. Since for Burke all language is metaphorical to some extent, he draws a distinction between metaphors that work through "as" and those that work through "as if." Because we primarily approach other humans "as" persons (a more literal form of metaphor), not "as if" they were machines or animals (a more fictional form), dramatism is the current best account for motivation. But because dramatism, as symbolic action, is undertaken on a scene that is nondramatistic, it might one day find itself outdated, with individuals approaching one another not "as" persons but only "as if" they were persons (Crable 336). At this point, we would need a new motivational calculus, and dramatism would no longer be literal.

9. Burke employs this strategy himself in "Questions and Answers about the Pentad," referring to his revision process in order to clarify a common misunderstanding about the pentad. Burke explains: "The revised version was such that Grammar begins with the pentad that my first draft had ended up with—and that's probably why the use of the pentad in the Irmscher Handbook differs from its use in Burke's Grammar, so that in one case the procedure leads to a text; in the other it starts from a text" ("Questions" 333). Burke's account of his composition process in this piece is discussed in greater detail by Dana Anderson and Debra Hawhee in their contributions to a CCC "Re/Visions" feature that revisited Burke's "Questions and Answers."

WORKS CITED

Anderson, Dana. "Burke Is Dead. Long Live Burke!" *College Composition and Communication* 60.2 (2008): 441–42+.

Biesecker, Barbara. *Addressing Postmodernity: Kenneth Burke, Rhetoric, and a Theory of Social Change.* Tuscaloosa: University of Alabama, 1997.

———. "Of Historicity, Rhetoric: The Archive as Scene of Invention." *Rhetoric and Public Affairs* 9.1 (2006): 124–31.

Brock, Bernard L. "Epistemology and Ontology in Kenneth Burke's Dramatism." *Communication Quarterly* 33.2 (1985): 94–104.

———. "The Evolution of Kenneth Burke's Philosophy of Rhetoric: Dialectic between Epistemology and Ontology." *Extensions of the Burkeian System.* Ed. James W. Chesebro. Tuscaloosa: University of Alabama Press, 1993. 309–28.

Brock, Bernard L., Kenneth Burke, Parke G. Burgess, and Herbert W. Simons. "Dramatism as Ontology or Epistemology: A Symposium." *Communication Quarterly* 33.1 (1985): 17–33.

Burke, Kenneth. "Dramatism." *The International Encyclopedia of the Social Sciences.* Ed. D. L. Sills. New York: Macmillan, 1968. 445–52.

———. "Dramatism talk." 1966. Kenneth Burke Papers, Penn State University, Burke-3, P.19.5.

———. *A Grammar of Motives.* Berkeley: University of California Press, 1945.

———. Letter to Matthew Josephson. Sept. 11, 1940. Matthew Josephson Papers. Beinecke Rare Book and Manuscript Library, Yale University, New Haven, Conn.

———. Letter to Matthew Josephson. Dec. 17, 1941. Matthew Josephson Papers. Beinecke Rare Book and Manuscript Library, Yale University, New Haven, Conn.

———. Letter to Norman Guterman. Nov. 25, 1939. Norman Guterman Papers. Butler Library, Columbia University, New York.

———. Letter to Richard McKeon. May 19, 1942. McKeon Papers. Joseph Regenstein Library, University of Chicago.

———. *The Philosophy of Literary Form.* Berkeley, University of California Press, 1973.

———. "Questions and Answers about the Pentad." *College Composition and Communication* 29.4 (1978): 330–35.

———. *The Rhetoric of Religion: Studies in Logology.* Berkeley: University of California Press, 1970.

Chesebro, James W. "Epistemology and Ontology as Dialectical Modes in the Writings of Kenneth Burke." *Communication Quarterly* 36 (1998): 175–91.

Crable, Bryan. "Defending Dramatism as Ontological and Literal." *Communication Quarterly* 48.3 (2000): 323–42.

Ferreira-Buckley, Linda. "Rescuing the Archives from Foucault." *College English* 61.5 (1999): 577–83.

Hawhee, Debra. "The Squirm." *College Composition and Communication* 60.2 (2008): 442–43+.

Rountree, Clarke. "Coming to Terms with Kenneth Burke's Pentad." *American Communications Journal* 1.3 (1998).

————. "Revisiting the Controversy over Dramatism as Literal." *KB Journal* 6.2 (2010): n. pag.

Wess, Robert. *Kenneth Burke: Rhetoric, Subjectivity, Postmodernism.* Cambridge: Cambridge University Press, 1996.

————. "Pentadic Terms and Master Tropes: Ontology of the Act and Epistemology of the Trope in *A Grammar of Motives.*" *Unending Conversations: New Writings by and about Kenneth Burke.* Ed. Greig E. Henderson and David Cratis Williams. Carbondale: Southern Illinois University Press, 2001. 154–75.

JODIE NICOTRA

NOTES FROM THE ABYSS

Variations on a (Mystical) Theme in Burke's Work

In notes for a review of John Peale and Edmund Wilson's book of short stories *The Undertaker's Garland* (1922), Kenneth Burke reported on a terrible dream: "I had died, yet still was living: I existed as a bit of disembodied mind, alone in the infiniteness of space, nothing but my own abstract identity, without flesh, without surrounding objects, with nothing but a vague sense of nothingness that stretched on forever, through endless space and endless time" (Note P5 2:22). The dream was so frightening and powerful that Burke could not "shake [himself] free" of it for days (P5 2:22). "Indeed," he wrote, "in one sense I shall never perhaps completely do so, for it seems to have been at the very core of me—a sense of the abyss that makes one henceforth take an over-avid delight in the society of living and breathing people, any people" (P5 2:22).[1]

Burke's interpretation of this dream succinctly captures the simultaneous terror and allure of the mystical orientation, recognizable here as the subject of the dream though not directly formulated as such. Even as an encounter with the vast expanse of the universe obliterates the individual human self, it prompts humans to overcome the confines of individuality by pursuing stronger social ties. Or as the familiar final line of *Permanence and Change* (1954) would have us remember, "men build their cultures by huddling together, nervously loquacious, at the edge of an abyss" (272). In fact, though clearly Burke's review of a 1922 book would have been written quite some time before *Permanence and Change*, the fact that the notes for this unpublished piece reside in a folder marked "Miscellaneous notes, *Permanence and Change*, discards, etc." in the Penn State Kenneth Burke Papers suggests that the famous last paragraph of *Permanence and Change*—and indeed Burke's career-long interest in mysticism—may have had decidedly personal underpinnings.

Burke himself was no mystic.[2] As his dream report suggests, he took too great a delight in the "society of living and breathing people" to spend too much time in the company of the universal and ineffable. Nonetheless mysticism as a concept haunted Burke's published work throughout his career; thus while cataloguing his ambiguous, complex, layered relation to mysticism can be "a daunting, vertiginous task," as Debra Hawhee writes (31), it is also certainly a fruitful one. Hawhee herself is one of the few who have written seriously about mysticism in Burke. Her book *Moving Bodies* (2009) examines Burke's use of mysticism in the 1920s and 1930s as a concept that "grew out of his regard for things bodily" (29)—notably from his interest (and that of his Greenwich Village intelligentsia circles) in the mystical dance performances of the Russian mystic G. I. Gurdjieff's Institute of Harmonious Movement, and also in the intellectual meliorism of William James. While Hart Crane, Waldo Frank, Jean Toomer, and other of Burke's contemporaries eventually left mysticism behind for other intellectual ventures, Burke "shaped a kind of political, intellectual, and bodily mysticism more slowly but perhaps more surely" than they (Hawhee 47).

While Hawhee focuses mainly on mysticism as it models Burke's "productivist" approach to bodies, and while other scholars have employed Burkean concepts of mystery and mysticism to explore contemporary communication phenomena,[3] I am more interested in how the rhetorical work that mysticism does for Burke shifts according to his own changing circumstances and orientations.[4] And it is clear throughout his career that, for Burke, mysticism in both its religious and secular guises has a unique persuasive power. As he wrote, along with Stanley Romaine Hopper, in an appendix to "Mysticism as a Solution to the Poet's Dilemma", "Rhetorically considered, Mystery is a major resource of persuasion. Endow a person, an institution, a thing with the glow or resonance of the Mystical, and you have set up a motivational appeal to which people spontaneously . . . respond" (105). But perhaps the most interesting dimension of Burke's treatment of the mystical is how it highlights the ambiguity inherent to mysticism itself. More than a vaguely intriguing "glow or resonance," the mystical can also function to create discord in the form of an alien perspective that helps to correct piety and to right faulty orientations. On a social or collective level, it can serve as a more fundamental solace when the state (or the market) demands unreasonable things from people in the name of patriotic sacrifice. However the ineffability associated with mysticism can also serve to *mystify*—to persuade those beholden to a system to acquiesce without protest. At various points in Burke's career, mysticism performs all of this rhetorical work. In other words, "mysticism" as a concept is contextual, functioning differently in different situations.

Archival work—the most basic aim of which is to unveil what is hidden from the sight of the typical reader—always brings with it a faint whiff of the occult. It seems especially appropriate, then, to employ the archives as a means of enriching and complicating the understanding of Burke's own often contradictory uses of the concept of mysticism. The letters, notes, marginalia, scrapped material, and unpublished essays that make up the Kenneth Burke Papers at the Pennsylvania State University reveal echoes and layers of other conversations that unfold alongside those works that have been editorially vetted, their contradictions at least partly resolved and smoothed over. Unstructured notes and whole chapters excised from

Permanence and Change; sheaves of annotated passages from thinkers (like Bertrand Russell, Sir James Frazer, D. H. Lawrence, and Maxime Laignel-Lavastine) who clearly influenced how Burke thought about the work of mysticism, but who never or rarely made it into the published work; a variety of correspondences, some showing an earlier Burke working through permutations of mysticism, and some amusingly detailing his unpleasant encounters later in life with the mysticism inherent to bureaucracies: these materials illustrate in much richer detail the development of Burke's thought about a single compelling concept—mysticism—that ultimately took on multiple connotations and performed sometimes contradictory rhetorical functions in his published work. Albeit written to describe a different phenomenon, an analogy by that mystical dabbler William James (whom Burke greatly admired) fittingly describes the relation between archival materials and published works: "The maple and the pine may whisper to each other with their leaves, and Conanicut and Newport hear each other's fog-horns. But the trees also commingle their roots in the darkness underground, and the islands also hang together through the ocean's bottom" ("Confidences" 374). This essay aims to delve into the fecund, messy territory of archival materials that exists beneath the surface of Burke's published works in order to explore these recondite relations. Doing so provides a more contradictory but ultimately richer understanding of a significant concept in Burke' work. But perhaps more important, it also underscores the rhetorical character of concepts, suggesting how we might reenvision them: not as static bits of thought, but as operations that work differently, even within a single thinker's *oeuvre,* according to the frames in which they are placed and the perspectives from which they can be seen.

SEEING AROUND CORNERS: MYSTICISM AS CREATIVE SKEPTICISM

As Ann George and Jack Selzer have pointed out, the primary focus of Burke's work in the 1930s was the concept of orientation. Habituated and often invisible frames of reference that shape thoughts, behaviors, and eventually entire social systems, orientations are inevitable but also dangerous. Considered within this framework, orientations thus necessitate correction. Burke's concepts of metabiology and mysticism both serve the primary purpose of righting faulty orientations. Thus while they function differently, it is useful to consider them together, as complementary. Archival materials, especially the excised chapters and Burke's handwritten and typed notes for *Permanence and Change,* help to clarify and strengthen the links between orientation, metabiology, and mysticism that exist only implicitly in his published work.

As Burke reassures us at the beginning of *Permanence and Change,* "all living things are critics." That is, they have the capacity to correct behaviors and orientations that have proven harmful or problematic—like the trout, which, having once bitten down on a hook, subsequently becomes choosier about its food. Humans of course also have this critical, corrective ability. But because human problems are so much more complex, owing to the "vast network of mutually sustained values and judgments," which "makes it more difficult for them to perceive the nature of the reorientation required, and to select their means accordingly" (*PC* 23), a human's faulty orientations prove to be far trickier to set aright than those of a fish.[5] The difficulty inherent in correcting maladaptive orientations, trained incapacities, faulty means-selection, and various occupational psychoses begat Burke's attempts to find something like a solid ground (that is, permanence) amidst the mutability and contingency of orientations in the rhythms and processes inherent to human biology and social systems.

As he wrote in an excised chapter of *Permanence and Change*, "the methodological questioning of all temporal dogma naturally leads one into the regions wherein is found the 'rock that supports the rock that supports the rock,' and these are the orthodoxes of the body itself" (P5 02:11). The "orthodoxes of the body" here, the immoveable reality of the corporeal, is recognizable as Burke's concept of metabiology—an island of permanence that echoes the mystical orientation. While here such methodological questioning is linked to the body's ostensible unchangeability, the language ("methodological questioning of all temporal dogma") also resonates with traditional practices of mysticism, many of which in fact attempt to deny or deprive the body in order to find a more lasting or transcendent truth.

In any case, while critics have frequently taken metabiology as evidence of Burke's biological essentialism (and indeed given quotations like the one above from the archives, such assessments seem reasonable), Burke himself insisted that this was a misreading. In the 1954 prologue to the second edition of *Permanence and Change* for instance, he wrote, "Even on an empirical basis, a 'Metabiology' needs the corrective of a concern with *social motives as such*. Thus, human kinds of domination and subjection must decidedly never be reduced to the strictly 'natural' or 'biological'" (li). Burke sympathizers have likewise used his published work and archival materials to prove that metabiology does not automatically equal reductive biological essentialism. Bryan Crable for instance demonstrates how Burke's concept of "recalcitrance"—the nonsymbolic aspects of the world that are left out of any orientation—rescues metabiology from charges of essentialism. Crable uses Burke's own case of the Pacific Northwest tribe whose culture has been perennially fishing-oriented as an example of how recalcitrance works. The sickening of the tribe from eating fish that are now being poisoned by the factories upstream serves as evidence of an orientation that has become defective, the recalcitrant element in the system being the poison itself. This recalcitrance, Crable argues, "is the critical edge to Burke's discussion of orientation and metabiology, the point which differentiates Burke's *Permanence and Change* from an extreme perspectivist position" (313). Though Burke went to great lengths to establish the variability of orientations, he was ultimately more concerned with providing tools to critique them. For him this necessitated finding some sort of solidity, even if that solidity was merely a recalcitrant element of a given orientation.

Mysticism occupies a position similar to the recalcitrance of metabiology in Burke's earlier work in that it provides an opportunity for critique. In a letter to Burke, the psychologist William Galt of the Lifwynn Foundation (various members of which had been corresponding with Burke) wrote, "You speak of feeling that the only way to avoid symbolic manipulation is in the study of the mystic trance. It seems to me that this position has much to recommend it if we can approach it free of the dissociative attitude of its habitual devotees" (WG to KB December 15, 1934). This and other appearances of mysticism in the Burke archives suggest that more than a recalcitrant, nonsymbolic element *within* the system, mysticism provides a stance or position *outside* of the earthly realm. In an unpublished discussion of a Sidney Hook article about the Young Hegelians, Burke argues that the problem with critiquing history from within is that one must rely on the same form of reasoning that constitutes the historical process itself, thus producing a tautology. This is where Burke sees mysticism as useful: "Again: we begin to see more clearly now that the so-called 'rational' movement really involved the criticism of history *from within,* whereas the 'mystic' reaction attempted to establish a point of reference *outside* the historical process" (P5 2:10). Though mystics' attempts to get "outside" of history were typically characterized as flight or escape (by Marxists, we can assume, given Burke's concerns of the time), Burke argued that "this is only true in the sense that one may 'flee' to a point or vantage from which to renew his attack with the protection of stronger entrenchments" (P5 2:10).

Part of what positions mysticism in its vantage point outside the historical process is its inherent skepticism. Mystics are always looking for what Burke called elsewhere a "beneath-which-not" (*PLF* 161). Distrusting the superficial, shifting contingencies of orientation and speech, mystics are therefore always attempting to "[see] around the corner of our accepted verbalizations" (*PC* 222). While Burke acknowledges later that this itch to see beyond or beneath accepted orientations or viewpoints might happen to anyone at any time, "even in an era that has great fixity for most people" (*ATH* 57), as an inherently skeptical perspective, mystical practice flourishes uniquely as a *collective* movement in times when "traditional ways of seeing and doing (with their accompanying verbalizations) have begun to lose their authority" (*PC* 223). Collective mysticism "belongs to periods marked by a great confusion of the cultural frame, requiring a radical shift in people's allegiance to symbols of authority" (*ATH* 57–58). Burke uses the examples of the Hellenistic period, the Reformation, and his own between-wars Depression era in *Attitudes toward History* in order to prove that skepticism (and along with it, mysticism) can be expected to increase exponentially in periods where orientations have been proven faulty.

But unlike that skepticism which can devolve into mere nihilism during times of social upheaval, the skepticism of the mystic is *creative*—or to use a more Burkean vocabulary, *poetic.* And what it creates are new orientations, new ways of seeing. As Burke explains, during periods of "a dying code," when old orientations are falling apart, the mystic's skepticism "is a scheme of 'organized doubt' developed and intensified, not for reasons of *complaint,* but for the ends of *practical guidance*" ("Ends and Means" 61).

Such a skeptical attitude of collective mysticism requires a specific mechanism in order to create new attitudes, however, and Burke terms this mechanism the *grotesque,* a transitional mode that "focuses in mysticism" (*ATH* 57). Mysticism and the grotesque go hand-in-hand during times of collective upheaval: the grotesque is at once both the manifestation of the mystical attitude and that which spurs the creation of new ways of seeing. The grotesque is always there but appears primarily "when confusion in forensic pattern gives more prominence to the subjective elements of imagery than to the objective, or public elements" (60). In other words, when the "public frame" or superstructure is strong and "rich with satisfaction," it sufficiently distracts from or suppresses the incongruities and discordances of the grotesque (*ATH* 61). But when the public frame is thrown into confusion, the symbolic or subjective elements of the grotesque come to the fore.

Unlike humor, which produces incongruities that are then relieved by laughter (a function that ultimately makes humor a conserver of the social order), in the grotesque "the perception of discordancies is cultivated without smile or laughter" (*ATH* 112). Above all the grotesque seems to be *uncomfortable*—an unresolved, irresolvable meshing of discordant elements, a gargoyle—and this is the basis of its revolutionary potential, Burke argues.[6] The discomfort of the grotesque spurs attempts to relieve it, many of which can be seen in artistic attempts: Burke explicitly mentions the surrealist paintings of unfunny "soft clocks," shocking in their depictions of a different symbolism or conception of the function of time. Others aim to create a physical sense of space that might resolve the dissonance of the grotesque: the "strange lonely landscapes" of the surrealists (*ATH* 58), and the attraction of poets to mountain imagery ("people atop magic mountains, or poets clambering over mother-mountains . . . or being drawn towards magnetic mountains" [*ATH* 62]).[7] By allowing clashing elements to remain unresolved, the grotesque can invoke a discord that might shake people out of habituated reactions; and in this way it is the creative tool of mysticism.

SEEING AROUND THE COMMERCIAL ETHIC: MYSTICISM AS "A MORE FUNDAMENTAL SOLACE"

But the archives reveal a still more specific need for the jangling discord of the mystical, one that barely appears in Burke's published works. The notes and unpublished chapters of *Permanence and Change* reveal that in Burke's earlier thinking, mystical skepticism proves to be most useful in times when institutions such as the state and the market actively attempt to veil their own greed-driven motives with noble-sounding calls for patriotism and self-dignity. And while the discord produced by the grotesque-mystical and the desire to "see around the corners" of established thought obviously helped with identifying the "real" motives of these institutions, mysticism in Burke's earlier thought also served as a kind of safety valve—a realm beyond rational thought that gave some recourse to citizens who felt that they could not escape the pressing-in of institutional agendas.

In one folder that contains his notes for *Permanence and Change* for instance, Burke has typed out a long passage by Sir James Frazer in which Frazer critiques the ancient Greeks as having allowed themselves to be "corrupted" by "the spread of Oriental religions," rejecting as heroes those patriots who would sacrifice themselves for their country and embracing those (like monks and recluses) who sought union with God. As a result, Frazer wrote, "the centre of gravity, so to say, was shifted from the present to a future life, and however much the other one would have gained, this one lost heavily by the change. A general disintegration of the body politic set in" (qtd. in Burke P5 02:09). In other words, says Frazer, by focusing on the otherworldly and the mystical, these citizens tended to elevate their own spiritual interests above the common good, resulting ultimately in the disintegration of the polis. But countering Frazer's assessment, Burke asked whether it might not be the reverse: that citizens turned to mysticism as "a more fundamental solace" because the state was demanding patriotic sacrifice from them for its own self-serving interests. That is, whereas Frazer viewed the Greeks' turn to mysticism as decadent and irresponsible, Burke saw it as a creative solution to an impossible situation in which the people of Greece knew they were being manipulated yet could do little as recourse except turn to the Beyond or extra-worldly.

The Greeks served as a historical analogy to the state in Burke's own era, which, as he wrote, "asks of a very man very much the kind of 'unselfish sacrifice' in the interests of private wealth as service to the Roman state seems to have done" (P5 02:09). Given these circumstances, Burke asked, "need we be surprised to note again the search for a 'rock' upon which one's objections to the demands of the circumambient ethic can be founded?" (P5 02:09). By focusing attention on that which was beyond the concerns of the immediate world with its compromised ethics, the creative skepticism of mystic practice provided a means by which citizens could reject manipulation or parasitism by the state.

But even more than the subterfuged aims of the state, Burke identifies the commercial ethic as that which in his own time necessitated the most solace and the biggest dose of mystic skepticism.[8] The folders of unstructured notes and unpublished chapters of *Permanence and Change* reveal a recurrent connection between Burke's discussions of mysticism and his analysis of the commercial ethic that is practically invisible in his published work. In notes for *Permanence and Change* for instance, Burke wrote: "The mystic is 'world-weary in precisely the sense that one could be called 'world-weary' if he set out to prove that an ethic is assinine [*sic*] which (a) compelled him to spend the best years of his life in some department-store slum, and (b) made it impossible for him to get a job there. . . . Such 'wounds' are now magnificently handed out to us in the very texture of our living. About us are bound the belts of nails called 'progress,' 'efficiency,' and 'profit.' We do not need as goading the 'inner voice' or strange exceptional sorrows-the neurological and emotional inadequacies in the very structure of living which the 'commercial ethic' imposes upon us are 'guidance' enough" ("Ends and Means" 65–66).

Perhaps the need for mystical skepticism *and* solace here has to do with the difficulty of shaking capitalist orientations, which are motivated by powerful drives toward personal gain. In another unpublished chapter of *Permanence and Change*, Burke uses the example of J. P. Morgan, who apparently during the Depression allowed food to rot and machines to sit idle while people were starving because he could not let go or "see around the corner" of his capitalist piety: "Mr. J. P. Morgan reaffirmed his faith in our earlier values, literally preserved in every detail. . . . In either the broader or the more economically applicable aspects of a 'given faith,' we may find such intensive reaffirmation precisely at the moment of collapse" (P5 02:11). The "earlier values" referred to here were those innate to capitalism: expand and make money at any cost. These worked fine at a time earlier in the century when a critical mass of the country was flush with cash and high on the concepts of expansion and progress. However such values make little sense once the social and historical situation radically changes as it did during the Depression. In this passage, Burke suggests that a strong dose of mystic skepticism would have served to shake the "given faith" of Morgan's capitalist piety.

Luckily, however, the very inanity of the commercial ethic is also what makes it so ripe for rethinking or reseeing. As Burke notes, "The moral superstructure of the 'commercial ethic' being complete, misleading, and inane, its very inadequacies can be turned into a benefit, if they drive us back to a concern with *sources*. These sources are in the body, the body's basic relationship to other bodies, and the relation of them all to the universal body" ("Ends and Means" 62). The commercial ethic is a temporal thing that pulls apart at the seams to reveal the flimsiness of the fabric. Thus, while compelling, it can prompt a mystical response, an attempt to see around the corner of the inanity of the commercial orientation and to seek solace in permanent things, or at least things on a larger scale. (By analogy, many contemporary critics of consumer capitalism—Thomas Frank, Stuart Ewen, Michael Moore—serve as secular mystics of the sort Burke diagnoses here.)

In general then the mystical in Burke's early work seems to serve a positive or useful purpose. As a perspective so alien to those of the earthly realm, mysticism provides a natural place for critique and an escape from the senseless piety of the commercial ethic. However even this early work contains intimations that mysticism is more troublesome than it would initially seem. As Burke discovered in the terrible dream recounted at the beginning of this essay, the abyss is not something external to us, but an "awful internal chasm (Eliot: 'we are the hollow men'), a sense of distance, division, or vertigo" (*PC* 146)—something that lies "at the very core" of one (P5 2:22). This sense of division within oneself, of not being fully unified, or being dwarfed by something that (though ironically it is inside oneself) is other-than-human, outside of human control. Thus the unknown realms of the mystical are potentially as dangerous as they are useful. And it is this danger inherent in the mystical that becomes more apparent in the work of Burke's later career, after a traumatic bodily encounter with the bureaucratic forces-that-be exposed him to a mysticism of a different (and less poetic) sort.

MYSTICISM AS MYSTIFICATION: THE ANAESTHETIC REVELATION OF KENNETH BURKE

Both financially and physiologically, 1956 was a difficult year for Burke. In October of that year, he underwent what was supposed to be only minor surgery for a hernia; or, as he put it rather more colorfully in a letter to David Mandel, "[I] was in the House of Hospitality, having my balls cut out, or thereabouts" (KB to DM November 22, 1956). As his sardonic characterization suggests, Burke's ostensibly "minor" surgery turned out to be fairly traumatic—a fact that he epistolarily grumbled about to any correspondents who would listen: Mandel, Virginia Holland, George Knox, Howard Nemerov, Salem Slobodkin, Daniel Fogarty, and James Sibley Watson, among others. First, as he explained to Watson, the "almost picturesquely forgetful" surgeon, having apparently forgotten about the scheduled surgery, was eating breakfast twenty miles away while Burke lay on the operating table, under anesthesia but still vaguely conscious of the situation—furious, as one might imagine, but prevented from expressing his anger by the anesthetics (KB to JSW October 9, 1956). To make matters worse, in his postoperative hospital stay, Burke experienced terrible insomnia, a combination of the toxic aftereffects of a larger-than-planned dose of anesthesia and insufficient doses of sleeping pills. "Despite my pleas for soporifics in the hospital," Burke wrote to Watson, "for some godam [*sic*] reason the bastard let me sweat it out—and I spent several days and nights when, at most, I must have slept in snatches." He consequently explained, "for several days thereafter, the world was [a] /damned queer place to me. What I thought was a neurosis was purely and simply one hell of a drug-laden hangover" (KB to JSW October 9,1956).

However the experience turned out to be productive in at least one sense. Being "still quite loaded with bits that need carrying off" and with "testicles . . . as purple as indelible ink" (KB to JSW October 9, 1956), Burke used his run-in with the bureaucratic powers-that-be to churn out "an 8,500 word monstrosity"(KB to HN October 16, 1956) called "The Anaesthetic Revelation of Herone Liddell." First published in the *Kenyon Review* in 1957, this fifty-nine-page piece was also included in Burke's 1958 book of short stories, *The Complete White Oxen*. Though clearly Burke intended for the piece to be read as fiction, "The Anaesthetic Revelation of Herone Liddell" might be better thought of as part diary entry and part essay, a venue in which Burke could use his own experience to further develop—and perhaps correct—his earlier thought about the rhetorical work of mysticism.

The title of Burke's "what-is-it," as he called "The Anaesthetic Revelation of Herone Liddell," alludes to a thirty-seven-page-pamphlet titled *The Anaesthetic*

Revelation and the Gist of Philosophy, written in 1874 by an amateur philosopher from upstate New York named Benjamin Paul Blood. Blood's pamphlet was his first brief attempt at creating a metaphysical system to account for a mystical awakening that he experienced upon coming out of a nitrous oxide stupor during a tooth extraction at the dentist's. A tireless promoter of his own work, Blood sent his pamphlet to a number of Victorian notables, including Alfred Tennyson, Ralph Waldo Emerson, and Henry James Sr., the father of William and Henry Jr. William James, having acquired Blood's pamphlet from his father, was intrigued enough to write a review of it for the *Atlantic Monthly* in 1874. Subsequent to the appearance of James's review of *The Anaesthetic Revelation and the Gist of Philosophy,* James and Blood struck up an epistolary friendship that spanned the length of James's career. Though Blood lacked the legitimacy of a connection with a scholarly institution, his work exerted a strange power over James, who later wrote of *The Anaesthetic Revelation,* "I forget how it fell into my hands, but it fascinated me so 'weirdly' that I am conscious of it having been one of the stepping-stones of my thinking ever since" ("A Pluralistic Mystic" 173). Indeed, James's last publication before his death in 1910 was an encomium to Blood in which he wrote, "Let *my* last word, then, speaking in the name of intellectual philosophy be *his* word" ("A Pluralistic Mystic" 190; emphasis in original), thus, ending his final piece of published writing with a cheeky quotation from Blood.[9]

Burke had been aware of Blood since the 1920s: an unpublished essay titled "Some Aspects of the Word," probably written around 1921 (Selzer 216 n64), refers to Blood as "our spotty native philosopher, our Walt Whitman of metaphysics" (6).[10] In brief Blood's anaesthetic revelation is what the mystical tradition calls a "unitive experience," where the individual experiences a feeling of profound and absolute connection to the universe. Blood claimed—in grand, though somewhat tortured prose—to have realized the shortcomings in philosophy's attempts to produce discursive knowledge about the universe, a way of knowing that automatically creates distance between the knower and the known. In the passage from which Burke undoubtedly gets the name "Herone Liddell" ("little hero"), Blood declared, "Faith comes not by doubtful tests, but is ever a foregone conclusion. It arrests us rather than is assumed by us. Its dignity and courage are simply divine, 'the gift of God,' and according to nought besides; especially may I say, not according to knowledge. Courage as by knowledge is in a sense of safety, in which courage has no part; for the more definite sense of safety, the less merit of courage. Your bully Samson, and Marcius, and Wallace, and Plantagenet, safe in their knowledge of superior strength and address, shall not be mentioned *with many a little hero* who, divinely resentful of accidental advantages, and having no hope of a successful battle, would yield only his life" (32–33; emphasis added). Here is mystical experience par excellence: the Truth of the universe comes not from rational knowledge or subjective will, but arrives from beyond, "arresting" us. The "little heroes" are those who have the courage to abandon this subjectively attained knowledge and rely on that which comes as a "gift of God." Or as James summarized Blood's point more pithily in his 1874 review of *The Anaesthetic Revelation:* "What we are, we are, whether we be aware of it or not! The stuff of which we and our universe are made cannot be helped by knowledge. . . . whether for weal or woe its inmost equality or meaning *is* already, nor can all our complacent recognition confirm or clinch it" (Review 627–28). What Blood's anaesthetic revelation revealed, in other words, was that our typical attempts to *understand* the world using our intellect and rationality were insufficient, if not altogether pointless. Blood argued that contrary to this traditional philosophical approach, a more effective mode of relation would be through a sort of prediscursive intuition that could enable an individual to grasp reality on a more affective, bodily level.

What seemed to strike James—and later Burke, though perhaps not quite so positively—about Blood's description was the idea of a prediscursive, ineffable relation to the universe. Drawing on Blood's description of the anaesthetic revelation and supplemented by his own experiences with nitrous oxide, James defined the primary characteristic of mystical experiences as their *ineffability,* or the inability for an individual who has experienced a mystical awakening to talk about it or describe the experience in a way that would make it accessible to another person's understanding. Of course the ostensible ineffability of experience has never stopped anyone from trying to convey it, a paradox summed up neatly by Joshua Gunn: "'The Truth is ineffable, but let me tell you about it anyway'" (50).

Burke's notes for *Permanence and Change* suggest that he was interested in such ideas of mysticism as an ineffable experience early on.[11] But in his published work, Burke barely mentions ineffability, having apparently decided to focus on the rhetorical and political functions of mystical skepticism and the grotesque. After the hernia operation however the ineffable does indeed have a much more pronounced presence in his discussions of mysticism—and it takes on a decidedly gloomier cast. While the title of "The Anaesthetic Revelation of Herone Liddell" might initially appear to pay homage to Blood's pamphlet, in the story (and the archival materials) it becomes clear that Burke ultimately rejects Blood's and James's enthusiasm for the intuitive, prelinguistic relation between the individual and the universe celebrated by Blood's pamphlet. Like Blood, the protagonist of Burke's story also experiences the inability to communicate under anesthetics. But far from delighting in the intoxicated individual's ability to bypass what both Blood and James would see as the flimsiness of human rationality or intellect in favor of a deeper, more intuitive grasp of reality, the inability to communicate in Herone Liddell's (a.k.a. Kenneth Burke's) case has serious ethical ramifications.

In Burke's story the protagonist Herone recounts the simultaneous rage and impotence that came from being strapped down, forced to stare at the harsh light above the operating room table, and completely unable to articulate himself. Most frustrating for the self-described "Word-man" was his inability at the moment to *communicate* his rage: "Outwardly, the resources of hating were reduced to mere

cursing—but even that outlet in turn was reduced, by the aphasic conditions resulting from the amount of anaesthetics already in his system, to ineffectual words that
somehow refused to come out right. Things were so set up that, if wanting to call
someone a filthy bastard, he would at most hear himself, as though from within
himself, shouting as though from outside himself, 'oo lya snar!'" (*Complete White
Oxen* 258). Burke's description of the aphasia produced by the anesthetics ironically
echoes James's catalogue of the characteristics of mystical experience (such as the
giddy aphasia produced by nitrous oxide inhalation). But while there was a nonlinguistic experience of reality here, it was not a very empowering one—certainly not
"a gift of God."

Language shapes Herone's experience in another way. Where Blood's encounter
with the anesthetic revelation produced a wordless knowledge, Herone's took the
form of what he called an "epistemological fever dream" in which language figured
very prominently. The dream consisted of a vision of symmetrically arranged rods
of white light, what in his dream Herone names a "Radiant Quincunx." Along with
the vision, Herone hears a solemnly pontificating voice providing the dreamer with
a "rock bottom explanation" of things; the glowing rods were intended not simply
to represent or to model the way the universe was constructed, but they were in the
dream "a revelation of the literal basic fact" of reality (*Complete White Oxen* 271). So
what immediately differentiates Herone's fictional revelation from Blood's has to do
with language.

While both Blood's and Herone's revelations could be described as "pedagogic,"
given that they teach the experiencer something about the nature of reality, only
Herone's revelation is *narrated*: it relies upon a Voice to explain what's happening.
Implicit in Burke's piece, then, is the idea that language is a necessary aspect of the
interpretation of experience and our understanding of reality. The Voice in Herone's dream goes on to explain that something went wrong with the functioning
of this device that reveals the very nature of reality; and in the course of repairing
the device, it became apparent that one could view it from many different angles
instead of just a single perspective. Hence the interpretation of reality suddenly
becomes more complicated. Though one might point out that this description still
assumes is the existence of a singular reality, this reality can no longer be viewed
objectively. Rather one suddenly becomes aware of the many other possible perspectives from which it might be interpreted: "One might become more exacting
still, and contend that realism could not prevail in its Simon Pure state except prior
not only to all taliation but even to all speech. Thus, the 'truly' realistic vision of the
Design was impaired as soon as the Absolute Voice entered the situation (which it
did almost at the very start of the dream as he remembered it). Implicit in the Voice
would be the *dialogue*; and implicit in the dialogue would be the *dramatic personae*
of different points of view, the 'perspectival' element" (*Complete White Oxen* 275).
In other words, as soon as one considers the social networks—the dialogue—in
which the symbol-using animal is inevitably immersed, the pure, nonlinguistic

individual grasp of reality falls apart. To admit that humans are social beings above all is to automatically complicate the pure, ineffable relation between the individual and the universe.

Burke's rewriting of the anaesthetic revelation thus contains an implicit critique of what he calls the "realist" philosophy of Blood and James because such realism disregards the individual's position as a social, symbol-using animal. By failing to take these social and economic networks into account, this realist philosophy ironically works in the favor of bureaucratic and institutional forces; bureaucracies by nature are grateful for anything that looks like silent compliance by those constituents whom they ostensibly serve. In other words, the mysticism inherent to the realist philosophy serves a *mystifying* function here. Or as Burke writes, "Where there is bureaucracy, 'realism' combines with absoluteness and authority, to suppress inspection. It requires, first of all, an act of *faith*. One must put himself trustingly in the hands of those who 'know best.' He must take things at face value" (277).

Bureaucracies thus thrive on mysticism. For example, as Burke points out, at some level actually curing a patient runs counter to a doctor's best interests because the doctor loses business when the patient is cured. However because the entire medical bureaucracy operates on the basis of this paradox, the patient has little choice but to go along with the charade and hope that the doctors will hold to their Hippocratic oath. Or as Burke told Watson, "As the little woman said, in connection with our experiences in this case, whereas the rules of the hospital are supposedly for the protection of the patient, they are actually used rather as a protection for the doctor" (KB to JSW October 9, 1956). With a system that relies upon the generation of mystery about itself in order to keep operating, rational examination of that system is strongly discouraged. Burke writes: "But insofar as the physician's professional manner (with all the corresponding hierarchy of attendance by interns and nurses) is accepted realistically, *simpliciter, uno intuito,* as equitable with the poise, authority, competence, dignity, and professional goodwill that it proclaims on its face, then the patient is enfolded in a Grand Mystique of Absoluteness, calling for silence, and obedience, and readiness to pay. Something untoward may have happened? Try and find it! Indeed, try by questioning even to prove to yourself that it did *not* happen—and the wall of the Grand Mystique was just as impenetrable" (*Complete White Oxen* 277–78). In this sense the ineffability of mystical experience described by Blood and James has a function that is detrimental to what we might call the individual subject of an institution. In Burke's eyes the notion that rational understanding or discursive explanations of reality should be bypassed in favor of a more intuitive, nonlinguistic grasp of reality is not only naïve, it is dangerous: it forgets the symbol-using animal's complete immersion in and imbrication with the social, institutional, and economic interests that so powerfully shape the individual's relation to reality.

Etymology here might also shed some light on the matter. *Mystes*, the Latin root of the word "mystic," literally means "to close the lips or eyes" (*OED*). Such a closing off of the human sensory equipment, according to the mystic tradition, is necessary to open the individual to the unearthly realms from which Truth emanates. However Burke's anaesthetic "revelation" cautions us that one closes oneself off to these worldly, human networks of symbolic interactions at one's peril. While you are off wordlessly communing with the universe, the hospital may be bilking you for everything you've got. While undoubtedly of a gloomier cast than Burke's previous uses of mysticism, then, this view provides a useful counterpoint, one that ultimately serves to enrich and complicate our understanding of this concept's rhetorical field of operations.

CONCLUSION: HAUNTED BY THE ECOLOGY OF CONCEPTS

I conclude by considering what might be gained by initiating a dialogue between archival materials and published work. I especially want to call attention to how such a dialogue can help us to see how a single concept such as mysticism can operate differently at different times over the course of one thinker's work. My interest is not to reconcile via some Hegelian synthesis the different ways that the concept of mysticism operates in Burke's work. Nor is it to connect Burke's changes in the use of mysticism with the details of his biography (though certainly we can see in the case of "Herone Liddell" that his experience perhaps drove home for him a different, less positive function of mysticism). Rather I believe an examination of this sort leads to a conclusion that Burke himself would likely endorse: the idea that concepts are not static and immobile entities but dynamic, operational bits of thought. Put another way, concepts like mysticism exist rhetorically, and they always contain within them the possibility of functioning *differently* in different circumstances—when inserted into different frameworks of thought and experience (orientations) for instance, or when seen from different perspectives.

Perhaps it is possible through a close reading of Burke's published work alone to appreciate how mysticism took on different roles over the course of his career. However when the published work is considered in a dialogue with all of that subterranean material that had been expurgated from, was supplementary to, or was simply tangential to the material that had been sanctioned by the publishing process (a process that is itself entirely dependent on place and historical circumstance), it offers us a way to "see around corners" of the accepted, certified readings of a concept—those of the author as well as the host of people who influenced the shape of the work as it wended its way toward publication. Indeed, could we not ascertain via the Kenneth Burke Papers that Burke's interest in mysticism stemmed not only from the nascence of his intellectual life but also from something as personal as a difficult-to-shake nightmare, we would risk overlooking a great deal. Especially given the plethora of concepts in Burke, it is understandable how we might see mysticism, as many Burke scholars indeed have, as just one more concept in the jumble. But studying the relationships between archival materials and published work concerning particular concepts can yield a clearer vision of the ecology with which these concepts are entangled and from which they are inseparable. It can provide a sense for how they are as enmeshed in a larger intellectual system's operation as the often-concealed networks that produce and make visible the food that sustains us, or as the root systems of trees that, though invisible from the surface, commingle in silent communication in the darkness underground.

NOTES

1. In good Hegelian fashion, Burke consciously invented a fiction to serve as a conscious "counter-myth" to the sense of the abyss that the dream left behind that suggests that even from early on he was "haunted by ecology": "I thought of living things as having their roots in nature, of these roots stretching out through all infinity, and of their taking satisfaction in the final, living affirmations of the particular earthly body with which they were associated. And I further assured myself that when that particular life, in which they were associated, had ended, they became parts of other systems, and thereby they always shared something of the earth's flesh and sunlight" (P5 2:22).

2. A fact bemoaned by Waldo Frank, who in a letter to Burke that contained a critique of Burke's manuscript of *Permanence and Change* wrote, "I realize, however, that all the 'criticism' of you comes down to my quarrel with you as not being a mystic" (Frank to Burke September 30, 1934).

3. Hawhee's focus on mysticism in Burke's earlier work is unique in that most Burke scholars who discuss the concept do so within the context of *A Grammar of Motives* (1945) and *A Rhetoric of Motives* (1950), the books that are perhaps most familiar to scholars of rhetoric. Bronwyn Law-Villjoen, for instance, writes about Burke's equation of mysticism with purpose in her unpublished dissertation "Haunted Itineraries" (2003). Other scholars, such as John Meyer (1996), use these concepts as tools to analyze contemporary communication phenomena. Meyer employs Burke's concept of "mystery" from the *Grammar* to suggest how communication might be improved within organizations. While mystery as described by Burke can impede communication by introducing an element of "strangeness," Meyer argues that organizations should actually embrace the ambiguity that this strangeness produces because it spurs the completion of tasks and the development of a group identity. Littlefield, Sellnow, and Attansey have shown how this ambiguity can be strategically employed by organizations to specific rhetorical ends—for example, in the Catholic Church's response to the 2004 tsunami. Ashley Mack uses Burke's concept of "mystery" to analyze the contemporary texts of Imam's "I Am African" campaign to raise funds for anti-AIDS vaccines in Africa. However she picks up more on Burke's positing of mystery in the *Rhetoric* as sustainer of social hierarchies, a function that Robert Heath had explored earlier in *Realism and Relativism* (1986).

4. As he moved from a modernist focus on aesthetics and form to an interest in Communist-inflected politics, the Burke of *Permanence and Change* called upon the function of mysticism that enables critique of systems (political and otherwise). In midlife however a perhaps more cynical Burke emphasizes how mysticism serves to produce and sustain ambiguities within organizations and social hierarchies; see Selzer 152–56.

5. Burke's agenda in showing how orientations were created was at least in part to critique what he saw as the too-easy Marxist adhesion to economic materialism as a

determining factor in human behavior. With such a critique, Burke aimed "to restore people's natural sense of themselves as agents" (George and Selzer 130); in this way he advocated "not passive resistance but active, poetic, and rhetorical resistance" (132).

6. Hawhee links the grotesque to Burke's interest in Gurdjieff's dancers. In their explicit attempts to uncover the automatisms of bodily habits, Hawhee points out, the dance performances explicitly aimed to "make the normal and everyday seem very, very strange" (40).

7. The only way to effect a "conversion downwards" of such an "internal chasm," Burke suggested, would be to actually recreate the effect of the abyss externally, by going to high places with sweeping perspectives: mountain-climbing and flight. Indeed the longing for such a perspective on the abyss may be part of the appeal of mountain-climbing literature: "And one who has read accounts of mountain-climbers . . . will have reason to believe that the 'visions' rewarding the seers do not derive merely from the view, but rather the constant dread that animates them as they pick their loose footing above the abyss" (*PC* 141).

8. Indeed in the margins of Burke's above comment about the rejection by the Greeks (via a flourishing interest in mystical practice) of the so-called "patriotic sacrifice" demanded by the Roman state is scribbled the note, "which forces us to question the [aims] of the commercial ethic today" (P5 02:09).

9. "There is no conclusion. What has concluded, that we might conclude in regard to it? There are no fortunes to be told, and there is no advice to be given—Farewell!" (190).

10. Burke of course was also obviously indebted to James, who was an important influence on Burke's earlier work. In fact as Hawhee points out, James begins *Attitudes toward History* more so than Burke, and despite the fact that the other two thinkers in the first chapter—Whitman and Emerson—come chronologically before James, Burke symbolically gives James the more important position by putting him first in the chapter. James's views on mysticism undoubtedly had influenced Burke. According to Hawhee, "James's work provided a handy way for Burke to establish what would be the main cluster of terms in *Attitudes toward History—language, action, frames of acceptance and rejection, attitudes*—and to cast them in the radiant light of mysticism" (48).

11. For instance several passages by Bertrand Russell typed out by Burke imply Burke's interest in the ways that a significant experience adds an affective charge to material that was already there, by a process that Russell calls "inessential secretions": "The definite beliefs at which mystics arrive are the result of reflection upon the inarticulate experiences gained in the moment of insight" (P5: 02:10).

WORKS CITED

Blood, Benjamin Paul. *The Anaesthetic Revelation and the Gist of Philosophy*. Amsterdam, N.Y., 1874.

Burke, Kenneth. *Attitudes toward History*. 3rd ed. Berkeley: University of California Press, 1937.

———. *The Complete White Oxen*. Berkeley: University of California Press, 1968.

———. "Ends and Means of Simplification," ts. Unpublished manuscript. Kenneth Burke Papers. P5, Box 02, Folder 11. Pennsylvania State University.

———. Letter to David Mandel. Nov. 22, 1956. Kenneth Burke Papers. Pennsylvania State University.

———. Letter to Howard Nemerov. Oct. 16, 1956. Kenneth Burke Papers. Pennsylvania State University.

———. Letter to James Sibley Watson. Oct. 9, 1956. Kenneth Burke Papers. Pennsylvania State University.

———. Note, "for Wilson article," ts. Kenneth Burke Papers. P9, Box 02, Folder 22. Pennsylvania State University.

———. Note, "insert towards end of 3," ts. Kenneth Burke Papers. P5, Box 02, Folder 10. Pennsylvania State University.

———. Note on Sir James Frazer, ts. Kenneth Burke Papers. P5, Box 02, Folder 09. Pennsylvania State University.

———. Note, "on Lawrence-Richards," ts. Kenneth Burke Papers. P5, Box 02, Folder 10.

———. Note on Bertrand Russell, ts. Kenneth Burke Papers. P5, Box 02, Folder 10. Pennsylvania State University.

———. *Permanence and Change: An Anatomy of Purpose.* 3rd ed. Berkeley: University of California Press, 1954.

———. *Philosophy of Literary Form.* 3rd ed. Berkeley: University of California Press, 1973.

———. "Some Aspects of the Word." Unpublished essay, 1921. Kenneth Burke Papers. Pennsylvania State University.

Burke, Kenneth, and Stanley Romaine Hopper. "Mysticism as a Solution to the Poet's Dilemma." *Spiritual Problems in Contemporary Literature.* Ed. Stanley Romaine Hopper. New York: Institute for Religious and Social Studies/Harper and Brothers, 1952. 95–115.

Crable, Bryan. "Ideology as 'Metabiology': Rereading Burke's *Permanence and Change.*" *Quarterly Journal of Speech* 84 (1998): 303–19.

Frank, Waldo. Letter to Kenneth Burke. Sept. 20, 1934. Kenneth Burke Papers. Pennsylvania State University.

Galt, William. Letter to Kenneth Burke. Dec. 15, 1934. Kenneth Burke Papers. Pennsylvania State University.

George, Ann, and Jack Selzer. *Kenneth Burke in the 1930s.* Columbia: University of South Carolina Press, 2007.

Gunn, Joshua. *Modern Occult Rhetoric: Mass Media and the Drama of Secrecy in the Twentieth Century.* Tuscaloosa: University of Alabama Press, 2005.

Hawhee, Debra. *Moving Bodies: Kenneth Burke at the Edges of Language.* Columbia: University of South Carolina Press, 2009.

Heath, Robert. *Realism and Relativism: A Perspective on Kenneth Burke.* Macon, Ga.: Mercer University Press, 1986.

James, William. "Confidences of a Psychical Researcher." *Essays in Psychical Research.* Ed. Frederick Y. Burkhardt. Cambridge, Mass.: Harvard University Press, 1986.

———. "A Pluralistic Mystic." *Essays in Philosophy.* Ed. Frederick Burkhardt et al. Cambridge, Mass: Harvard University Press, 1978.

———. Review of *The Anaesthetic Revelation and the Gist of Philosophy. Atlantic Monthly* 33:205 (1874): 627–28.

Law-Villjoen, Bronwyn. "Haunted Itineraries: Tracing Mysticism in William James, Kenneth Burke, and Michel de Certeau." Ph.D. diss., New York University, 2003.

Littlefield, Robert, Timothy Sellnow, and Matthew Attansey. "Mysticism and Crisis Communication: The Use of Ambiguity as a Strategy by the Roman Catholic Church in Response to the 2004 Tsunami." *KB Journal* 3:1 (Fall 2006).

Mack, Ashley. "Keeping the Mystery Alive: Divine and Exotic Discourses in the 'I AM AF-RICAN' Campaign." Conference Papers—National Communication Association. Communication and Mass Media Complete. 2008.

Meyer, John. "Seeking Organizational Unity: Building Bridges in Response to Unity." *Southern Communication Journal* 61 (1996): 210–19.

Selzer, Jack. *Kenneth Burke in Greenwich Village: Conversing with the Moderns, 1915–1931.* Madison: University of Wisconsin, 1996.

Tymoczko, Dmitri. "The Nitrous Oxide Philosopher." *Atlantic Monthly* 277:5 (1996): 93–101.

SCOTT WIBLE

"TALK ABOUT HOW YOUR LANGUAGE IS CONSTRUCTED"

Kenneth Burke's Vision for University-wide Dialogue

In her contribution to this collection, Ann George troubles the claim frequently made by rhetoric scholars that "Kenneth Burke was ahead of his time." George demonstrates that rather than being "dismissed, embattled, misunderstood" by his contemporaries Burke instead prompted vigorous responses from critics and admirers alike who "typically did not perceive his work as irrelevant or inscrutable." George uses archival materials, then, to redefine Burke not as a theorist who "belongs in no time" but rather as one who read, wrote, and organized within specific political and cultural scenes (29–30).

Like George's examination of Burke in the 1930s, this essay leverages archival materials to explore Burke at work within another of his contemporary scenes: the college campus of the 1950s. From 1943 to 1961, Burke served on the literature faculty—teaching every other year—at Bennington College, a liberal arts college in southwestern Vermont that was guided by several key principles of the progressive education movement. The archive at Penn State University holds a host of valuable materials regarding Burke's teaching life, including Burke's 1959 letters to Bennington economics professor George Soule, his comments on student papers, and minutes from a 1950 literature department faculty meeting. These materials can usefully inform recent scholarly efforts to understand the pedagogical relevance of Burke's theories of symbolic action (Enoch; Smudde; Wible). The 2010 essay collection *Humanistic Critique of Education: Teaching and Learning as Symbolic Practice* (Smudde) in particular draws on Burke's published writings as a means for composing educational philosophies, designing progressive curricula, and inventing teaching strategies appropriate for our present political and cultural scenes. The present essay adds depth to these efforts to apply Burke's theories to educational policy and practice, as it uses archival materials to depict Burke teaching and theorizing in his professional scene at Bennington in the 1950s. These archival materials help one to see Burke working in the classroom and in department meetings to foster interdisciplinary dialogue throughout Bennington College, a goal he tried to achieve by enacting the same analytical methods he illustrates in such texts as *Attitudes toward History, The Philosophy of Literary Form, A Grammar of Motives,* and his 1955 essay "Linguistic Approach to Problems in Education."

In his day-to-day life at Bennington, Burke worked strenuously to translate his theories into the college's everyday practice, as he saw his analytical methods having the potential to reshape the routine nature of academic work inside the classroom, within his department, and across the entire college. Burke identified academic specialization in particular as a problem. He perceived scholars and students to be so narrowly focused on mastering a specific discipline's theories and methods that they were unable to examine critically what the discipline's terminology enabled and disabled them from seeing. In both his 1959 letters to Soule and his contribution to the 1950 faculty meeting, Burke proposed his methods of terministic analysis as tools that could unify the university curriculum through an attention to language, helping scholars to see their common ground—as symbol-users—with colleagues in other disciplines.

This essay, then, captures Burke's vision of university life, focusing particularly on Burke's attempts to put his theories into practice. The essay proceeds by first examining two of Burke's theoretical concepts that would ultimately inform his critique of contemporary education. It considers both the "bureaucratization of the imaginative," a formula Burke introduced in *Attitudes toward History,* and Burke's methods of terministic analysis developed in part 2 of *A Grammar of Motives* and, to a lesser extent, in *The Philosophy of Literary Form.* After outlining these two Burkean concepts about how language shapes social action, the essay then draws on archival materials to consider how Burke used these concepts to articulate an alternative theory of education, a vision in which these linguistic theories were brought to life in the space of the classroom and the university. The essay concludes by imagining how Burke's vision of the university might inform and invigorate university life today.

"AN ATTITUDE OF HUMANISTIC CONTEMPLATION": DISRUPTING TERMINISTIC ROUTINE

Burke's critique of modern schooling is grounded in his theory of the "bureaucratization of the imaginative" (*ATH* 225). In *Attitudes toward History,* Burke defines "imaginative" as a term that "suggests pliancy, liquidity, the vernal"—in other words, the potential for a social situation to be arranged in any number of different ways (225). He asserts that the imaginative gets "bureaucratized," however, when one particular possibility is carried out, thereby restricting the chances for other possibilities to unfold. "An imaginative possibility is bureaucratized," Burke explains, "when it is embodied in the realities of a social texture, in all the complexity of language and habits" (225). When "the imaginative" gets bureaucratized, other possibilities are restricted from emerging (225–26). By way of example, Burke discusses how the emergence of the scientific method had bureaucratized the possibilities for discovery about the natural world:

> In the modern laboratory, the procedure of *invention* itself (the very essence of the imaginative) has been bureaucratized. Since the time of the Renaissance, the West has been accumulating and perfecting a *methodology* of invention, so that improvements can now be coached by routine. Science, knowledge, is the bureaucratization of wisdom (228).

Burke's primary concern here is not simply that one particular idea or process gets bureaucratized. Rather Burke worries about the intellectual and cultural consequences of people not being aware that alternative possibilities could exist and that different insights and ways of life could be explored.

Burke draws attention to how people use language to do this work of bureaucratization. As he explains in *A Grammar of Motives,* language is involved at "the 'critical moment' at which human motives take form" (317). These motives direct a person's attention toward particular aspects of a situation and necessarily away from other aspects. For Burke it is important to study how any group uses a discourse rooted in key terms that shape their motivational stances toward situations, toward ideas, and toward other people. In short he believes that people use language without reflecting on how it forms their attitudes and motivations. Burke imagines an alternative possibility for living, then, in which humans heighten their "consciousness of linguistic action generally" (317), so that they remain ever attentive to how linguistic action influences their understanding of the physical and social world.

Burke demonstrates a strategy for heightening "consciousness of linguistic action" in part 2 of *A Grammar of Motives,* a section titled "The Philosophic Schools." In part 1 of the *Grammar,* Burke introduces the analytical terminology of dramatism: Act, Scene, Agent, Agency, and Purpose. In part 2 he explains how five different strands of the discipline of philosophy—Realism, Materialism, Idealism, Pragmatism, and Mysticism—each place a different dramatistic term at the center of their respective terminologies, and he then analyzes how each philosophy's entire terminology gets described in ways that closely relate to the primary grounding term. For example Burke shows how "pragmatist philosophies are generated by the featuring of the term, Agency" (275). He contends that when a pragmatist philosopher considers matters related to Purpose, he will "derive the nature of his terms" for discussing Purpose from the nature of his terms for Agency (128). In other words, because critics strive to create an internally consistent philosophy, the shades of meaning they give to all of their philosophy's terms will be influenced by the primary term they select. Thus Burke sets up a dialectic among the philosophic schools in part 2 of *A Grammar of Motives* to demonstrate how any discipline's central terms influence the meaning of its other key terms and how, in turn, these terms shape the types of statements that scholars in that discipline are likely to make.

This dialectical analysis develops one's "consciousness of linguistic action" (317) by tracing the "*dis*position and *trans*position of terms" as they manifest themselves in different disciplines' vocabularies (402).

Burke provides another glimpse of what it means to sharpen a discipline's understanding of linguistic action in *The Philosophy of Literary Form*. Here Burke examines how the terminology used by literary scholars had effectively bureaucratized the discipline. He describes how the traditional approach to analyzing literature is so narrowly focused on abstractions such as "Truth" and "Beauty" and on studying a literary text "purely within itself ('in terms of' its internal consistency)" (ix) that it encourages people to view literature in only one way: as texts that emerge from writers "poetizing in the middle of nowhere" (ix). As a result scholars rarely perceive how literary discourse, like all forms of language use, makes statements about human motives and persuades readers to make judgments about economic, political, and cultural realities. Burke's project in *The Philosophy of Literary Form*, then, in part involves positioning the terminology of literary studies alongside that of disciplines such as sociology, psychology, and economics. Burke believes that two things could result from such a disciplinary dialectic: one, an alternative theory of how literature operates, namely as "the act of an agent in a non-literary scene" (ix); and two, an alternative terminology for analyzing literature, one that examines "the relationship between literary 'strategies' and extra-literary 'situations'" (ix). Fostering interdisciplinary dialogue, then, enables literary scholars to develop a more rounded approach to analyzing how and why writers use language.

Burke believed the benefits of carrying out this disciplinary dialectic went beyond building more intellectually probing, more linguistically slanted theories of the social world. Burke thought that his analytical method could prompt greater self-reflection among scholars and, through both their scholarly and pedagogical work, ultimately improve human relations. From Burke's perspective, human motives too often take shape as "absurd ambitions," ambitions that necessarily "have their source in faulty terminology" (*GM* 317–18). Rather than being open to analysis of their own "interpretive vocabularies" (Crusius 189), scholars had, in Burke's words, become "zealous in [their] attempt to destroy" the ideas and perspectives of other thinkers (Burke, Response to Louis Carty's essay on realism, 1955). As Timothy Crusius contends, Burke set up this disciplinary dialectic, then, in order to make "any voice in the dialogue 'response-able' to critique" (189). No voice would attempt to destroy any other, and no voice would come under threat of being destroyed. Instead, by situating every discipline's terminology within the dialectic, scholars would come to better understand what each disciplinary perspective affords in relation to others and how together they might help one to create more rounded-out statements about the world.

Equally as important, Burke had faith that this method of terministic analysis would help to foster an attitude of tolerance, cooperativeness, and patience rather than defensiveness and hostility among scholars from different disciplines. Indeed, as Burke contends in *A Grammar of Motives*, "whereas an *attitude* of humanistic contemplation is in itself more important by far than any *method*, only by method could it be given the body necessary for its existence even as an attitude" (319). Carrying out this method, Burke argues, can disrupt the routine use of disciplinary terms and the satisfied, assured attitude that scholars develop through it. Consistently examining each discipline's terministic nature can help scholars discover opportunities for creatively synthesizing analytical frameworks even while being aware of the possibilities for more linguistic foibles to emerge.

It is significant that Burke did not stop at the printed page in his efforts to create a cross-disciplinary dialogue that carefully traces the "disposition and transposition of terms" in each discipline (*GM* 402). Archival materials show how he translated this theory from the pages of *Attitudes toward History*, *The Philosophy of Literary Form*, and *A Grammar of Motives* into his practice as a teacher and faculty member at Bennington College. He taught his analytical techniques to undergraduates at the school and proposed ways for faculty members in all disciplines to undertake this dialectical analysis of disciplinary terminology. He believed such dialogue would develop scholars' awareness of the essentially linguistic nature of the academic enterprise and enable them to examine the social and political motivations embedded within their field's key terms. Moreover he saw this dialogue as a means for all scholars to realize a common intellectual and social purpose, what he describes in *A Grammar of Motives* as "the obligation" for each discipline "to recognize its own presence and . . . influence upon the orbits of our thoughts" (226).

UN-BUREAUCRATIZING THE EDUCATIONAL ROUTINE:

Putting Theory into Practice

Burke viewed schools as bureaucracies, and as a result, he thought of schools, like all bureaucracies, as "diseases, however necessary" (KB to GS February 21, 1959, 11). In a February 21, 1959, letter to his colleague George Soule, Burke declared that "Routine is King" in American schooling (4). He uses this phrase to suggest just how thoroughly this single, school-centered "imaginative possibility" shapes the "language and habits" of education (*ATH* 225). Burke argues in his letter that educational policy focuses on routine to such an extent that schools seem designed simply to help "potentially disorganized citizens keep in line during this essentially chaotic period" of adolescence (KB to GS February 21, 1959, 2). Students and teachers had settled into a patterned educational practice that focused on instilling discipline and rudimentary skills rather than fostering teacher innovation and student creativity.

To highlight the intellectual opportunities that get lost through this bureaucratization of schooling, Burke writes to Soule about an alternative possibility for education: "A teacher is working at something. His project keeps developing. Also, he has a bell. If, at a certain time, he suddenly makes a 'break-through' into some new stage of his theory, and if he feels that he can best tell about it exactly then, he rings his bell, and the students must come running to class. If it's three o'clock in the morning, well—that's that. They must be there, or give the reason why. (They can stand this hardship, they're young. And as a result of this arrangement, they'll participate in the project, exactly when it's vital)" (KB to GS February 12, 1959, 3). Even as he acknowledges "how absurd it is as guidance for an educational policy," Burke maintains that this imagined possibility for schooling might be "the nearest ideal in our complicated structure" (4). Certainly Burke's educational model is an extremely teacher-centered one, with the teachers, not the students, making the intellectual discoveries; the students "participate in the project" only inasmuch as they listen to the teacher lecture about his emerging theories and, when they can, pose questions and offer feedback. Nevertheless, the spur-of-the-moment intellectual development Burke describes here reflects his emphasis on "pliancy" and "the vernal" in his definition of "imaginative" (*ATH* 225). Burke believes it is just this sort of "pliancy" that educational policy needs as a "comic corrective" to schooling's overemphasis on routine. Schools would adhere to a loose schedule that best enables teachers to produce new insights and to foster student creativity by exposing them to these models of emerging innovation.

Beyond this admittedly absurd idea for educational change, however, Burke also offered more pragmatic critiques and approaches to the routinized educational paradigm at work, and it is here that one sees how Burke tried to directly translate his theories of disciplinary dialectic into practice for university life. Extending the arguments he was then making in his published scholarship, Burke sought to address the routine ways that most scholars and students used their discipline's terminology. Each discipline is necessarily grounded in terms that effectively serve as tools scholars use to identify, describe, and analyze phenomena. He believed that many scholars thoroughly assimilated their discipline's vocabulary and then leveraged its theoretical power to churn out one analysis after another. For Burke a fundamental problem was that scholars, and by extension their students, were too often unaware of their respective discipline's terministic grounding and the motivations embedded in the statements scholars within that field could produce. Moreover scholars also lacked awareness of how the language itself enabled them to see the world in only one particular way. To address these concerns, Burke proposed another "imaginative possibility" for schooling, one that promotes more widespread examination of how language use shapes intellectual activity in the university and in the larger social world. Archival materials reveal that Burke proposed solutions to this problem in two ways: through his teaching and through his recommendations for faculty programs.

Burke's Pedagogy for Increasing Awareness of Disciplinary Terminology

During his first eight years of teaching (over a sixteen-year period) at Bennington College, Burke's "Principles of Literary Criticism" and "Language as Symbolic Action" courses focused on teaching students how to analyze language use. Students in Burke's courses wrote essays in which they practiced using methods such as indexing and charting and theoretical concepts such as the dramatistic pentad and terministic screens in order to analyze both literary and critical texts. The Penn State archives include several folders stuffed with Burke's extensive comments on student essays from these courses. These teaching materials show that Burke used his lectures and feedback on writing assignments to help students re-see texts not as arguments to be defended or picked apart but rather as useful artifacts for "study[ing] the problem of language in its bearing upon human relations generally" (Burke, "Language").

While the Principles of Literary Criticism and Language as Symbolic Action courses gave Burke the freedom to teach his analytical methods to students, his experience teaching Prose Writing in the spring 1959 semester lends greater insight to Burke's critique of the work of literary studies and literature departments. A catalog description of the course suggests that Burke's students were not only learning to read and analyze expository texts but also to write creative ones: "PROSE WRITING. To develop precision and variety of expression. At first the emphasis will be upon style, with particular emphasis on modes for condensation. Later the emphasis will be on form, the ways of developing a theme. Both fiction and expository prose will be practiced, and if necessary the class will be subdivided to take care of specific preferences" (*Bennington College Bulletin* 1958–1959, 41). While none of Burke's teaching materials from this particular course appear in the Penn State archives, he did reflect on his experience teaching it in a May 16, 1959 letter to Soule. These remarks reveal that teaching creative writing presented Burke with a different problem than the one he faced in his earlier classes: students used traditional aesthetic principles to talk about what they were trying to do in their writing but did not reflect on the cultural values and meanings these terms carried with them. Burke's comments on teaching Prose Writing provide a useful frame for understanding how he put his theories and methods to use in the classroom as a means to revitalize the university's imaginative energies.

In his May 16, 1959 letter to Soule, Burke expressed his frustration with the fact that so many students in his Prose Writing course tried to produce creative texts that fit aesthetic standards of "beauty" or "truth" but were at the same time unwilling to examine these abstract terms.[1] The Prose Writing students, Burke observed, seemed to believe that creative writing "must traffic in a kind of delicate, half-secretive, half-confessional charades whereby ideas that might be made clear are stated rather in terms of fuzzy images" (1). As a result, "whereas imagery was once used as a way of making ideas more salient, it now becomes used as a way of hiding even a very simple idea behind an imposing veil whereby some trivial peccadillo can look as though it were near the very core of the universe" (1). In other words, students were trying to produce creative writing that escaped the real world and probed seemingly big, important, universal truths. In so doing however they suffered from the same disciplinary blindness that Burke critiqued in *Philosophy of*

Literary Form and *Grammar of Motives;* they fail to acknowledge how their writing emerges from a specific social context.

Burke thought the reason students tried to do this work was clear: they had long been taught to see literature as a unique type of text that emerges wholly within the mental realm, untouched by social and material conditions. Literary scholars and language arts teachers gave students terminology such as "beauty" and "imagination" as tools to evaluate and even guide their composition of creative texts, but in presenting these key terms as abstract aesthetic principles, they failed to prompt students to consider the motivational statements inscribed into literary discourse. Burke argued that the teaching of seemingly universal aesthetic principles had produced "a *categorical* way of closing the mind to the *economics* of sentiment" (Letter to Soule, May 16, 1959, 4). By way of example, Burke explained that at the same time that literary scholars considered "market" to be "a dirtier word than all the four-letter words in the deck," they ignored how they nevertheless promoted literary study "as a kind of intellectual hair-do, to prepare the educatee for the market" (4). Burke was greatly discouraged by the fact that his students seemed to have developed—through both classroom instruction and the majority culture's reverence for literature—an unwillingness to consider literary discourse as language of the "real world." What was necessary was teaching scholars and students how to put literary terminology into the disciplinary dialectic, making it response-able to critique.

To carry out this project, Burke envisioned his Prose Writing course as a space for teaching students about the ways literary discourse, like all forms of language use, makes statements about human motives and persuades readers to make specific judgments about economic, political, and cultural realities. Thus he revised the course by asking students to critically examine the aesthetic principles that inform literary studies. He described to Soule the assumptions guiding his alternative approach to the course: "In any case, it all adds up to my firm conviction, (1) That creative writing should be studied not just as a craft but as a way into the contemplation of man in all his complexity; (2) that such contemplation requires an explicit, systematic concern with the ways in which political and economic factors help shape the nature of our imagination and secretly participate in our imagery, no matter how 'pure" of such elements it may seem to be on its face; . . . and (3) that the current esthetic, with its norms of taste uncritically taken for granted, automatically blocks such an approach. The younger people simply resist, without knowing why" (KB to GS May 16, 1959, 3). While Burke's teaching materials for this particular course have not been found, his reflections here as well as his approach in other courses (see Wible 268–78) suggest that he likely would have used two different types of assignments to help students re-see creative writing as a tool for contemplating "man in all his complexity." First, of course, students would compose creative texts that more explicitly engaged with the social world. As he described his overall course goal to Soule, Burke wanted students "to think of man's social-political-economic problems in general when writing a story or a poem" (KB to GS May 16, 1959, 1). Second, students would compose analytical essays that charted the key terms in their creative works as a means "to inspect the socio-political implications of their sensitivities" (3). Through this second project, students would examine how their creative texts' key terms reveal their own motivational stances.

Examples of this latter type of assignment can be seen in other courses Burke taught at Bennington. In his 1955 Language as Symbolic Action course, students performed the same type of disciplinary dialectic that Burke created in the "Philosophic Schools" section of *A Grammar of Motives*. Students read five essays from the 1955 collection *Modern Philosophies and Education* (to which Burke had contributed "Linguistic Approach to Problems in Education") and composed four writing assignments on them. For each assignment, students first used Burke's indexing methods to identify the key terms in an essay from the collection and the relationship among these terms. They then used his methods of dialectical analysis to capture the dynamism within the text by describing how a text's "titular terms" put into motion a series of associations between these terms that led readers to form specific logical or emotional conclusions about the essay's main subject, education. Burke's comments on student essays reveal that he was more interested in having students work through difficult problems in understanding how each critic develops and employs a terministic screen rather than having them parse out the nuances of each philosophy.

While these types of assignments were ones that Burke used in his Language as Symbolic Action course, they likely would have been assigned to his Prose Writing students, as well, in order to help them develop "maximum consciousness" of the linguistic operations of their texts (*ATH* 170). In creating linked assignments that asked students first to compose fiction and then to analyze its terministic grounding and movement, Burke would have been working to address the disciplinary blindness that comes from using a specific terminology in routine, or unreflexive, ways. Students ideally would have left Burke's Prose Writing course, then, with a better understanding of how their creative writing both explicitly and implicitly made assertions about human motives as well as how these motivational statements gave "cues that place [others] with relation to them" (170).[2]

Burke's notes on student writing suggest however that his concerns were not only relegated to his classroom. In fact he often pushed students to apply the kind of thinking they developed in his courses to the work they were doing in other disciplines. One sees this cross-disciplinary concern in Burke's comments on Ruth Goldstone's final essay for his 1955 Language as Symbolic Action course. Goldstone was a dance major at Bennington, and Burke writes in response to her essay on the linguistic operations of Thomist and Marxist philosophies of education that his "main regret has been that she has not, by comments or questions, forced us to find at just how many points (*mutatis mutandis*) the terministic emphasis considered in this course might have its analogues in the field of dance." For Burke, Goldtsone's paper exemplified the educational "routine" that disabled students from drawing connections between courses they took in different fields. The following section discusses how Burke worked through this concern by exploring ways for students and their teachers to put disciplines in dialogue. His overarching goal was to unify the curriculum through a linguistic approach to the disciplines. This goal, however, required that Burke demonstrate to faculty across the college what such analysis looks like and explain what this theoretical perspective affords.

Burke's Vision for University-Wide Terministic Dialogue

Burke's assignments in his Language as Symbolic Action course and his reflections on teaching Prose Writing show him translating his educational theory into peda-gogical practice, as he guided students through the process of using his methods of terministic analysis. These archival materials establish that Burke had clear ideas about what he wanted faculty to be doing inside the classroom in their role as teachers. Equally as important, other documents reveal how Burke's theories of disciplinary dialectic informed his arguments about the kinds of critical work he wanted faculty to perform in their role as scholars both at Bennington College and within the wider world of academia. These ideas can best be seen through his 1955 published essay "Linguistic Approaches to Problems in Education" (LAPE) and the minutes from a 1950 faculty meeting in Bennington College's literature department. The latter document in particular reveals Burke's plan to initiate inter-disciplinary dialogue at the school, the same type of dialectical analysis of termi-nology that Burke himself carried out in part two of *A Grammar of Motives*. Burke wanted faculty in all disciplines to practice and make habitual the critical methods he illustrates in *Grammar*, all toward the end of disrupting educational routine and cultivating a greater appreciation for how language use shapes the insights each discipline makes about the natural or social world.

In LAPE Burke composes his vision for scholarly practice grounded in his belief that all academic disciplines are linked through their use of language. Even dis-ciplines whose "subject matter is exclusively the realm of nonsymbolic motion," such a physics, chemistry, astronomy, and geology, are nevertheless "buil[t]. . . in the realm of symbolic action" ("Linguistic" 279). For this reason Burke argued that even scholars in disciplines not thought of as being concerned with language neces-sarily "must criticize their own terminology" (279).

Certainly Burke acknowledges that individual disciplines should continue to pursue the types of pressing questions that have traditionally defined them ("Lin-guistic" 282 n4). But Burke suggests that they should also acknowledge their con-nection to all other disciplines—and indeed to all human activity—through the realm of symbolic action. According to Burke, "Whereas we would divide the curric-ulum in ways that allow for the traditional autonomy of the various disciplines, we would so conduct our investigations that we might glimpse, brooding over the lot, a lore of the *universal pageantry* in which all men necessarily and somewhat som-nambulistically take part, by reason of their symbol-using natures" (282). Burke's use of "we" here reflects his belief that scholars from all disciplines should attend to issues of symbolic action, particularly in terms of tracing how a discipline's termi-nology reflects a particular motivational stance toward the phenomena it tradition-ally studies.

Burke's vision for the university, then, brings together scholars to engage in interdisciplinary inquiry as a means of exploring the strengths and shortcomings of each field's terminology. Burke describes this type of critical practice in LAPE when he refers to disciplines—or, to be more specific, the statements that different disci-plines make about a related subject—as "voices in a dialogue" (283). Burke stresses that in the ideal dialogue, each voice "deemed relevant to the particular issue or controversy" would be given its say, and no voice "would be inadequately repre-sented (as were one to portray it by stating only its more vulnerable arguments)" (283). As this emphasis on accurately and fairly representing different disciplinary positions suggests, Burke did not want scholars to approach this dialogue in the spirit of either demanding "scientific accuracy" or defending one's own field (283). Instead they would remain open to the possibility that such analysis could correct some shortcomings in their own disciplinary perspectives, infusing humility into critical practice: "One hopes for ways whereby the various voices, in mutually cor-recting one another, will lead toward a position better than any one singly. That is one does not want merely to outwit the opponent, or to study him; one wants to be affected by him, in some degree to incorporate him, to so act that his ways can help perfect one's own—in brief, to learn from him" (284). This type of interdisciplin-ary dialogue, then, would require scholars to "analyze the structure of [each disci-pline's] statements, considered as symbolic acts" (284). Burke believed that through such linguistic analysis, scholars would come to acknowledge their own discipline's linguistic foibles, and through such interdisciplinary dialogue, they would identify places where the motivational statements embedded in different disciplinary termi-nologies could be brought together to make more rounded analyses.

Burke believed the type of dialogue he outlines in LAPE and demonstrates in *A Grammar of Motives* should be brought to life within the university—so much so that he made specific suggestions about how to do it at Bennington. On Sep-tember 10, 1950, faculty in the Bennington College literature department met to discuss "possible and desirable activities over and beyond our regular activities in classes" that the department might pursue (1). During the faculty meeting, Burke made a number of suggestions that reveal his attempts to put his theory into prac-tice. Burke's first proposal reimagined the work of the student literary magazine, the *Silo*. Here Burke suggested that the undergraduate magazine broaden its focus to initiate a university-wide conversation wherein students from different majors would approach the same topic from their respective disciplinary angles. He was concerned that many Bennington faculty members viewed *Silo* as "just a special organ for English in the narrow sense," so he suggested that inviting students from other disciplines to contribute could be a way to "invigorate" the undergraduate journal (Bennington College Literature Department, meeting minutes). While one faculty member critiqued the proposal, claiming that Burke simply did not think *Silo* was good enough (2), Burke's suggestion reveals his attempt to put theory into practice by composing *Silo* as a space for students from different disciplines to explore a single common topic and to examine what each discipline can enable other fields to understand. Just as important as the insights students could gain through such dialogue were the intellectual habits they could develop through routinely participating in it, becoming, as Burke describes in *The Philosophy of Literary Form*, more "pliant" in their theorizing and more "likely to see around the corner of their received ideas" (13).

Rather than belabor his points about redefining *Silo* as a multidisciplinary journal, however, Burke offered at the same meeting a second recommendation for a program to which all Bennington faculty ideally would contribute. "Here's an extension of the idea of getting all departments in the magazine," he said. "Suppose, if we had a reading of poems, we sent copies to Social Science people, too, and asked them to attend, too. Let them bring in their angles" (2). As he elaborated on this proposal for interdisciplinary dialogue around the analysis of a particular poem, Burke repeatedly emphasized the fact that scholars should approach this conversation with openness to the attitude formation that can come through systematic, patient analysis. For example when literature colleague Thomas Wilcox tried to clarify Burke's suggestion by saying, "The proposal then is that we have meetings in competition with other departments. And discussions with other faculty" (3), Burke quickly clarified his position: "Not competition. Getting together" (3). Later in the meeting, Burke reemphasized this point, stressing, "We don't want to compete. We just say: Talk to us. Talk about how your language is constructed" (3½).

Burke's emphasis here reveals that he saw the university-wide dialogue as a means to temper the combative ambitions that led many scholars to expend energy defending and justifying their respective disciplines rather than making themselves open to learning from others. This part of the program was crucial to Burke, as he believed the benefits of such interdisciplinary dialogue could and should extend beyond the realm of academics and university life. As Burke would put it five years later, the practice of participating in dialectical analysis could habituate people to the practice of "stopping to analyze an exhortation precisely at the moment when the exhortation would otherwise set us to swinging violently" ("Linguistic" 284).

This concern to revise scholarly interaction from competition to conversation emerged again and again in Burke's proposal to his colleagues. The department meeting minutes, written in a secretarial shorthand, show Burke taking yet another moment to clarify the assumptions informing his ideas: "We are in languages. Languages are the basis for unifying a curriculum. All teaching a language. Everything taught here basically a language. Out of that a special skill distinct within that field. You turn out of the language into a special realm. The fundamental principles would of course be through a theory of language. I was going to try to get the whole works in—to the glory of the whole of Bennington, not just of our department" (3). At the end of this statement, Burke expressed his belief that even the literature department had much to learn from colleagues in other disciplines. Wilcox nevertheless suggested that the "frankest way" to set up the university-wide dialogue would be to "tell the others they need to know more about language" (3). Wilcox's response implied that literature faculty members were already aware of the insights about language that could emerge from these forums. Burke, on the other hand, read Wilcox's response as evidence that even scholars of language and literature lacked a sensitivity to how each and every discipline could benefit from collective linguistic analysis.

Thus Burke did not stop with the two proposals to revise *Silo* and to create university-wide discussion through the analysis of a poem. At the department meeting, he offered yet another more general idea for interdisciplinary discussion at Bennington. Here he suggested that members of different disciplines gather together to engage in an investigation of symbolic action that could best be framed in terms of the theme "composition and division." As he explained, "Every discipline has to begin with that: Putting things together and taking them apart" (3½). He envisioned this iteration of university-wide dialogue beginning with a representative from each academic department examining how his or her discipline uses composition and division when selecting or shaping the definitions of its grounding terms. Burke provided an example from literary studies to illustrate how scholars use composition and division to generate new principles within a discipline. In this case he discusses "a purely aesthetic problem," one that "concern[s] matters of 'beauty' and the 'sublime'": "Consider [the] example of man observing a mountain, and feeling satisfied thereat. In contrast with mountain (division) he feels infinitesimally weaker. But in imaginative identification with it, 'emphatically' letting eye soar with it & range along its lines (composition), he feels assertive, 'free'" (5). For Burke the term "Sublimity" emerges from the "mixture of the two principles" (5). He asserted that composition and division is the most traditional method for analyzing a specialized body of subject matter, so he considered that particular angle as the most logical way to approach this interdisciplinary dialectical analysis.

Burke also offered a more thorough description of how these analyses of discipline-specific symbolic action could proceed. Each participating scholar would trace the logical relationships that necessarily follow from each discipline's selection of its key terms and that move the discipline's arguments toward their conclusions. Here scholars would identify titular terms in their discipline and then trace "how they are connected by 'therefore,' 'however,' or 'and'" (3½). Burke saw these three words as the means through which disciplines create seemingly logical relationships between their key terms. Indeed these three words are central to

Burke's methodology in *The Philosophy of Literary Form* and *A Grammar of Motives*, as he focuses on how they shape the progression and transformation of terms in clusters. As Burke contends in the *Grammar,* there are always "conclusions implicit in key terms or propositions used as generating principle" (403). The scholar's job is to make these conclusions more explicit by tracing "the spinning of terms out of terms" (403). To perform this analytical work, he or she identifies which terms and propositions are given particular meanings by being linked together by "therefore" statements, which by "however" statements, and which by "and" statements (406).

Burke's proposal to have scholars across campus at Bennington analyze their respective terminology is significant, then, for it would bring to life his theory of "Dialectic in General" as articulated in *A Grammar of Motives.* For Burke, "dialectics" means the study of "the possibilities of linguistic transformation," and he distinguishes the study of "particular instances" of linguistic transformation from the possibilities of linguistic transformation "in general" (402). The university-wide dialectic Burke proposed for Bennington would bring together numerous studies of "particular instances" of linguistic transformation within each discipline. These individual studies then would be considered together as a way to work toward the primary goal of Burke's overarching scholarly project, namely building and continually refining an overall theory of linguistic transformation.

Burke saw this type of dialectical approach as the "only way to unify academic discourse and the university curriculum" (3½), for it emphasizes not how disciplines are divided in terms of the ways they build knowledge but rather how they merge in terms of being shaped through symbolic action. As this discussion demonstrates, Burke believed his own colleagues at Bennington would more likely pay attention to work in other disciplines were they able to see how their "differences emerge in the various structures of symbols" (3½) rather than in fundamentally different approaches to the same object of study. Burke's proposals to the department ultimately argue for a more language-sensitive—and thus more motivation-sensitive—university and educational enterprise.

"WE COULD GET A VERY ZESTFUL GOINGS-ON": THE QUEST FOR TRUE INTERDISCIPLINARITY

Three months after he made his proposal to literature department colleagues, Burke raised the topic again in a December 26, 1950, letter to department chair Tom Brockway: "And I'd like to repeat my suggestion: That a series be started in which each department states, in lectures before the assembled multitude, what its basic terms are, what its basic purposes are, what its basic propositions are. Say the word, and I'll be glad to prepare such a talk, in behalf of my asseverations. If this were done right, we could get a very zestful goings-on." But academic routine won the day. Despite Burke's numerous attempts, the university-wide dialogue he dreamed of initiating at Bennington College never materialized.

Just as Burke the teacher hoped his analytical methods would disrupt the bureaucratized educational routine in which students learned to use but did not reflect on their academic major's key terms, Burke the faculty member viewed interdisciplinary dialogue as an unexplored alterative for university life that could foster cooperation among scholars who too often focused on fortifying the boundaries of their discipline from perceived outside attacks. Indeed Burke believed that all scholars had a greater capacity to "fearsomely *appreciate*" man's use (and misuse) of symbolic resources ("Linguistic" 301). He wanted his colleagues across Bennington College to become more attuned to how institutional routine did not allow them to develop greater awareness of the common ground—language—that all disciplines share.

Burke saw this project as significant because he viewed his own educational moment as one when schools, bureaucratized as they were by routine, were busy preparing students for a marketplace ruled by logics of speed and competition and for an international political scene in which "new weapons . . . threaten not only our chances of living well but even our chances of living at all" (301). Given these social conditions, Burke viewed the university instead as a space where patience and collaboration could be cultivated through a critical method of linguistic analysis. His plan for bringing his rhetorical theories of dialectic and terministic analysis to life in the institutional space of the university underscores his commitment to broadly cultivating an attitude of goodwill toward others.

Burke's proposal to translate his theories and methods for dialectical analysis into concrete practice is no less relevant in the present moment when scholars and university administrators alike argue over both the need for interdisciplinary work and the best strategies for putting it into practice. As we all know, many institutions' strategic plans now feature statements on fostering more collaboration across disciplines, and many have taken steps to implement these plans by creating research centers and academic units focused on interdisciplinary topics. This increasing scholarly practice and institutional emphasis has emerged with the realization that complex intellectual and practical problems, such as those dealing with disease prevention and treatment, climate change, intellectual property, and literacy acquisition, do not sit neatly within the boundary of any one field. As such, interdisciplinary work allows scholars to assemble a diverse set of "tools for inquiry" that are necessary to examine these multifaceted problems (Hood, Letter, Jan. 10, 2010).

Even as institutions recognize the increasing complexity of research questions, however, there is disagreement over what interdisciplinary research can and should look like. For example writing studies scholar Carra Leah Hood sees opportunities for productive research and pedagogical collaboration among academics whose disciplines "share vocabulary, conceptual approaches, notions of facts and evidence, and methods for producing knowledge" (Letter, July 6, 2007). Disability studies scholar Lennard Davis, on the other hand, doubts the possibility for " true interdisciplinarity" on the grounds that disciplines operate according to such different sets of assumptions. "A truly interdisciplinary approach is potentially dangerous," Davis contends, because "it would involve subjecting disciplines and the rules by which they operate to a thorough scrutiny, and it would require scholars to listen to those critiques."

Burke's vision of a university-wide dialectic provides a useful frame for thinking through contemporary debates about interdisciplinarity. His proposal suggests that despite Hood's and Davis's different perspectives on the possibility for interdisciplinary research and teaching, they both foreground two important aspects of such work: method and attitude. Hood believes most scholars are open to collaboration when they can identify shared vocabulary and conceptual approaches; Davis similarly considers the need to analyze disciplinary assumptions informing knowledge production, even as he supposes that such investigations will put scholars in a defensive mode, sensing the need to protect their disciplinary turf. In contrast to these positions, Burke maintained in *A Grammar of Motives* that the attitude necessary for cooperation was "embodied" in his analytical method (441). Indeed Burke believed it simply was not good enough to tell scholars or students to be tolerant of others' analytical frameworks. Instead scholars needed to practice "systematically suffering" a discipline's key texts before critiquing them, carefully studying linguistic transformation within these texts to the point that patience and humility became habituated (276). The archival materials examined here illustrate Burke's efforts to translate his theories and methods of dialectic into a university-wide practice. The archives provide a unique glimpse of Professor Burke putting on his administrator's cap. Even more important, these materials might aid us all in envisioning new ways to foster dialogue across departments and to facilitate more—and more productive—interdisciplinary scholarship and teaching.

NOTES

1. In Burke's two 1959 letters to Soule, he was responding to Soule's inquiries about university life at Bennington. Soule was interviewing faculty members as part of a Carnegie Foundation–supported study of Bennington's progressive education experiment. Two years after corresponding with Burke, Soule published his study under the title *Educational Experimentation: A Study Focused on Bennington College.*

2. It is interesting that while Burke pushed his Prose Writing students to consider the motivational statements implicit in their creative texts, he took a different approach when serving as Judith Greenhill's senior thesis advisor in 1955. Greenhill wrote either a novel or novella for her senior thesis (Burke's typed notes from an advising session suggest that the work contained chapters), and Burke made this comment concerning his advisory role for such a culminating, extended creative text: "in a project of this sort, . . . certain important questions of motivation cannot be considered en route, lest they throw the project out of gear by introducing new matter. Accordingly, as I see it, a

counselor's advice must be reduced to a minimum and must in no case question a work's basic assumptions (as regards the writer's esthetic or sociological presuppositions). Such matters must be left in abeyance, except insofar as the writer herself feels moved to consider them." In earlier advising meetings with Greenhill, Burke did in fact suggest that she attend more closely to the social motivations emerging through her literary discourse, but Greenhill countered that he was "trying to discourage her as much as possible, trying to make her task as difficult and unappetizing for her as possible."

WORKS CITED

Bennington College. *Bennington College Bulletin, 1958–1959.* Bennington, Vt.: Bennington College Publications Office, 1958.

Bennington College Literature Department. Meeting minutes. Sept. 10, 1950. Bennington, Vt. Kenneth Burke Papers, Penn State University.

Burke, Kenneth. *Attitudes toward History.* 1937. 3rd ed. Berkeley: University of California Press, 1984.

———. Advising notes on Judith Greenhill's senior thesis. 1955. Kenneth Burke Papers, Penn State University.

———. *A Grammar of Motives.* 1945. 3rd ed. Berkeley: University of California Press, 1969.

———. Letter to George Soule. Feb. 21, 1959. Kenneth Burke Papers, Penn State University.

———. Letter to George Soule. May 16, 1959. Kenneth Burke Papers, Penn State University.

———. Letter to Thomas Brockway. Dec. 26, 1950. Kenneth Burke Papers, Penn State University.

———. "Linguistic Approach to Problems in Education." *Modern Philosophies and Education: The Fifty-Fourth Yearbook of the National Society for the Study of Education.* Pt. 1. Ed. Nelson B. Henry. Chicago: University of Chicago Press, 1955.

———. *The Philosophy of Literary Form: Studies in Symbolic Action.* 1941. 3rd ed. Berkeley: University of California Press, 1973.

———. Response to Louis Carty's essay on realism. 1955. Kenneth Burke Papers, Penn State University.

———. Response to Ruth Goldstone's final essay. 1955. Kenneth Burke Papers, Penn State University.

Crusius, Timothy W. *Kenneth Burke and the Conversation after Philosophy.* Carbondale: Southern Illinois University Press, 1999.

Davis, Lennard. "A Grand, Unified Theory of Interdisciplinarity." *Chronicle of Higher Education.* June 8, 2007.

Enoch, Jessica. "Becoming Symbol-Wise: Kenneth Burke's Pedagogy of Critical Reflection." *College Composition and Communication* 56.2 (2004): 272–96.

George, Ann. "Finding the Time for Burke." *Burke in the Archives: Using the Past to Transform the Future of Burkean Studies.* Ed. Dana Anderson and Jessica Enoch. Columbia: University of South Carolina Press, 2013: 29–49.

————. "Language as Symbolic Action." Course description. *Bennington College Bulletin, 1953–54.* 39.

Hood, Carra Leah. Letter. *Chronicle of Higher Education.* July 6, 2007.

————. Letter. *Chronicle of Higher Education.* Jan. 10, 2010.

Smudde, Peter M., ed. *Humanistic Critique of Education: Teaching and Learning as Symbolic Action.* West Lafayette, Ind.: Parlor Press, 2010.

Soule, George. *Educational Experimentation: A Study Focused on Bennington College.* Bennington: Bennington College Press, 1961.

Wible, Scott. "Professor Burke's 'Bennington Project.'" *Rhetoric Society Quarterly* 38.3 (2008): 259–82.

DEBRA HAWHEE

HISTORIOGRAPHY BY INCONGRUITY

In the spring of 1932 Burke traded letters with Elizabeth Parker, the widow of Dr. George M. Parker, a well-regarded New York psychiatrist who for a time served as the psychiatric examiner for the Prison Association of New York and who became an outspoken opponent of prison overcrowding.[1] Burke had been recommended to Mrs. Parker as a good candidate to complete her husband's unfinished manuscript, a treatise on psychology. According to the letters that remain, Mrs. Parker paid Burke at least two installments for the work he agreed to do and sent him about a dozen books from Dr. Parker's collection, including Russell's *Analysis of the Mind* and Rivers's *Instinct and the Unconscious* (EP to KB May 23, 1932). By October, though, none of the work had been done. Burke wrote to Mrs. Parker that he had been "worrying for a considerable length of time over the book of my own which I was trying to write this summer," and now that he had "hammered out a fair copy" he was "free to begin work on the chapters of Dr. Parker" (KB to EP October 3, 1932).[2] In December Burke sent Mrs. Parker an annotated outline, for which she sent him $150, the second installment.

From that point the archives bear not a trace of any progress on the posthumous book that Burke was to have completed, and not a word between Burke and Mrs. Parker for nearly seven years. And then in 1939 they apparently traded correspondence again, though what appears to be the final letter between the two is all that remains in the archive. Earlier that year Mrs. Parker had telegraphed Burke to "keep the manuscript" (EP to KB September 11, 1939). Either this telegraph or an additional letter from Mrs. Parker put Burke on the defensive, for his reply, quoted in Parker's reply, protested that he was not "the sort of writer who needs to pilfer" (qtd. in EP to KB September 11, 1939). What apparently set Burke off is an intriguing hint that Parker noticed Burke's use of the term "chart" (most likely in *Attitudes toward History,* which Burke had published subsequent to their initial exchanges). Chart is a term Mrs. Parker's husband had apparently developed in the notes toward his own manuscript. Mrs. Parker's follow-up letter is quite amicable, and she notes with regret that the intervening years since their original agreement have not been kind and that she is no longer able to "keep to the original financial agreement" (EP to KB September 11, 1939). Nevertheless Parker expresses hope that Burke will write some sort of "In Memoriam" article someday if he sees fit, and that he really ought to keep the manuscript, because, as she writes, "if it came back into my hands, what could I do but eventually burn it up?"

With that final extant letter, the archive falls silent on the matter. I discovered this exchange when I was in the middle of researching Burke's bodily theories, theories that he frequently developed while performing odd jobs much like this contractual one.[3] *Permanence and Change,* which I argue is Burke's "most bodily book" (*Moving* 167), is obviously engaged with psychological theories, some of which Burke discusses with names attached. Others are less easily identifiable. The letters from Dr. Parker's widow provided, I thought, a considerable lead. I spent months trying to fill in the archival silences, searching for information about Dr. Parker's theories, even attempting to recover the manuscript that Mrs. Parker left with Burke, to find out more about what this book had to say, and how specifically Dr. Parker's work might have seeped into Burke's methods and his thinking on bodies and language. How did Dr. Parker use the term "chart"? What was his take on W. H. R. Rivers, whose book Mrs. Parker promised to lend Burke, and whose work with soldiers and trauma Burke discusses in *Permanence and Change*?[4] Having done some productive work with Burke's other ghostwriting, I was hopeful that I could fill out that picture by locating the Parker book. I searched the Library of Congress for a posthumously published book by George M. Parker to no avail. In the end I was left with a smattering of *New York Times* articles from the 1910s in which Parker is consulted as a trial lawyer; a 1902 book edited and partially authored by Boris Sidis to which Parker contributed several chapters on mental dissociation; an obituary; and six letters chronicling the agreement between Burke and Mrs. Parker, an agreement that never came to fruition. This material, promising as it seemed when I first discovered it, never made it into my published work, but the unanswered questions it prompts still remain with me.

Archives are furtive things. They blurt and withhold; they offer information that directs, redirects, perplexes. Those of us who write archival histories are well familiar with archival dead-ends such as the one I have just described, unsolvable puzzles that raise more questions than they answer. Such findings haunt us long after our studies—crafted as though such dead-ends were never encountered—are in print. Archives, that is, are records of breakdown and failure as much as they are of the intellectual activities and practices that offer the historian and her readers insight into the fully formed theories, performances, or practices by the thinkers or movements that draw historians to archives in the first place.

In this essay I explore the archive as a record of breakdown by articulating an approach to history I call "historiography by incongruity." The method is informed by two key Burkean concepts, the well-known "perspective by incongruity" combined with his lesser-known notion of "the Beauty Clinic," both of which I describe later in the essay. Together these terms help us to trouble the smooth narrative arcs that often fill the pages of history (especially Burkean histories). The idea of historiography by incongruity is meant to draw out—and to encourage productive use of—the necessary unevenness of archival work. I offer historiography by incongruity not necessarily as a method for doing history, though I will describe an instance of using it as both a method and a theme later in this piece. Rather its more useful function might well be as a method for reflecting on the history we do, by which I simply mean that historiography by incongruity offers a kind of check on the tidy narratives historians end up producing, acknowledging the necessarily messy, incomplete, surprising, and often stubbornly befuddling nature of archival work.

Historiography by incongruity, with all its holes and gaps, serves as a helpful reminder of the repression involved in writing history, even as it encourages us to slow down in the archive, to consider items that do not obviously and immediately fit our narrative. The perplexing dead-ends, the falling into silence of certain correspondents, the visible dwindling of intellectual paths or social movements, the inexplicable note jotted in the margin of a manuscript, all mark the archive as a place of excess. In that excess inhere instructive stories as well, for as Burke teaches us better than just about anyone else, that which is not used forms the very contours of that which is.

"A FALLING TOGETHER OF THINGS FORMERLY APART": ENACTING INCONGRUITY

As I mentioned, two of Burke's concepts inform the metahistorical method I am proposing here. First and most obvious is his method of "perspective by incongruity."[5] The second, "the Beauty Clinic," is more descriptive than methodological, but my aim is to try to cull a methodological stance from it. Perspective by incongruity and the Beauty Clinic have not to my knowledge been theorized together before, but this is likely because few people have noticed or written about the Beauty Clinic, given that it is buried in Burke's lesser-known work from the 1950s and 60s, and the one self-reference Burke offers proves rather elusive.[6] The terms come from very different points in Burke's career, with perspective by incongruity serving as one of the core methods outlined in his 1935 *Permanence and Change*. Both terms, however, edge toward breakdown.

Perspective by incongruity breaks down existing associations between words and/or objects. Nietzsche is Burke's model here; in Burke's words, "Nietzsche establishes his perspectives by a constant juxtaposing of incongruous words, attaching to some name a qualifying epithet which had heretofore gone with a different order of names" (*PC* 90). At the heart of such a move is a rebuilding through destruction: "Nietzsche knew that probably every linkage was open to destruction by the perspectives of a planned incongruity" (*PC* 91). Likewise "the humorists, the satirists, the writers of the grotesque, all contributed to this work with varying degrees of systematization, giving us new insights by such deliberate misfits" (91). Burke takes scientific discourse—"scientific revelations" is his phrase—as "evidence that Perspective by Incongruity is both needed and extensively practiced" (119). "Were we to summarize the totality of its effects," he continues, "we might say that planned incongruity should be deliberately cultivated for the purpose of experimentally wrenching apart all those molecular combinations of adjective and noun, substantive and verb, which still remain with us. It should subject language to the same 'cracking' process that chemists now use in their refining of oil" (119). The point, then, of perspective by incongruity is to wrench apart status-quo associations and to form new ones by making jarring conceptual alliances.

Burke's reflection on scientific processes launches him into the exhortative mode, whereby he delineates perspective by incongruity in terms of what critics "should" or ought to be doing. The excited tone of the passage as well as its concrete examples make it worth quoting at length:

An idea which commonly carries with it diminutive modifiers, for instance, should be treated by magnification, as were one to discuss the heinousness of an extra slice of beef, or the brain storm that rules when one has stumped one's toe. One should be prepared to chart the genesis, the flourishing, and decay of a family witticism, precisely as though he were concerned with the broadest processes of cultural change, basic patterns of psychology and history thus being conveniently brought within the scope of the laboratory. One should study one's dog for his *Napoleonic* qualities, or observe mosquitoes for signs of wisdom to which we are forever closed. One should discuss sneezing in the terms heretofore reserved for the analysis of a brilliant invention, as if it were a creative act, a vast synthesis uniting in its simple self a multitude of prior factors.

Conversely, where the accepted linkages have been of an imposing sort, one should establish perspective by looking through the reverse end of his glass, converting mastodons into microbes, or human beings into vermin upon the face of the earth. Or perhaps writing a history of medicine by a careful study of the quacks, one should, by the principle of the *lex continui*, extend his observations until they threw light upon the processes of a Pasteur. . . . Or by a schematic shift in the locus of judgment, supply eulogistic words to characterize events usually characterized dyslogistically, or vice versa, or supplement both eulogistic and dyslogistic by words that will be neutral, having no censorious quality whatsoever, but purely indicative of a process. (*PC* 119–20)

Perspective by incongruity is at once a style, an attitude, and an act. It is a style of interacting with the world, a rupturing of existing attitudes and the creation of a new one, and an act of taking existing modes of questioning and turning them sideways. It can simultaneously entail a kind of strangification—a defamiliarizing of the familiar—and deprivation; as Burke writes in the same long passage, "let us even deliberately deprive ourselves of available knowledge in the search for new knowledge. . . . In this you will have deliberately discarded available data in the interests of a fresh point of view, the heuristic or perspective value of a planned incongruity" (121). Such incongruous methods, wholly antithetical to an approach whose aim is truth or certainty, serve as a means of invention, or what Burke calls a heuristic. As he puts it, "The doctrine of perspective would suggest that perspective is heuristic insofar as we see close at hand the things we had formerly seen from afar and vice versa" (122–23). Perspective by incongruity, then, involves a stretching, a distorting, and ultimately a breaking down of prevailing habits and attitudes, an embracing of that which would usually be discarded or ignored.

The act of revaluation also motivates Burke's use of the term "Beauty Clinic," which he conceived as something of an ironic designation for the phenomenon by which stuff—and here "stuff" can mean anything from an academic argument to clothing—is valued only when it is pristine, scrubbed of grime, cleansed of its own production. Burke offers his 1963 article "The Thinking of the Body" as a "contribution" to the Beauty Clinic (25), but only after noting: "Persons who insist on keeping the subject of the poetic imagination *salonfähig* (or, as the dictionary might put it, 'suitable for discussion in the drawing room') will resent such analysis" (25). That article—and Burke's cloacal criticism of which it is a part—might also be understood as enacting perspective by incongruity insofar as it openly flouts the Beauty Clinic's values and tendencies, discussing the excrement and rot that underlies most literature.[7]

For most of "Thinking of the Body," Burke is toying with "the possibility that, in Freudian theory, talk of a 'death-instinct' could serve stylistically as tragic dignification of an 'excretion instinct.'" He continues, "Dramatic grandeur here sneaks into the Beauty Clinic, transforming bathos into pathos . . . in the very midst of the Clinic, we find tricks of poetic 'miraculism' intruding, by the unrecognized transforming of lowly physical functions into terms quite pretentious" (65). By "transforming . . . lowly physical functions into terms quite pretentious and lovely to consider," the Beauty Clinic inspires the reversal of such incongruous perspectives—an incongruity of an incongruity—that Burke offers in "The Thinking of the Body," whereby the word "faces" morphs into faeces, the word "towards" into turds. For Burke, then, the Beauty Clinic, with its insistence on whitewashing, on sweeping misfit phrases under the carpet, ought to be broken down, exposed, and resisted in order to undo its deadening effect. It's important to note too that the Beauty Clinic does not begin and end with literature or literary criticism. Indeed, in the conclusion of "The Thinking of the Body," Burke observes several instances of this kind of thinking. Here are two: "There is, for instance, the ideal of floor wax that does not 'yellow,' when the floors are compulsively kept polished to the point where they become a major menace to life and limb (a kind of dream-life that matches the military man's ideal of fighting his dirty wars with 'clean' bombs). Or there are the millions of dollars spent on detergents that add disgracefully to the pollution of our waters, and all for some slight extra edge of white in our fabrics that is wholly worthless except as the obedient response to a commercially stimulated idea of purely ritual cleanliness" (67). This passage vividly details the ironic, incongruous conditions—bright clothes lead to filthy rivers, clean wars to dirty bombs—that Burke struggles against in his mid-century writings and that he folds into his critical methods under the irreverent heading "The Beauty Clinic."

So how do these two terms relate to archival research, or to research in Burke's archives in particular? How, that is, do they feed into what I'm calling historiography by incongruity? Here's how: archival research demands that we select archival materials and fashion them into a neat argument. And yet as David Gold aptly observes in reflecting on his experiences in multiple archives, "we never know where an archive will lead" (18). Anyone who has worked with the Kenneth Burke Papers similarly knows that not only is it impossible to know where the materials will lead—this element of surprise is part of the joy of such research—but there are materials in that archive that do not necessarily support a "cleaned-up" version of Burke, materials ranging from Burke's phobic emendation of Hart Crane's epistolary nickname for him ("Butter-Tail"[8]), to his lackluster response to Dewey.[9] And then there are the incomplete tasks. So much of Burke's work, like the Parker book discussed at the beginning of this essay, did not get finished. He was busy; he overcommitted and was charmingly disorganized, a constant state captured rather humorously in an epistolary line to Cowley, "I am as busy as an abortionist six weeks after a holiday" (KB to MC October 9, 1955).

All of these conditions—the messiness, ideological and material—conspire to make it difficult indeed to extract a tidy and coherent thirty- to forty-page argument about Burke's life vis-à-vis his theoretical contributions to our discipline. Those articles and essays—prime candidates for Burke's Beauty Clinic (and I have written my fair share!)—are made possible by a hefty dose of repression. And yet my recent work in Burke's archives has prepared me to suggest that an abiding awareness of the archive as a record of breakdown might bolster archival work on Burke, forcing researchers to slow down and attend to the documents that do not immediately seem to fit. In other words, practicing historiography by incongruity encourages a recognition, and perhaps a strategic suspension, of the scholarly drive toward the Beauty Clinic. Such awareness would in turn enable researchers to pause and consider the incongruities masked by the Beauty Clinic: the stories of failure so often swept beneath the clean narrative of intellectual development. Historiography by incongruity, that is, entails both a wrangly awareness of Burke's critiques of the Beauty Clinic as well as an enactment of perspective by incongruity. Historians of Burkean rhetoric might do well to resist subjecting Burke to the Beauty Clinic, to let the archive lead to incongruous—and not tidily congruous—perspectives. In the next section I describe the archival experiences that led to an articulation of this incongruous historiographic method, including an archivally induced revelation by which the notion of breakdown suddenly became quite central to a chapter I was researching, and to my view of Burke in general.

A TALE OF THREE BREAKDOWNS

Sometimes archival dead-ends, like the one I shared at the outset of this essay, pop up out of nowhere, demanding—but ultimately not obviously rewarding—the researcher's attention. At other times they are presented by the archival subject itself, in this case by Burke. I turn now to an account of the process (if it can be called a process) by which I researched and composed the final chapter of my book on Burke's bodily theories. It was a process of following Burke's own detours, failures, and dead-ends. It was a process, in other words, of breaking down along with Burke, of having perspective by incongruity block my quest for the Beauty Clinic.

In its previous life as a tidy paragraph-long description that was tucked into book proposals, tenure files, and the like, that last chapter had nothing to do with breakdown. Instead it was going to focus mainly on Burke's last piece of fiction, "The Anaesthetic Revelation of Herone Liddell," a sprawling work that John Crowe Ransom published in the pages of *Kenyon Review* (1957).[10] The story promised to be a neat capstone to my book's chapters on Burke's bodily theories, for in it Burke revisits nearly every perspective considered in the book's first six chapters. Having already visited the John Crowe Ransom papers at Vanderbilt University, I had a stack of letters the two traded about the story's publication, and I also had extensive notes about how the perspectives were manifest in that key story. Unaware of it at the time, I had made my appointment at the Beauty Clinic, and I thought all I needed to do was show up—that is, write a tidy analysis of the story to conclude my book neatly.

And yet even before I began to write that chapter, something happened to it. The first precipitating event occurred during the fall of 2006 in my graduate seminar on bodies and rhetoric. For that seminar I had planned a day that I titled "figural studies," in which seminar participants would read a handful of studies focusing on the bodily conditions of important historical figures, studies I would later group under the term "body biography" (a term discussed later in this essay). The figures under consideration in the pieces I assigned were Kant, Darwin, Franklin Roosevelt, and Burke. The first four readings take the form of scholarly considerations of these figures' health vis-à-vis their theories, work, and/or rhetorical performance, but for Burke I settled on the aforementioned short story.[11] The fictional piece is rather incongruous when set against the four scholarly examinations of biographical details. And yet given that the story is quasi-autobiographical—Burke himself endured a botched hernia operation with the same details as those attributed to his story's main character—it fit rather well, and it offered seminarians a way to imagine writing about Burke in the same vein as the other writers wrote about their subjects.

Four things emerged from this set of readings. One, men's bodies seem only to become apparent—to themselves and to others—in moments of breakdown, disability, or illness. Two, breakdown can be productive. As an example, Janet Browne's piece on Charles Darwin's well-known poor health, what she calls his "very public life of the shawl" (318), demonstrates how Darwin's ailing body served as something of what Browne calls a "professional resource" (319), enabling him to avoid extensive social engagements and otherwise cultivate his life of the mind. Three, Browne and the other authors could not arrive at these conclusions about their subjects without access to life narratives offered only by archives. No genre of writing chronicles bodily maladies like letters, diaries, and personal notes, the very stuff of archives. And finally, in order to engage Burke's story sufficiently, to compose a body biography of my own, I had to get myself back into the archive. Together all these observations set both my hypothesis and my research agenda for the coming year, and while both were still on track for the Beauty Clinic, they were nevertheless coming under the influence of scholars who were not afraid to engage the incongruity of unhealthy bodies sporting otherwise seemingly healthy minds. These scholars were effectively resisting the ultimate call of the scholarly Beauty Clinic, which is to disentangle ideas from messy, broken down bodies.[12] They were resisting, that is, a pristine narrative of intellectual development and scientific, intellectual, or rhetorical discovery and success. After reading and discussing these body biographies, I realized I could no longer rely on the wispy snippets of bodily breakdown found in Paul Jay's necessarily truncated version of the Burke-Cowley letters. I had to explore the full record further, in order to fill out my account of the hernia operation on which the Herone Liddell story was based. The most suitable destination would be the Newberry Library in Chicago.

As many Burke scholars know, Burke and his lifelong friend Malcolm Cowley traded letters from the 1910s up until Cowley's death in 1981. Cowley's papers are held in the Newberry's Midwest Manuscript Collection, a collection that contains an impressive eighty-two cubic feet of papers, correspondence, and news clippings that Cowley accumulated during his long and productive intellectual-literary life. The collection is neatly organized into series, and series 5, called "The Kenneth Burke Files," is where my research focused.[13] This subcollection is crucial because it contains both sides of correspondence between the lifelong friends, four boxes in all, and it is therefore the most complete record of extant letters between the two thinkers. A few hours in the collection was enough to make me appreciate the enormous feat accomplished by Jay, when he edited his collection on Burke and Cowley correspondence.

I went to the archive intent on filling out some of the details of Burke's own hernia operation. Still in pursuit of that Beauty-Clinic-worthy conclusion for the book, I presumed that the archive could help fill in any gaps in my research and scrub clean any imperfections. I had a clear hunch going in, based on a mention in Jay's selection of the Cowley-Burke correspondence (MC to KB 1956), that the archive would have more to say about the relationship between Burke's operation and the development of his theories. Archives can sometimes exceed our wildest hunches, and the Newberry guided me to a new level of historiographical incongruity. The letters at the Newberry revealed an astonishing chronicle of spurts and sputters, a decade-long record of Burke's struggles to keep things going both health-wise and work-wise, and a chapter plan (my own) in shambles.

The most intriguing thing about Burke's documenting of his health problems, which mostly stemmed from his difficulty catching his breath, what he repeatedly called his "gulpo-gaspo-gaggo," is how details of his bodily struggle were interspersed with details of his struggle to complete the book he was working on during the 1950s, what he called his "Symbolic," the planned completion of the Motives trilogy. The bodily and theoretical ailments at times themselves muddle together in the letters, presenting an even more direct tie between Burke's body and his work than Browne offers of Darwin. For example, as I note in the book, Burke directly connects the breathing problem with a problem of writing (134). His struggle with completing the "Symbolic" also drives him to a bizarre cocktail of Aristotle and alcohol, which I pursue at some length (135–36). The image of Liddell/Burke, pinned and wriggling on the operating table, powerful as it is, could no longer lie at the core of this chapter. Instead the chapter needed to be about Burke's own practice of embodied theorizing, and about the utterly crucial role played by physical breakdown itself. In other words, this chapter could not merely be about the neat correlation between Burke's body and his ideas. And though I did not realize it in the haze of the archival research, the chapter ultimately needed to be about failure; it needed to use the archive as a record of breakdown to disrupt its own pull toward the perfection of the Beauty Clinic. And not unlike the unfinished project of George Parker's posthumous book, Burke's own unfinished project, "The Symbolic of Motives," became the new puzzle.

A CONTROVERSY

Away from the archive and back home, now in search of a way to put things back together again, I began to reread the existing arguments about what exactly happened with Burke's "Symbolic of Motives," a book that Burke was hammering away on during the 1950s, the same decade in which he developed his bilateral hernia and a host of other physical ailments, and during which he published "The Anaesthetic Revelation of Herone Liddell." For the past several years, scholars have been trying to reconstruct what would have been published under this title, to finish the book that Burke toiled over for nearly two decades. He reportedly generated close to a thousand manuscript pages for the "Symbolic," and a good deal of that was published in article-form or delivered as lectures.[14] Some scholars, working in the biographical mode, blame the declining health and death in 1968 of Burke's wife, Libbie. A letter to Malcolm Cowley in 1975 supports this angle. Here Burke writes,

"The thing is, Malcolm, since Libbie cleared out, I have quit putting out my books" (KB to MC June 9, 1975).

William Rueckert and Richard Thames, however, make a different argument. They believe that Burke never finished his "Symbolic" because, as they both put it, he was a "victim of his own genius" (Thames " Gordian" part 2; Rueckert, *Essays* xv). These recuperative efforts tend to take a somewhat mournful approach, insisting on salvaging Burke's "lost" work, on saving Burke, as it were, from himself. To be sure, both of these scholars know Burke and his work rather thoroughly. Even so, the time I had spent in the archive, reading anguished letters about an ailing body and an ailing book, had convinced me that the issue was not Burke's genius.[15] Instead my reading of the archival material from that period suggested that the lessons his ailing body was teaching him about the abiding relationship between body and thought, and ultimately between body and language, undermined Burke's effort to isolate a theory of symbolic language from rhetoric and ultimately from bodies. In other words, I began to suspect that Burke deliberately abandoned the project simply because it was no longer a fruitful or even theoretically tenable direction. It might be that he had said all there was to say about motives in the *Grammar* and the *Rhetoric*, and that beginning the "Symbolic" was a mistake. Such a claim—that Burke's own movement toward the Beauty Clinic, his plan for a tidy trilogy, imploded in the face of his theory and his physical state—is incongruous at best, irreverent at worst. Mobilizing such a claim, that is, required a suspension of the Beauty Clinic on at least two levels: first, on the level of my own chapter, which was no longer this neat and easily summarizable set of claims, and—more riskily—on the level of Burke himself. My new argument required a layering of the archive over the preexisting, loric speculations that depend so much on reverence for Burke's program.

But there is more to the argument than simply refuting Thames and Rueckert. Indeed, to me, their blaming of Burke's genius presents a compelling case of what can go wrong with archival research when it focuses on a single figure: researchers can become so devoted to their subjects that it is impossible to notice, let alone write about, that subject's breakdowns and failures. Spending hours of every day immersed in Burke's words, his worldviews, his charming, self-deprecating (and other-deprecating) remarks, and his spirited arguments with close friends, makes it difficult, if not impossible, not to become affectively attached to the quirky character behind all those words. And yet such intense devotion as many Burkeans have for Burke might lead to lopsided, overly worshipful scholarship about him. Such emotive screens tend to filter out the failures and failings that dot the archives. It becomes difficult, if not impossible, to say a word about Burke that might be construed as critical.

And so beneath the question about whether or not scholars should revive the book that was to be Burke's "Symbolic of Motives" lies a potentially more serious controversy: the possibility that a profound admiration for Burke and the insistence that anything he was doing is worth pursuing—what I call "Burkophilia"—is under-mining the field of Burke studies itself.[16] Here it is worth noting that the archives do not provide all the answers; my own conclusions about Burke's "Symbolic," much like the others mine resists, began as a hunch, and a certain way of encountering archival evidence—an attitude or perspective informed by the archival materials with which I was working.

BACK TO METHOD

Such is the gnawing controversy that ultimately drew me to "the Beauty Clinic," a term I end up foregrounding in that chapter's title. My hunch was that there is something important to be gleaned from this rather underdeveloped concept, something about academic discourse and its insistence on weaving together pris-tine, disembodied ideas. Burke scholars have tended to ignore Burke's ailments, to include them as—at most—spare footnotes or asides about his love for the bottle. Doing so disarticulates Burke's theories from the material, embodied conditions that helped form them. My main task in the chapter, then, became a re-embodying effort, one built around bodily breakdown and its effects on Burke's work. The re-sult was this idea of "body biography," which took me back to that initial cluster of readings about individual thinkers and their ill health. Body biography, too, can be called something of a method, given that it is modeled after existing work (that of Browne, Benbow, and Houck and Kiewe), and that it ended up being one of the main ideas of the chapter.

And yet I could have never gotten there if not for the incongruous approach I ended up taking vis-à-vis the archive. The basic incongruity here is pairing Burke with breakdown, resisting the lure of the hero, and looking to the archive as a re-cord of failures and not just—or in addition to—a positive record of productivity, a lively index to a great thinker. As I have discussed, such an incongruous approach might be deemed irreverent. It might also lead to frustrating dead-ends. But in this instance, when followed through the archive, the cumulative stallings of the 1950s added up to something: a Burke with a renewed reverence for bodily processes and their role in communication and thought. But getting to that point took about nine months of sputtering and stalling of my own, multiple visits to archives, and uneven toggling between archival material, Burke's published work, and existing scholarship on this period of Burke's life and work.

Once the chapter came this far, I could finally include a brief reading of "The Anaesthetic Revelation of Herone Liddell," the story that was originally supposed to fill the entire chapter. In that story, the main character's body, immobilized from prematurely administered anaesthesia, nevertheless tries to speak. The character's body approximates language (or so Herone observes) by forming knots in its sinews and muscles, by building up such frustration that it finally forces its vocal chords into a tangle of jibberish. "The Anaesthetic Revelation" became something other than the tidy capstone of the book's previous chapters. Instead this story became one of revelation-through-breakdown, just exactly the kind of thing I'd been after all along, without fully realizing it. The chapter I thought would take me seven or eight weeks ended up taking ten months. The most salient lesson from those months is this: the archive does not make scholarly works, it remakes them.

As most archival researchers know too well, archives offer a surplus of narrative possibilities that can be overwhelming, contradictory, and impossibly stumping. The idea of historiography by incongruity might help researchers to suspend their preexisting hopes and hunches, their wills-to-perfection, encouraging instead an openness to the violent breakdown of archival preconceptions. Even tales of breakdown themselves offered by the archive, while typically left to the side, pursued briefly and then abandoned, or (most often) skimmed over, might render moot the researcher's prearchival conclusions. The result might be work that is less trim or prim, even less clinical. Such work would take seriously Burke's scattered criticisms of the Beauty Clinic and linger more comfortably, more lastingly, in the delightfully incongruous world of archives.

NOTES

1. For prison overcrowding, see "Overcrowding in the Tombs"; for a discussion of Parker as an expert on criminal psychology, see Marshall and "To Test Belling's Sanity."

2. The book he's referring to having completed is most likely *Auscultation, Creation, and Revision,* which he wrote that summer.

3. For instance his work as a ghostwriter at John D. Rockefeller's Bureau for Social Hygiene yielded a number of lengthy arguments about why hormones and endocrine glands might matter for a theory of communication (see Hawhee, *Moving Bodies* 79–83). Jordynn Jack has also demonstrated how that part-time job led Burke to develop theories of what he terms "constabulary function" ("Kenneth Burke's Constabulary Rhetoric"). Burke's work as a translator also appears to have formed a longstanding interest in bodily constitutions. See *Moving Bodies* 94–97 for a discussion of that job.

4. See pages 136–39 of *Permanence and Change* for Burke's discussion of some of Rivers's theories with special attention to his use of Freud's notion of "active forgetting" (137).

5. The title of this section is quoted from *PC* 158.

6. The most explicit reference appears in Burke's 1963 essay "The Thinking of the Body," also reprinted in *Language as Symbolic Action.* Burke also mentions the Beauty Clinic in a letter to John Crowe Ransom when, after a nearly four-page engagement with Ransom's book *The World's Body,* in relation to his own views on the human body, Burke concludes abruptly, "So much for the Beauty Clinic at present" (KB to JCR January–February 1957, 4)

7. The readings Burke offers here are performed in the Freudian vein, as established by Ellen Quandahl.

8. In the early sixties when Burke's wife, Libbie, was gathering his materials together, Burke emended this letter to say, "To save my honor I must make haste to explain the epithet. Bill Brown used to write me as "Beurre-que" a kind of "French" for "Burke." From

that the joke developed in bilingual punning to 'butter-that.' And Hart added the further development, as per the epithet. K.B." (Thanks to Michael Faris for the sleuthing on the question of when the explanatory note was added.)

9. He writes to Cowley: "I am progressing steadily with Dewey, the first half of whose book has not greatly thrilled me. He seems too external to his subject, so far at least" (KB to MC March 30, 1934).

10. For an extensive treatment of that story, see Nicotra, this volume.

11. Written by Benbow, Browne, and Houck and Kiewe respectively. (The Houck and Kiewe reading was an excerpted chapter from their book on FDR.)

12. See my discussion of this phenomenon in *Moving Bodies*, 126–27.

13. The Cowley papers are helpfully inventoried online at <http://www.newberry .org/collections/FindingAids/cowley/Cowley.html>.

14. For Rueckert's reconstruction of the Symbolic, see *Essays toward a Symbolic of Motives*. Williams, too, proposes a table of contents in his "Toward Rounding Out the *Motivorum Trilogy*." Additional commentary can be found in Rueckert's "Kenneth Burke's 'Symbolic of Motives' and 'Poetics, Dramatistically Considered,'" as well as Thames's "The Gordian Not" and Wess's "Looking for the Figure."

15. For details, see my discussion of the letters in *Moving Bodies*, 129–36. One powerful instance occurs in a November 16, 1950, letter to Cowley:

> All this [the "Symbolic"] has been written, while I squirm and gasp, nearly below the surface of the mud, at one moment my legs heavy; at another, pains in my left arm; again and again and again, my lungs only half as ample as they should be—and then, lo! Ecstatically, a full breath incipit vita nova. O, on the edge of the abyss. O, by the seashore at night, the waves ripping. (KB to MC November 11, 1950)

16. The Burkophilia argument didn't make it into my chapter, but it formed the teeth of at least one part of that chapter, and they gnawed at me, so much so that I presented a polemic about Burkophilia at the 2007 Rhetoric Society of America meeting.

WORKS CITED

Benbow, Heather Merle. "Ways In, Ways Out: Theorizing the Kantian Body." *Body and Society* 9.1 (2003): 57–72.

Browne, Janet. "I Could Have Retched All Night: Charles Darwin and His Body." *Feminism and the Body*. Ed. Londa Schiebinger. New York: Oxford University Press, 2000. 317–54.

Burke, Kenneth. "The Anaesthetic Revelation of Herone Liddell." *Kenyon Review* 19 (1957): 505–59.

———. *Permanence and Change: An Anatomy of Purpose*. 3rd ed. Berkeley: University of California Press, 1984.

Gold, David. "The Accidental Archivist: Embracing Chance and Confusion in Historical Scholarship." *Beyond the Archives: Research as a Lived Process*. Ed. Gesa E. Kirsch and Liz Rohan. Carbondale: Southern Illinois University Press, 13–19.

Hawhee, Debra. *Moving Bodies: Kenneth Burke at the Edges of Language.* Columbia: University of South Carolina Press, 2009.

Houck, Davis W., and Amos Kiewe. *FDR's Body Politics: The Rhetoric of Disability.* College Station: Texas A&M University Press, 2003.

Jack, Jordynn. "Kenneth Burke's Constabulary Rhetoric: Sociorhetorical Critique in *Attitudes Toward History.*" *Rhetoric Society Quarterly* 38 (Winter 2008): 66–81.

———. "'The Piety of Degradation': Kenneth Burke, the Bureau of Social Hygiene, and *Permanence and Change.*" *Quarterly Journal of Speech* 90 (2004): 446–68.

Jay, Pual. *Burke and Cowley: Selected Correspondence.* New York: Viking, 1988.

Marshall, Edward. "Large Proportion of Crime Might Be Eliminated." *New York Times* Dec. 17, 1911: SM8.

"Overcrowding in the Tombs." *New York Times* Dec. 3, 1911: 14.

Parker, George. "Mental Dissociation in Functional Motor Disturbances." *Psychopathological Researches: Studies in Mental Dissociation.* Ed. Boris Sidis. New York: G. E. Stechert, 1902. 255–79.

———. "Mental Dissociation in Psychomotor Epilepsy." *Psychopathological Researches: Studies in Mental Dissociation.* Ed. Boris Sidis. New York: G. E. Stechert, 1902. 280–320.

Quandahl, Ellen. "'More than Lessons in How to Read': Burke, Freud, and the Resources of Symbolic Transformation" *College English* 63.5 (May 2001): 633–54.

Rueckert, William, ed. *Essays toward a Symbolic of Motives.* West Lafayette, Ind.: Parlor, 2007.

———. "Kenneth Burke's 'Symbolic of Motives' and 'Poetics, Dramatistically Considered.'" *Unending Conversations: New Writings by and about Kenneth Burke,* ed. Greig Henderson and David Cratis Williams, 99–124. Carbondale: Southern Illinois, University Press, 2001.

Thames, Richard. "The Gordian Not: Untangling the Motivorum." *KB Journal* 3 (2007).

"To Test Belling's Sanity." *New York Times* Dec. 24, 1910: 6.

Wess, Robert. "Looking for the Figure in the Carptet of the Symbolic of Motives." *KB Journal* 3:2 (Spring 2007).

Williams, David Cratis. "Toward Rounding Out the *Motivorum Trilogy:* A Textual Introduction." *Unending Conversations: New Writings by and about Kenneth Burke.* Ed. Greig Henderson and David Cratis Williams. Carbondale: Southern Illinois, University Press, 2001. 3–34.

AFTERWORD

My Archival Habit

My graduate school roommate, Bob Kruger, loves fishing. (I don't.) When I once asked Bob to explain his fondness for sitting in a small boat for hours, casting time after time (after time) in the hope of hooking something, he fell back on his psychology studies as an explanation: "It's called 'selective reinforcement,' Jack," he explained. When I looked puzzled, he put it into concrete terms so that even I could get it: "If I could catch a fish with every cast, then I'd never fish. There would be no challenge, no suspense, no point. And if I could *never* catch a fish, then obviously I wouldn't do it either—it would be pointless. But the fact that *sometimes* I catch a fish, and that you can never predict when: that's what makes it irresistible; that's what makes fishing an addiction."

Catching a fish at unpredictable intervals: that's selective reinforcement; and Bob says that it's just about the most powerful motivator around. It explains why people play slot machines or gamble more generally: the lure of an occasional, unpredictable payoff can make for an irresistible addiction. And it explains why people play golf despite its maddening difficulty: if you hit a great shot every time, you'd give it up quickly, and if you never hit a great shot, you'd quit too. But if you hit just a half dozen good shots out of a hundred: omigosh, that can make you into a golf junkie. (Bob Kruger incidentally likes golf and low-stakes gambling as well as fishing. One of his life goals is to visit every horse racing track in the United States. No wonder we're still friends after all these years.)

Anyway: While Bob can't stay away from fishing, I now can't stay away from archives, and I think that selective reinforcement explains why. When you enter into an archive, you've really gone fishing. Whether it's deep sea fishing or looking for small fry, it's all the same: you troll with a general idea of what you're looking for, but you're open to whatever hits the line; you put in long hours looking at maddeningly routine things, but you can't give it up because once in a while—you can't predict when—you'll come across something wonderful, something so interesting and enlightening that you can't wait to look some more. And that means you'll be back again the next day or the next week, trolling for more—just in case you might catch a big one.

So the archive has become my addiction, my habit, even since my first experiences in Penn State's Kenneth Burke Papers two decades ago. And this essay is a set of fish stories, if you will. It's a chance to share some of my favorite expeditions and memories—about some of the ones that got away, but mainly my favorite catches (and by "catches" I mean people that I met as well as information that I've gathered). Along the way it will give me a chance to explain some of the values associated with archival research, and a chance to counteract some myths about it. If it all works out, I'll be persuading some of you to join me.

THE FIND

The most obvious attraction to archival research is the lure of hooking and then landing something new, the satisfaction of clearing up once and for all a vexing, longstanding problem. These come along less often than one would wish because lots of problems have been taken care of by previous scholars: Kenneth Burke studies in particular have attracted the efforts of many excellent scholars over many years, with the result that anyone puzzled by a Burkean passage can usually get enlightenment just by doing some scholarly reading. But not every problem has been solved, believe me, and not every Burkean archive has been fished over or even discovered.

A favorite that that comes to mind is uncovering the inside story behind Kenneth Burke's celebrated feud with Sidney Hook, recounted (in part) by Ann George and me in *Kenneth Burke in the 1930s*. (Maybe it's the name "Hook" that reminds me of him in this tale about hooking a big fish?) It has always been well known that Hook fell out of Burke's favor, fully and forever, when the philosopher brutally and unfairly savaged Burke's *Attitudes toward History* in a December 1937 review in *Partisan Review*. Hook made fun of Burke's "amateurish" scholarship and "obscure" writing style, called him a moral nihilist, and polished him off as a "weak man of minor talent."

But why did Hook write that review? After all, Burke and Hook had started out as respectful leftist comrades and kindred spirits: Hook was a fervent Marxist who nevertheless detested Stalin and Stalinism, and Burke had advertised his own analogous misgivings about Communist Party USA hegemony in "The Nature of Art under Capitalism" and in other essays of the early 1930s. True, when Hook's fierce anti-Stalinism got him barred from the First American Writers' Congress in May 1935, he was disappointed when Burke decided to participate and to take a leadership role in the League of American Writers because the Popular Front agenda of the Congress and of LAW sustained Stalin's regime and muted criticism of the Soviet Union. But Burke was not alone in staying generally true to the CPUSA main line, he had nothing to do with Hook's being blacklisted from the congress, and his gently dissident *Permanence and Change* (published in April, 1935) expressed viewpoints that could easily be perceived as in general sympathy with Hook's outright apostasy. And of course Burke's famous address at the congress, "Revolutionary Symbolism in America," was dissident enough to merit outrage and condemnation, a reaction which Hook surely would have been aware of. So when Hook's review eighteen months later instead of praising *Attitudes toward History* savaged it as "opaque" and "disorganized," as immature in its criticism of Dewey and in its "home-baked objective relativism," and when it castigated Burke for writing a positive review of Henri Barbusse's book *Stalin,* Burke was both blindsided and enraged.

Why had Hook so fiercely turned on Burke, and what was Hook referring to when he mentioned Burke's own review of *Stalin*? Burke scholars had already noted that Hook seemingly had motive enough when he observed Burke's apparent forgiveness of the notorious Moscow show trials in the pages of *Attitudes Toward History;* and yet the trials actually became public only after the book was finished and in press. So what was Hook's real problem with Burke, particularly with Burke's review of Stalin, and where was that review, anyway? It was not to be found by fishing around in the standard bibliographies or trolling through the magazines that Burke usually patronized and it was a continuing open question to the committed Burkeans that I was encountering at conferences.

The Sidney Hook Papers at Stanford's Hoover Institution cleared it all up. I had come to Stanford to research the details on Burke's famous participation in the First American Writers' Congress in 1935 because that story was still incompletely understood, it seemed to me, despite its fame. I had already learned plenty from the Penn State Kenneth Burke Papers and from navigating archives related to the American Left at Syracuse University (including the Granville Hicks Papers), and I had gone to Stanford to explore what perspectives the Joseph Freeman Papers might add, since Freeman's famous encounter with Burke was central to the Writers' Congress story. (Freeman, past editor of *New Masses,* cofounder of *Partisan Review,* proletarian poet, and leading figure in the CPUSA, is a fascinating figure in his own right, and his papers did indeed contribute to my understanding of the Writers' Congress.) To be honest, I didn't even know that Hook's papers were at Stanford until I got there, finished my work with the Freeman Papers, and (having some additional time on my hands) began fishing around to see what else might be at the Hoover Institution besides Freeman's papers.

The Hook Papers contained more than I could have imagined. Most important, the files contained a copy of Burke's lost review of *Stalin,* which had been published in an obscure backwater known as the Book Union newsletter. The Book Union was a short-lived quasi–Book of the Month Club, intended for people interested in left-leaning reading. Every month beginning in 1935 (and ending the following year) its newsletter described new books that had a proletarian commitment—fiction, poetry, history, economics—and offered them at a discount to club members. In that newsletter Burke had indeed penned a purely descriptive review of Barbusse's *Stalin,* the one that Hook took to be so appreciative (because it was not explicitly unfavorable), and the one, the Hook Papers make it clear, that Hook took definite offense to.[1] That is because Hook himself, at the precise time that Burke was reviewing the book, was in the process of savaging *Stalin* in an in-press review slated for the November 16, 1935, *Saturday Review*. An off-print of the review is included in Hook's papers: in the margins of his manuscript review he wrote to Burke, "I have just read your review of Barbusse's *Stalin* in the Book-Union circular and am wondering whether there are two different books by Barbusse on Stalin or whether your review and mine just illustrate the law of selective reference. Don't think I don't appreciate the real skill that went into the writing of your review but I am grieved that you did not dare to write a single critical line about a book which—despite your review—I know in your heart you regard as thoroughly bad. Excuse the 'bad taste' of this note but you are the only 'mind' whose defection to Stalinism I mourn." In other words, Hook felt that Burke had thoroughly whitewashed, for the sake of party loyalty, a book that itself was covering up Stalin's monstrosity.

The trouble is, Hook for whatever reason never actually sent his furious marginal comments to Burke. Hook's remarks remained in his files and later in the archive, and so Burke remained unaware of Hook's disappointed venom and unable to explain to Hook his side of the story—notably (as Burke's papers demonstrate), that the Book Union editors had edited out some of Burke's most critical comments about *Stalin*. And so when *Attitudes toward History* arrived, again with a forgiving attitude toward Stalin, and when a newly Trotskyist version of *Partisan Review* was hatched by Hook and some of his anti-Stalin-but-pro-Marxist colleagues late in 1937, Hook was primed to perform a literary assassination on unsuspecting Burke, one that was so vicious that Burke never got over it. Burke everlastingly would refer to Sidney Hook as Shitney Hook, and he even vowed to piss on Hook's grave if he ever had the chance; but Hook lived to be 86—passing away only in 1989, when Burke was 92 and past the age of pissing expeditions. (When I mentioned this story to Burke's son Michael one day, Michael, who knew his father's attitude to Hook very well indeed, expressed genuine regret that had had failed to get Burke over to the site of Hook's grave to perform his ministrations before Burke died in 1993.)

While the Hook story was a particularly satisfying and conclusive strike, the archives have supplied many, many others—less elaborate and conclusive almost always, but also always enlightening in their own way: enough to keep me hooked, in other words. As one consequence, archives around the country that contain Burke letters have permitted me to construct a reliable chronology of Burke's life. The Informal Chronologies that I've put together with Ann George, in *Kenneth Burke in Greenwich Village* and *Kenneth Burke in the 1930s*, are the feature that is most often mentioned when someone commends those books. (Perhaps that tells you about what they think about the other parts of those books.) In any event, documenting what Burke was reading and writing, and when he was doing it: such basic scholarship is something that is very much needed—you never know when it might come in handy—at least until some hardy soul has the gumption and long life enough to take up the task of writing a Burke biography. Moreover, the archives have consistently enabled me and others to supplement the bibliographies of Burke's writings with some new finds—like the review of Barbusse's *Stalin* for instance; or Ann George's finding of Burke's essay "On 'Must' and 'Take Care'"; or the unpublished essay on economics that I turned up in the Milton Friedman Papers at Stanford last spring; or the remarkably detailed letters from Burke to James Sibley Watson that I came across in the New York Public Library's Berg Collection last spring and summer—letters that bear on the development of *A Rhetoric of Motives* as well as on the thinking that was consuming Burke as he pondered *A Symbolic of Motives, A Rhetoric of Motives,* and other late projects.

One postscript will close this segment: While at the Newberry Library in the fall of 2010, I was reading the full correspondence between Burke and Cowley, which includes a great many letters that Paul Jay was not able to include in his fantastic selection of Burke-Cowley letters, when I came across some poetry by Burke that I'm pretty sure has never found its way into any of the collections of KB verse. In Burke's letter to Cowley of December 15, 1961, he memorialized some of his intellectual adversaries with this short sonnet-of-a-sort:

> All the arts and crafts are tricky.
> Writing is a funny bizz.
> Should we say of poet Dickey
> That he plays with his?
>
> If you are minded to exhume
> The bones of litry Preussentum,
> Then know: At Yale there lies a relic,
> Herr Professor Rene Wellek.
>
> Cockneys get their aitches wrong
> But if you would get yours true,
> Join the ever-growing throng
> That puts an aitch in P( )artisan Review.
>
> Of all the kinds of academic crook,
> Imagine one who's picked the name of "Hook"!

You already know why he was still sore at Hook nearly twenty-five years after the *Partisan Review* episode. But you now, courtesy of the archives, know that Burke was also steamed because Wellek had been ripping Burke in a recent article in the *Yale Review.* And as for why he was upset at Dickey, I don't yet know: perhaps you can hook the answer in a trip to an archive yourself.

A RIVER RUNS THROUGH IT

If you've read the book or seen the movie by Norman Maclean (and incidentally Maclean figures into the Burke archives too), you've experienced what many regard as the best fishing story of all: *A River Runs through It.* (Then again, it may be the only fishing story I've ever read, unless you include as fishing stories *Moby-Dick* or *The Old Man and the Sea* or *The Book of Job* or "Big Two-Hearted River.") Part of Maclean's book is about *consubstantiality,* actually, as in the novel's final scene in which the tragically but irresistibly rebellious younger son becomes one with the river while chasing a magnificent trout—and we in turn become consubstantial with him. Here's the way the story ends: "Eventually, all things merge into one, and a river runs through it. The river was cut by the world's great flood and runs over rocks from the basement of time." Maclean's book is about life's uncertainty and flux, about ambiguity and ceaseless change: "On some of the rocks are timeless raindrops. Under the rocks are the words, and some of the words are theirs. I am haunted by waters."

Maclean's observations about process and flux, about epistemological ambiguity in the search for meaning, hold for archival research, too, I've found. It might seem that archives are closed, static resources, meant to resolve issues once and for all; and I've already given you a case in which material in an archive cleared up a puzzling conundrum once and for all. Sometimes archives do resolve something, as I've indicated, and when that's so, it can be intoxicating. But more often the findings are not final; the evidence, unreliable and partial, only complicates things; the dynamic flux and flow of interpretation continue, intriguingly; and it's the search that matters most of all.

Let's take a simple example. Those who habituate the *KB Journal* will recall recent contributions by Michael Halloran, Scott Wible, and Jim Zappen concerning Burke's famous epigraph to *A Grammar of Motives: "Ad bellum purificandum."* The ambiguities of the Latin have always intrigued Burke's readers, and many scholars have commented on the phrase, usually translated "toward the purification of war" or words to that general effect. Sometimes scholars have built entire systems of interpretation on the motto, as when Phillip Tompkins indicated that "Burke's entire system of thought was based on his outrage toward war" (121). A few years ago Halloran, Wibel, and Zappen came across an inscription on the wall of a small closet at Burke's Andover farm, an inscription that prompted further meditation because it included within it Burke's famous phrase: "potius convincere quam conviciari / ad bellum purificandi." "Better to debate than berate" or "better to demonstrate than revile": Based on that inscription, Zappen indicated that *"ad bellum purificandi"* amounted to "the hope of an end to war through an order that encompasses competing points of view and the understanding that this hope will never be realized." A few months ago I found a letter in the New York Public Library from KB to James Sibley Watson, his perennial patron, dated July 15, 1942. In it Burke commented on the motto for the book he was completing: "'Ad Purificationem Belli' or 'Ad Bellum Purificandum'? . . . Probably the former would be better, since 'purificatio' is not Augustan anyhow. Or should I say simply 'For the purification of war'? . . . I should think that the essentially liberal version would be: 'For the elimination of war.'" There you have it: Burke's own testimony indicates that the phrase should be translated, "For the elimination of war." Or does it? Does the discovery of Burke's self-translation mean that we should now simply accept the phrase as meaning "For the elimination of war," once and for all? Of course not. It doesn't cancel out the scratching on Burke's windowsill, and it doesn't end speculation. What does "not Augustan" mean, anyhow? What does it mean when Burke uses the phrase "the essentially liberal version," and what is wrong with the simpler "purificationem"? Recounting the details of Burke's letter to Watson only complicates the matter further, and intriguingly so. What I have come to do with what I find in the archive is just what Bryan Crable does in his recent book on Burke and Ellison and what many of the contributors to this book have also done: we treat the letters and documents in the archives as another set of Burkean texts, fully as authoritative and as worthy of analysis and interpretation (and fully as elusive and stimulating) as anything Burke ever published.

Like all great works, the letters and other documents in Burke's archives do not resolve or shut down acts of interpretation or understanding; they just add complexity, nuance, interpretive stimulation, and ambiguity. They make the search for understanding endlessly intriguing. I once recounted in some detail the amusing particulars related to a fistfight that involved Burke's friends Gorham Munson and Matty Josephson on November 10, 1923. It made a good story because it offered a way to discuss the workings of two early little magazines that Burke was involved with (*Broom* and *Secession*), but I also included it for epistemological reasons. While we know a fight took place that day, and know where it took place and even why, we don't know much more than that because the multiple accounts of the fight, recounted in letters to Burke and to others, all disagree in their details. What was the outcome of the fight? Who won? Who bloodied whom? To me the archives often create intriguing and addictive moments that point to the act of interpretation as everlastingly open and ongoing—and human. "A way of seeing is also a way of not seeing," we all know because of Burke (and because of Charles Sanders Peirce's sobering reminder, "We are blind to our own blindnesses"); and so one way of recounting an event is not conclusive. Archival evidence is always partial, never authoritative, and you cannot interpret the contents of a letter to or from Burke as more credible than a diary entry or other interested testimony. It makes searching the archive all the more addictive in that it provides no tidy narratives, only partial ones, no Beauty Clinic (to use Debra Hawhee's phrase) but more often a tide of mystery whose attractions are akin to those of fine detective tales.

I used to think that the archival work of Ann George and Krista Van Dyk had resolved, once and for all, the key ambiguities associated with Burke's novel *Towards a Better Life.* George settled many of the more biographical readings of the novel by turning up sent and unsent letters between Burke and Malcolm Cowley on the occasion of Cowley's 1932 review of John Dos Passos's novel *1919:* she established that Cowley's review was actually a commentary on *Towards a Better Life* (not *1919* at all), actually a diagnosis of Burke's own marital and personal stresses at a time when he was just publishing the book, and actually a warning that Burke should take steps to avoid the motives that had recently led their mutual friend Hart Crane to commit suicide. And Van Dyk found notes and commentaries by and about Burke in the archive that allowed her to resolve a host of interpretive puzzles, proving the novel's balance and coherence and clarifying its themes and arguments.

Except that no one has stopped arguing about *Towards a Better Life,* in spite of George's and Van Dyk's excellent work. Readers remain un-concluded—as they should, because the archives only add additional interpretive texture to Burke's narrative. Another letter from Burke to Watson in the New York Public Library, for example, responds to Watson's questions about the novel. Burke frankly admits to the effects of alcohol on his work, claims that "the movies were a tremendous help to me" (particularly movies involving Claudette Colbert and Ginger Rogers), discloses that "it became interwoven with elements of symbolic homosexuality," and offers his own account of how the novel is a response to various situations: his marital problems, his financial problems, his physical exhaustion, and the philosophical and esthetic problems he was encountering—all of it "helped by my firm belief in the rationality of the economic approach as the central gravitational force of cultural developments" (February 2, 1941). We aren't going to plumb the bottoms of Burke's novel anytime soon, and further archival findings, I predict, will only drive us back to Burke's published text for further readings and ruminations that will never be exhausted.

In short, while archival findings can contribute vital insights into Burke's elusive published works, they rarely will remove the elusiveness. Indeed part of the fascination of the archive is that Burke's unpublished letters and manuscripts and notes contribute their own ideas to the canon, becoming in the process of discovery as intriguing, perplexing, suggestive, and stimulating as the published works themselves. Archives unsettle as much as they settle. And there is as much room for interpretation of What Burke Meant in the archival record, and as much communion with him, as there is in the act of interpreting the unfathomable flux at the heart of *A River Runs through It.*

THE THRILL OF THE CHASE

It's not just the landing of the fish or its subsequent scrutiny that makes fishing addictive, though. The chase as well is a big part of the fun, especially if the search takes you through captivating territory. An exploration of the archive can be profoundly gratifying when the adventure brings you into contact with fascinating individuals, circles, and intellectual movements. In this respect the various archives related to Kenneth Burke have few or no matches: As Sandy Stelts and Jeannette Sabre indicate in their essay, the list of those that Burke engaged with amounts to a Who's Who in twentieth-century American intellectual and cultural history. And so the experience of fishing in Kenneth Burke's waters is a profound, sustained, inexhaustible, and intensely pleasurable educational expedition.

Some of the pleasure can be personal and voyeuristic, I must confess. What a kick it gave me to hear about the time that Peggy Cowley got bitten by a snake at Andover, or about the arrival of phone service there in 1952. Or about the various human foibles of Marianne Moore, Hart Crane, William Carlos Williams, Robert Penn Warren, Ralph Ellison, Shirley Jackson, or any number of other literary giants who visited Andover and swam in Lake Bottom. Or about the frustrations Burke had with a host of indifferent Bennington students and the satisfaction he took at the successes of others. Or to hear about what it was like for KB to live in the same rollicking Bennington cottage with Theodore Roethke. Or, more personally still, to hear about KB's tussles with those McCarthyite blackballers who were banning him from teaching at Washington, or about son Butchie's finishing third in the New Jersey math contest in April 1954, or about Michael's work atop a Hawaiian observatory, or KB's loving and lengthy portraits of his sons off at Harvard in the mid-1950s. For the sheer pleasure of it I published in *Kenneth Burke in Greenwich Village* Burke's absolutely delightful description of his outing to a Maine strawberry patch with his wife and daughter in 1921, and I agonized with KB as he wrote to others about the progress of Libby Burke's Lou Gehrig's disease during the 1960s. Burke's celebrated hypochondria, his insomnia and indigestion and irritating "gulpo-gaggo-gaspo" reflex, his hearing problems and hypertension, the struggles with and enjoyment of alcohol: all are documented and described in KB's letters. What a shock it was to discover that Burke's common law sister-in-law Dorothy Day had once had an abortion—I worried that the secret, if I revealed it, would scotch her chances for official sainthood in the Catholic Church, until I learned that Vatican sleuths already knew all about it. And what a pleasure it was to follow the details of Burke's lectures and visiting appointments at my own Penn State, including information about people who later became my colleagues. Burke (I learned) once earned $1,500 for a nine-day stint of lectures, parties, classes, and receptions in 1960 (KB to MC May 31, 1960), and he spent ten weeks in 1963 living in a house right down the street from where I would live two decades later in State College.

But I must resist the temptation even while acknowledging it, for it's a little like the guilty pleasure associated with reading someone else's diary, someone you've come to know and admire: fascinating, to be sure, but snooping nevertheless. Fortunately Burke knew that his papers would be seen by others for he was constructing his archive quite self-consciously as he worked. And if the bigotry of some of his acquaintances is often on display in their letters—I won't name names—it's seldom on display in Burke's. Letters about Sidney Hook to the contrary, Burke's missives are characterized by what he called "the comic corrective": he tended to regard people as mistaken rather than evil, and his letters typically reveal a generosity of spirit that is impressive to behold, especially because he was often addressing people with wildly divergent political and artistic beliefs and commitments and because he had a persistent commitment to intellectual agonism. I have already used the term "consubstantiality" here, but now I must use it again: there are moments when the exchanges between Burke and his interlocutors offer a movement toward human communion that is both inspiring and instructive. And as I read I grow consubstantial with these people too.

But most of what I refer to here has to do with the pleasures of learning the details of larger literary and cultural moments and movements. What teachers Kenneth Burke and his colleagues have been! "Teaching has become an integral part of my work," KB told Cowley in 1952 (September 6), and the letters he sent (and received) amount to a sustained and sophisticated tutorial for any reader interested in every important intellectual movement of the past century. The letters offer an in-process, insider's perspective on everything from post-Nietzchean philosophy to developments within the "new" social sciences after 1940. Before undertaking the research that became *Kenneth Burke in Greenwich Village* I had only the most general feel for the esthetic tenets that we call "modernism," for example, but Burke's sustained conversations with Marianne Moore, Crane, Cowley, Watson, Munson, Williams, and so many others taught me so much about the range and vitality (and difference) that accompany intellectual movements. When I took up the 1930s project with Ann George, by means of an immersion into Burke's letters to and from Cowley, Hook, R. P. Blackmur, James T. Farrell, Cleanth Brooks, Granville Hicks, Richard McKeon, Katherine Anne Porter, Allen Tate, and Robert Penn Warren—among many others only slightly less accomplished and celebrated—it introduced me to the intricacies and textures of 1930s literary and political thought, especially within the American Left, as nothing else could. And throughout his later career Burke remained not just current but thoroughly engaged with the debates that defined linguistics, psychology, New Criticism, poststructuralism, and New Rhetoric after World War II. To engage with Burkean archives is to hook yourself to particular times and places and personalities of exceptional interest. You enter an era, get swept up in its discourses, and begin living in a different time and place with different people. It's another kind of consubstantiation, and the pleasures of witnessing and experiencing firsthand the discourses peculiar to important intellectual movements are heady, intoxicating, addictive.[2]

FISHING WITHOUT FISH

Fishing, after all, isn't really about fish. Usually the addiction means the pure pleasure of the activity itself, particularly when the weather is fine and the company is good. In the case of archival research, the environment is nearly always fine and the company can be spectacular.

Getting immersed in a specific time and place and getting to know interesting strangers with unusual intimacy: these make for an unusually addictive and pleasurable mix. Not that the people Burke communicated with were perfect; far from it. Nor were they always especially noteworthy or interesting or their correspondence gripping or intoxicating. On the contrary, most of the details included in correspondence between Burke and his friends are banal and quotidian, and the friends themselves typically are anything but noteworthy. For every "Cowley, Malcolm" in the Burke correspondence there is also a Arthur Cox, David Cox, Mary Cox, and G. Armour Craig; for every Hart Crane and R. S. Crane there is Sue Crane, John Crawford, Robert Crowell, and Margaret Cuff.

And yet that's the point. Familiarity breeds intimacy; intimacy breeds its own fascinations; and obscure people from a lost moment jump back into the group portrait when their words are read against those of many contemporary others. A trip through Burke's correspondence makes you a participant in a particular place at a particular time, and the details and particulars bring those times and personalities to life in a way that is truly pleasurable and definitely addictive.

But it's not just a matter of meeting ghosts. Just as fishing often seems to be a solitary activity, you would think that archival research might be isolating, too. The stereotypical portrait of the researcher in an archive has been pretty vividly sketched: a lonely individual, presumably far from home, spends hours locked in solitary and secure library spaces, sitting at a table alone, silently poring over the papers and emerging from the cloister only at the end of the day—or week, or month. But in my experience the stereotype is completely false. Archives are highly social spaces. They have connected me not only with the words of vivid personalities who have left the scene long ago but also with a host of convivial, generous, living-and-breathing colleagues and associates who have enriched my professional and personal life.

Take the people who oversee the archives. Librarians, it turns out, love nothing more than meeting new people. They have work to do and that can give you the impression that you are intruding, but after a while you come to understand them: they are eager to help people out, the more perplexed the better. I came into my archival work knowing nothing about how to proceed, but Charlie Mann at Penn State made me welcome and answered my every question without ever implying that I was making rookie mistakes. A noted scholar himself as well as the head of rare books and special collections, everlastingly surrounded by stacks of Things To Do that might have intimidated me into withdrawing, Charlie nevertheless was always interruptible and patient (not to mention informed and funny). After a few months of guiding me along, Charlie pretty much gave me the run of his place, even dispensing with some of the security checks and letting me browse to my heart's content. It made me feel like a professional. In the process of working with Charlie I met Sandy Stelts, now the curator of rare books and manuscripts, who had been working closely with Charlie long before I came along and who is now one of my best friends—as well as a colleague who has never said No to a request, even if it means coming in after hours or on weekends, or going on the road to Andover (or Pocono Downs). I've spent other hours picking the brain of Jeannette Sabre, who knows every inch of the Burke papers, as her essay in this collection demonstrates, and I know of any number of others around the country who are benefiting regularly from her care and expertise.

And the Penn Staters, while unique, aren't alone in their professionalism and hospitality. On the road I've come to value the helpfulness of every librarian I've met—people who have given me tips and pointers, who have stayed after hours at times and gone extraordinary lengths to accommodate spontaneous needs, and who unfailingly try to do everything they can to sustain my explorations. Anne Garner at the New York Public Library has been my most recent benefactor: one minute she was patiently orienting a newcomer to the remarkable Burke holdings in the Berg Collection at NYPL; by the end of the day she was recommending ways that I might apply for financial support to sustain my studies.

Archival research connects you with other scholars, too. I'm hesitant to begin naming names because I'll forget many of them, but I'm pleased to have been able to share archival tales over the years with Jim Zappen, Robert Wess, Miriam Marty Clark, Bryan Crable, Steve Mailloux, Greg Clark, Bill Fitzgerald, William Rueckert, and Ben Giamo, among many others, not to mention unforgettable personalities that I've met via permissions and publications processes. Far from isolating me, the Burke papers have connected me with a host of like-minded others.

Most notable among the experts on Kenneth Burke are members of the Burke family. At first Michael Burke was the patient recipient of my permissions requests. Then he and Julie Whitaker invited me and my daughters and spouse to dinner at their New York City loft—and before the evening was over, they were putting us up for the night! That led to trips to Andover, half a dozen of them by now, and all of them have been social occasions, too: occasions to connect with Anthony "Butchie" Burke, with Michael and Julie's kids, Shannon and Brendon, and with other members of the extended and accomplished Burke family, often at a big barbecue dinner. What a professional and personal pleasure it has been to connect with this remarkable tribe, and to enjoy the unmatched hospitality that Kenneth Burke himself patented. The Kenneth Burke I've come to know through his archives was basically a shy person uncomfortable in large settings, I've come to believe; but in small gatherings (or in the one-to-one exchanges on display in his truly capacious letters) he was a captivating and charismatic host.

Michael and Julie also have always welcomed the graduate students that I've brought along to Andover and New York, and that brings me to my conclusion. Ultimately it's people you are fishing for, and my good fortune at getting involved with Kenneth Burke is most fundamentally this: it has given me an opportunity to work closely with a succession of talented graduate students who have continued our collaborations over the years. The dozen or so people represented in this volume stand in for two dozen others: without question the most deeply satisfying part of my professional career has been having a chance to bring people into graduate seminars on Kenneth Burke, to involve them in our mutual and interdependent explorations of the Burke papers, and then to watch many of them continue their independent studies of Burke in faculty positions—as they have in this collection.

It all reminds me of another inevitable feature of fishing: luck. No one in my profession has been as fortunate as I have been, for my chance encounter with the Burke archives two decades ago has given me pearls of great price: meaningful work to enjoy, and a succession of tremendous friends and colleagues to enjoy it all with. Their essays here continue to enlighten me and to inspire me to think further about the possibilities that are provided by archival research. Ultimately people are the things you fish for, that you hook if you are lucky, that you stay hooked to and become addicted to. I wanted to hook Kenneth Burke but ultimately I got myself hooked. To so much else and so many others.

NOTES

1. You can judge for yourself: Burke's review is included on pages 174–75 of *Kenneth Burke in the 1930s*.

2. I do not want to give the impression that everything about archival research is addictive, though. There are plenty of unsuccessful searches to discourage you, many promising leads come only to frustrating dead ends, and difficult heirs can sometimes withhold their permission to publish something very interesting that has been turned up in an archive. And once I had a near-death experience, as Steve Mailloux and Greg Clark can attest too, on a research trip to Andover.

WORKS CITED

Crable, Bryan. *Ralph Ellison and Kenneth Burke: At the Roots of the Racial Divide.* Charlottesville: University of Virginia Press, 2011.

George, Ann. "Kenneth Burke's 'On Must' and 'Take Care'": An Edition of His Reply to Parker's Review of *Attitudes toward History.*" *Rhetoric Society Quarterly* 29 (Fall 1999): 21–39.

George, Ann, and Jack Selzer. *Kenneth Burke in the 1930s.* Columbia: University of South Carolina Press, 2007.

Jay, Paul. *The Selected Correspondence of Kenneth Burke and Malcolm Cowley.* New York: Viking, 1988.

Maclean, Norman. *A River Runs Through It.* Twenty-fifth Anniversary ed. Chicago: University of Chicago Press, 2001.

Tompkins, Phillip. "On Hegemony—'He Gave It No Name'—and Critical Structuralism in the Work of Kenneth Burke." *Quarterly Journal of Speech* 71 (1985): 119–31.

Van Dyk, Krista. "From the Plaint to the Comic: Kenneth Burke's Towards a Better Life." *Rhetoric Society Quarterly* 36 (Winter 2006): 30–55.

Zappen, Jim, S., Michael Halloran, and Scott Wible. "Some Notes on 'ad bellum purificandum.'" *KB Journal* 3.2 (Spring 2007).

CONTRIBUTORS

DANA ANDERSON is an associate professor of English at Indiana University. A former editor of *KB Journal*, he is the author of *Identity's Strategy: Rhetorical Selves in Conversion* (2007) as well as articles about Burke, identity, and agency in *Philosophy and Rhetoric* and *College Composition and Communication*.

JESSICA ENOCH is an associate professor of English at the University of Maryland, where she teaches courses in first-year writing, rhetorical theory, history, and pedagogy, as well as feminist rhetoric. She published *Refiguring Rhetorical Education: Women Teaching African American, Native American, and Chicana/o Students, 1865–1911* (2008). Her current book project is titled *Claiming Space: Feminist Rhetorical Investigations of Educational Geographies*.

ANN GEORGE is an associate professor of English at Texas Christian University where she teaches undergraduate and graduate courses in rhetoric and writing. She is co-editor of *Women and Rhetoric Between the Wars* (2013) and co-author of *Kenneth Burke in the 1930s* (South Carolina, 2007).

KEITH GIBSON is an associate professor at Utah State University, where he directs the Ph.D. program in the theory and practice of professional communication. His research focuses on the rhetoric of science and technology, and he has published in *Technical Communication Quarterly*, *KB Journal*, and *The Writing Instructor*.

DEBRA HAWHEE is a professor of English at Penn State University, where she teaches the history of rhetoric (ancient and modern) and oral and written communication. She is the author of *Bodily Arts: Rhetoric and Athletics in Ancient Greece* and *Moving Bodies: Kenneth Burke at the Edges of Language* and is a coauthor, with Sharon Crowley, of *Ancient Rhetorics for Contemporary Students*.

IAN E. J. HILL is an assistant professor in the history and theory of rhetoric in the Department of English at the University of British Columbia, where he is also affiliated with the Graduate Program in Science and Technology Studies. He has previously authored an article about Burke in *KB Journal* titled "'The Human Barnyard' and Kenneth Burke's Philosophy of Technology."

JORDYNN JACK is an associate professor of English at the University of North Carolina at Chapel Hill. She is the author of *Science on the Home Front: American Women Scientists in World War II* and has published articles about Burke, rhetoric of science, and feminist rhetoric in *Rhetoric Review, College English, College Composition and Communication,* and *Rhetoric Society Quarterly.*

JODIE NICOTRA is an associate professor of English at the University of Idaho. Her scholarly areas of interest include material rhetorics and posthumanism, and she has published articles on, among other things, Burke and general semantics, urban foraging, climate change, and rhetorical agency.

NED O'GORMAN is an associate professor of communication at the University of Illinois, Urbana–Champaign. He is author of *Spirits of the Cold War: Contesting Worldviews in the Classical Age of American Security Strategy* and former president of the American Society for the History of Rhetoric.

JEFF PRUCHNIC is an assistant professor of English at Wayne State University. His articles on rhetorical and critical theory have appeared in such journals as *Rhetoric Society Quarterly, Rhetoric Review, JAC,* and *Configurations.*

JEANNETTE SABRE is an information resources and services support specialist in the Special Collections Library at the Pennsylvania State University Libraries. She created the Kenneth Burke Papers website, has written guides for several Burke collections, and coauthored an article about issues in processing the second Burke collection.

JACK SELZER is a professor of English and Barry Director of the Paterno Fellows Program at Pennsylvania State University, where he has taught since 1978 (his students including nearly all of the contributors to this book). Recently president of the Rhetoric Society of America, he is currently at work on a third book on the career of Kenneth Burke, focused on the years after World War II and tentatively entitled *Kenneth Burke in the University.*

MICHELLE SMITH is an assistant professor of English at Marist College. Her research, published in *Rhetoric Society Quarterly* and *Communal Societies,* considers the rhetoric of intentional (utopian) communities in nineteenth-century America, focusing on rhetorics of identity, place, and gender.

SANDRA STELTS is curator of rare books and manuscripts at the Pennsylvania State University Libraries, where she has curated two exhibitions on Kenneth Burke in the Special Collections Library. She has been a copresenter (with Jeannette Sabre) at meetings of the Kenneth Burke Society and the Penn State Conference on Rhetoric and Composition.

DAVE TELL is an associate professor of communication studies at the University of Kansas. He is the author of *Confessional Crises and Cultural Politics in Twentieth-Century America.* He has also published articles about Burke, Foucault, Augustine, and Rousseau in such places as *Philosophy and Rhetoric,* the *Quarterly Journal of Speech, Rhetoric Society Quarterly,* and *Rhetorica.*

SCOTT WIBLE is an associate professor of English and director of the professional writing program at the University of Maryland. He is the author of *Shaping Language Policy in the U.S.: The Role of Composition Studies* (2013) as well as articles appearing in *College Composition and Communication, College English, Cultural Studies,* and *Rhetoric Society Quarterly.*

INDEX

Abel, Lionel, 35, 36, 37, 38, 44n13
ableism, 84, 91. *See also* disability studies
abyss, 160, 167–68, 174n1, 175n7
academic debate, 69, 71, 80–81
act: action versus, 157n5; as term of pentad, 143, 145–48, 150–51, 153, 157n5, 180
action: act versus, 157n5; consciousness of linguistic action, 180–81; dichotomy of motion and, 73–75, 94, 118n2, 147–48, 157n5. *See also* symbolic action
action/motion dichotomy, 73–75, 94, 118n2, 147–48, 157n5
Addressing Postmodernity: Kenneth Burke, Rhetoric, and a Theory of Social Change (Biesecker), 149
advocacy, 124, 215
aesthetics, 133, 184–85
affect, 2, 9, 130–31, 135, 136–37
agency: Burke's skepticism about, 120, 133; and pentad, 143, 148, 150–51, 180; and pragmatism, 180
Agrarians, 33, 34, 43n2, 44n7
Alexander, Ben, 27n3
American Journal of Sociology, 35, 45n20
American Review, 35, 44n7
American Sociological Review, 45n20
American Sociologist, 20
American Writers' Congress, 31, 32, 34, 43n2, 44n7, 52, 63n1, 211, 212
Anaesthetic Revelation and the Gist of Philosophy, The (Blood), 168–72

"Anaesthetic Revelation of Herone Liddell, The" (Burke), 168–73, 202–4, 206–7
Analysis of the Mind (Russell), 196
Anderson, Dana, ix–x, 1–13, 11n1, 157n9
Andover, N.J., home archive of Burke, 6–7, 16–22, 26, 27n3, 215, 218, 221, 222n2
animality studies, 95
"Animals, Anomalies, and Inorganic Others" (Braidotti), 96n6
"Appeal to Progressives, An" (Wilson), 129
"Approaches to Communism" (Burke), 124–25, 129, 139nn4–5
archetypes, 74
archival event, 6, 7–8, 68, 81
archival provocation, 6, 7, 51, 63
archival research: and archival event, 6, 7–8, 68, 81; and archival provocation, 6, 7, 51, 63; and "Burkophilia," 205–6, 208n16; complexity and ambiguities in, 215–17; electronic resources for, 23; George on perspectives offered by, 30; and historiography by incongruity, 10, 196–207; Patrick Joyce on, 6; librarians' assistance with, 220–21; on mysticism, 9, 161–62; Osborne on, 3, 5, 10; overview of different roles of, 6–12; and pentad as "terministic" ontology, 154–56; pieties in, 2–6, 9; pleasure of, 217–20; and privileged status of archival materials, 155–56; on publication